New Chinese Cinemas analyzes the changing forms and significance of filmmaking in the People's Republic, Taiwan, and Hong Kong, emphasizing the way film commented on the profound social changes that occurred in East Asia in the 1980s. These original essays offer extended analyses of the important trends, themes, and styles that define contemporary Chinese filmmaking. They demonstrate that film is an important aesthetic form and social document in the interpretation of these ongoing changes.

NEW CHINESE CINEMAS

New Chinese Cinemas

Forms, Identities, Politics

Edited by

NICK BROWNE, *University of California, Los Angeles*
PAUL G. PICKOWICZ, *University of California, San Diego*
VIVIAN SOBCHACK, *University of California, Los Angeles*
ESTHER YAU, *Occidental College*

CAMBRIDGE
UNIVERSITY PRESS

PUBLISHED BY THE PRESS SYNDICATE OF THE UNIVERSITY OF CAMBRIDGE
The Pitt Building, Trumpington Street, Cambridge, United Kingdom

CAMBRIDGE UNIVERSITY PRESS
The Edinburgh Building, Cambridge CB2 2RU, UK   www.cup.cam.ac.uk
40 West 20th Street, New York, NY 10011-4211, USA   www.cup.org
10 Stamford Road, Oakleigh, Melbourne 3166, Australia
Ruiz de Alarcón 13, 28014 Madrid, Spain

First published 1994
First paperback edition 1996
Reprinted 1997, 1999

Typeset in Times

A catalog record for this book is available from the British Library

Library of Congress Cataloging in Publication Data is available

ISBN 0 521 44877 8 paperback

Transferred to digital printing 2003

CONTENTS

ILLUSTRATIONS

CONTRIBUTORS

Chris Berry is a lecturer in Cinema Studies at La Trobe University in Australia. He worked in Beijing as a subtitler and translator for the China Film Export between 1985 and 1987. He is the editor of *Perspectives on Chinese Cinema* (British Film Institute, 1991) and has published articles in *Camera Obscura, China Screen, Cinema Journal, East–West Film Journal,* and *Jump Cut.* He is completing his doctoral dissertation on Chinese film at the University of California, Los Angeles.

Nick Browne is Professor of Critical Studies in the Department of Film and Television at the University of California, Los Angeles. He is the author of *The Rhetoric of Filmic Narration* (UMI Press, 1982) and editor of *The Politics of Representation: Perspectives from "Cahiers du Cinema," 1969–72* (Harvard University Press, 1991) and *American Television: Economies, Sexualities, Forms* (Gordon and Breach, 1993). His lectures at the Beijing Film Institute, entitled "Film Theory: An Historical and Critical Perspective," are to be published in Chinese in Beijing.

Fredric Jameson is Professor of Comparative Literature and Director of the Graduate Program at Duke University. He is the author of *The Prison House of Language* (Princeton University Press, 1972), *The Political Unconscious* (Cornell University Press, 1981), *The Ideologies of Theory* (University of Minnesota Press, 1988), *Postmodernism, Or, the Cultural Logic of Late Capitalism* (Duke University Press, 1991), and *The Geopolitical Aesthetic: Cinema and Space in the World-System* (BFI / Indiana University Press, 1992).

Leo Ou-fan Lee is Professor of East Asian Languages and Civilizations at Harvard University. He is the author of *The Romantic Generation of Modern Chinese Writers* (Harvard University Press, 1973) and *Voices from the Iron House: A Study of Lu Xun* (Indiana University Press, 1987) and editor of *Lu Xun and His Legacy* (University of California Press, 1985). He is currently working on a study of modernist literature in Republican China.

Li Cheuk-to is a well-known film critic in Hong Kong and was editor of the *Dianying shuang zhou kan* [Film Biweekly] from 1980 to 1987. As program coordinator of the Hong Kong International Film Festival, he has edited the festival's seven retrospectives, which include *A Study of Hong Kong Cinema in the Seventies* (1984), *Cantonese Melodrama (1950–1969)* (1968), *and The China Factor in Hong Kong Cinema* (1990). He is the author of *Bashi niandai Xianggang dianying biji* [Notes on Hong Kong Cinema of the 1980s], 2 vols. (Chuangjin, 1990). His two-volume *Guan ni ji (Xianggang dianying pian; Zhongwai dianying pian)* [Viewing Against the Grain: Hong Kong Cinema; Chinese and Foreign Cinema] (Ci wenhua tang, 1993) was published recently in Hong Kong.

Li Huai is a visual artist whose studio is in La Jolla, California. She graduated from the Beijing Film Institute in 1982 and completed her master of fine arts degree at the California Institute of the Arts in 1990. Her work has been shown in Los Angeles, San Diego, Montreal, and Yokohama.

Ma Ning has published in *China Screen, Wide Angle, East–West Film Journal,* and *Journal of University Film and Video.* He has recently completed his doctoral dissertation, "Culture and Politics in Chinese Film Melodrama," at Monash University in Australia.

Paul G. Pickowicz is Professor of History and Chinese Studies at the University of California, San Diego. He is the author of *Marxist Literary Thought in China: The Influence of Ch'ü Ch'iu-pai* (University of California Press, 1981), coauthor of *Chinese Village, Socialist State* (Yale University Press, 1991), and coeditor of *Unofficial China: Popular Culture and Thought in the People's Republic* (Westview, 1989). He is presently completing a book on cinema and society in late Republican China.

Vivian Sobchack is Professor of Film Studies and Associate Dean of the School of Theater, Film and Television at the University of California, Los Angeles. She is the author of *An Introduction to Film* (Little, Brown, 1987), *Screening Space: The American Science Fiction Film* (Unger, 1987), and *The Address of the Eye: A Phenomenology of Film Experience* (Princeton University Press, 1992). She is past president of the Society for Cinema Studies and is a trustee of the American Film Institute.

William Tay is Professor of Literature at the University of California, San Diego, where he teaches courses on Taiwan cinema. His recent publications include the five-volume *Xiandai Zhongguo xiaoshuo xuan* [An Anthology of Modern Chinese Fiction] (Hongfen, 1989), a critical anthology, *Zhang Ailing de shijie* [The Worlds of Eileen Chang] (Yuchen, 1989), a collection of critical essays, *Wenxue yinyuan* [Relations of Literature] (Dongda, 1987), and individual articles on Wang Meng, post-Mao avant-garde theater, and Mei Lanfang's influence on American drama. A book on Chinese literature and Western theories is forthcoming.

Esther C. M. Yau is Assistant Professor of Film in the Department of Art History and the Visual Arts at Occidental College. She has published in *Dangdai dianying* (Beijing), *Film Quarterly, Wide Angle, Discourse,* and *Quarterly Review of Film and Video* and has contributed to *World Cinema Since 1945* (Unger, 1987) and *Women in Film: An International Guide* (Ballantine Books, 1991). She completed her dissertation, "Filmic Discourse on Chinese Women (1945–1965): Art, Ideology and Social Relations," at the University of California, Los Angeles.

ACKNOWLEDGMENTS

This book is a product of the University of California's steady support for a multicampus research project on Chinese film. The project originated with Nick Browne at the Pacific Rim Study Center at the University of California, Los Angeles. In 1988 a research and conference proposal titled "Cinema and Social Change in Three Chinese Societies," submitted by Professor Browne, Professor Donald Gibbs (University of California, Davis), Professor Paul G. Pickowicz (University of California, San Diego), and Professor Vivian Sobchack (University of California, Santa Cruz), was funded by the University of California President's System-Wide Pacific Rim Research Committee. Additional support was provided by the dean of humanities and the Program in Chinese Studies at UCSD. Esther Yau served as project coordinator.

In early January 1990, two dozen leading scholars of Chinese film from around the world came together at UCLA for a three-day conference. Presenters, in addition to those whose essays are published in this book, included Cai Shiyong, Cheng Jihua, Peggy Chiao, Paul Clark, Paul Fonoroff, Jenny Lau, Lee Tain-dow, Lin Nien-tung, Shao Mujun, Sergei Toroptsev, Wong Kin-yip, and Wu Tianming. Hu Ke and Ni Zhen were unable to attend.

The organizers of the project are grateful to Ms. Sue Fan and Professor Luci Cheng of the UCLA Pacific Rim Center and to Ms. Martha Winnacker of the Office of the President. Professor Donald Gibbs provided valuable advice. We thank as well Xiao Zhiwei of the Department of History at UCSD for preparing the glossary, Shannon Morris of the School of Theater, Film and Television at UCLA for typing the manuscript, and June Tang of the China Film Import and Export Corporation, Los Angeles, for assistance with photographs. Finally, we recognize the dedicated efforts of John Kim, Beatrice Rehl, and Mary Racine of Cambridge University Press on behalf of this book.

NOTE ON THE ROMANIZATION OF CHINESE

Generally speaking, this book employs the *hanyu pinyin* system of romanization used in the People's Republic of China. This system is employed almost exclusively in Chapters 1 through 4, in the list of scholarly works on Chinese filmmaking, and in all references to Chinese-language publications in the notes. However, in the chapters on Taiwan and Hong Kong, and in the portions of the introduction and chronologies that deal with Taiwan and Hong Kong, it did not seem appropriate to adhere rigidly to the *hanyu pinyin* system, since it is not used widely in those regions to identify people and places. Thus in the portions of the book that concern Taiwan and Hong Kong, the systems of romanization are local ones. Whenever a local system is used for the first time to identify a person or place, the *hanyu pinyin* equivalent follows in parentheses: for example, Hou Hsiao-hsien (Hou Xiaoxian). The glossary is alphabetized according to the *hanyu pinyin* system.

INTRODUCTION

Nick Browne

For a Western audience, the presentation of essays on Chinese cinema of the 1980s implies a distance of both culture and interpretation. This distance for film scholars may have a paradoxical aspect – disclosing a fascinating spectacle of another world under a familiar form of analysis. For scholars of Chinese history and literature, a book that takes Chinese film as a central instance of popular culture – one, moreover, that approaches its object through the languages of Western critical theory – may seem novel and strange. Nonetheless, the critical space created by this necessary crossing of perspectives provides a way to come to terms with the forms and meanings of Chinese filmmaking of the 1980s and to examine the way film occupies, within the sphere of Chinese popular culture, the contested space between art, entertainment, and national politics.

The presumption that Chinese cinema is the monolithic cultural expression of a Chinese nation has been dramatically undercut by history. "China" appears today largely as the consequence of the 1949 Communist revolution, forming an interregional social and economic network defined and sustained by politics. The People's Republic, Taiwan, and Hong Kong and their cinemas are marked as socialist, capitalist, and colonialist, respectively. Yet to exaggerate these differences would be to overlook a common cultural tradition of social, ideological, and aesthetic forms that stands behind and informs Chinese cinema as a whole. This book locates the Chinese cinemas of the People's Republic, Taiwan, and Hong Kong between the elements of a common culture and the differences of form and significance wrought by history and political division.

As a technology, of course, film has a Western origin. In this respect, the introduction of film into China is part of the history of "modernization," that large theme of the West's impact on Asia, linked in the contemporary period (in often misleading ways) to the vast transformation of social life in the region. Indeed, with the end of the Cultural Revolution and the dismantling of Maoism in the late 1970s, it was precisely mainland China's relation to the West and its commitment to resume modernization, first inaugurated in the late nineteenth century, that returned to the national agenda. Thus, as an art form, instrument of political communication, and medium of mass entertainment, Chinese film of the 1980s is deeply embedded in the process of political and social change across the region in a period marked by the cultural deconstruction of Mao's socialism and the new recognition of the possibilities and limits of Western-style modernization. Chinese cinema in the 1980s, inevitably caught up in the project of renegotiating China's past, enacts this cultural dilemma in different ways, according to its situation. Contemporary Chinese cinema, in other words, is a part of the continuing and convulsive efforts, ongoing through this century, at remaking China socially and economically.

Thus, the cultural critique of Chinese film in this period must be historical. The challenge is to map the changes of aesthetic form and sensibility upon the resistances and incursions, displacements, and reinscriptions of political power as it seeks to shape the social body. In this way, the critique of film form can register the local perturbations of form and affect, identify the points of discursive condensation around which semantic systems are established and revalued, note the distinctive re-marking of the problem of social and national identity, and recognize the changing significances of setting, style, narration, and genre in the presentation and revision of the culture's present relation to the past. That is, we can trace the changing relation of aesthetic form to political power in modes ranging from cultural reaffirmation to negation. The appended chronologies (see p. 217) seek to embed film in the larger social context. The essays that comprise this volume are analyses of Chinese film's efforts to express and reconsider the complex and long-standing theme of modernization in the post–Cultural Revolution period from both a Western and a Chinese perspective.

Traditionally, the aesthetic instance in Chinese culture has been supported by and derived from ethical precepts. Thus, well before the time of the founding of the People's Republic, the process of politicizing film art depended on recruiting and revising the tenets of traditional Confucian ideology for both reformist and radical aesthetic programs. The dislocations of the Cultural Revolution led at its conclusion in the late 1970s to an interrogation within certain elements of the film circle of the Party's insistence on congruence of art and politics and, by implication and consequence, to efforts to reconceptualize the status of film as an autonomous form distinct not only from politics but also from the other arts, most notably theater. Chinese film theory was one coded locus of the argument that explored the parameters of aesthetic autonomy in relation to the political instance.

The reinterpretation of the past in the major achievements of mainland cinema, as these essays show, took one of two dominant forms. The first reasserted the pre-Maoist ethical foundations of social life implicit in the narrative structures and conventions of melodramatic form and its historical retrospective mode of narration (as in the work of Xie Jin); the second adopted a modernist examination of the urban present in a flattened, synchronic mode, as in *The Black Cannon Incident* [*Heipao shijian,* 1986], or, alternatively, examined the rural past in a new light, as in Chen Kaige's *Yellow Earth* [*Huang tudi,* 1985]. In the first genre, as Ma Ning's essay shows, the conventions of melodrama serve both to critique the Party's role in the Cultural Revolution and to justify or legitimate the terms of the new sociopolitical order. It is a critique, I argue in my essay, that proceeds in the name of a new, depoliticized humanism, drawing on Confucianism for an ethical appraisal of the economic foundations of Maoism and its political program of class struggle. At the semantic center of this melodramatic mode is the in-mixing of the patriarchal order and the system of political economy that regularly installs the human being in a charged and overdetermined place – politically, economically, sexually – within the discourse of reform, private enterprise, and modernization. Post-1949 socialist ideology adopted the traditional figure of the countrywoman as the victim of feudalist patriarchy and sought by her liberation to constitute her as the beneficiary and bearer of the socialist program through narrative proof and visual spectacle. In this way, the relationship of the woman to the Party was inscribed as the setting of a didactic political lesson, and this figure took form as a significant political category. The post–Cultural Revolution cinema of the melodramatic type, however, explored in a number of its notable works the political victimization of men by the regime and dramatized masculine psychology, ranging from passive suffering to cowardice. *Red Sorghum* [*Hong gaoliang,* 1987], by contrast, showed the reverse side of masculine political castration by retrieval and restoration of an idealized masculine virility. Related shifts of form and valence in the writings of the young, Westernized Chinese critics indicate an account of the cultural and historical inscription of gender in Chinese cinema that shows it per se to be incidental to the genealogy, function, and meaning of the 1980s discourse on reform.

Rather, the aesthetic and ethical project of the new, post–Cultural Revolution cinema in the People's Republic is the depoliticization of the rhetoric and modes of signification of socialist cinema by contesting film's relation to official socialist historiography and by renegotiating the relation of film form to this official history by innovations in both modes of narration and style. For example, *Yellow Earth*'s reinsertion of nature into the coded semiotic system of Chinese film syntax, its reinterpretation of landscape, and its strategy of emptying space constitute, as Esther Yau has shown, the Daoist terms for the political reinstatement of a classical mode of the Chinese aesthetics. Thus, the film's style and form contest the founding myths of socialist political culture. Taken as a figuration of a possible way toward the future, the fate of the old farmer's children, especially the drowning of the daughter, contests the agency of the Party. The film evaluates the changes the Party has (not) worked on the patterns of Chinese history. The film's "modernist" form, in particular its silences, its absences, and its suspension of evident causality, stands in a negative relation to the cultural presumptions that had previously governed the correspondence of fictional and historical narratives. Likewise, the metropolitan version of this revisionist project, *The Black Cannon Incident,* treats contemporary Chinese life in that sector where the new industrial order and socialist administration converge and shows it as having reached paralysis, a historical impasse. The film argues that antiquated modes of bureaucratic regulation actively impede economic modernization, giving rise to what Paul Pickowicz calls a "postsocialist" malaise. Pickowicz treats these urban films of Huang Jianxin as documents of socialist disappointment and delegitimation. Like the melodramatic mode, they are meditations on the intractable, cyclical patterns of Chinese history, an acknowledgment of the limitations of Western ways in China, and testimony to the collapse of the utopian vision of the socialist world. Films of this type abandon the retrospective double narrative focalization of now *and* then found in melodrama, in favor of now *or* then, a strategy of flattening and compressing narrative focus in a way that restricts the rhetoric of change and of reform implied by the comparative aspect of temporal distance to the synchronic description and apprehension of a sensibility, an effective mode, marked by the dominant figures of impossibility and confinement. This strategy is not that of apology, justification, or reform, but the articulation of a radical cultural question about the impossibility of imagining a future different from present. As cultural critique, what these two modes of post–Cultural Revolution cinema have in common is a reconceptualization of the person, a historical process of rehumanization intended to invert and negate the victimization imposed by the technologies of political power.

In this regard, the correspondence of "subjectivity" (the technical term for the representation of inner or emotional life by film syntax) and society was a fundamental tenet of "classical" 1950s socialist realist film, linking the affective roots of individual life to the public sphere through socialist doctrine. The new Chinese cinema marks a historical break. What is undergoing renegotiation in the Chinese cinema is the historical reappearance of the "self," an analysis of its historical negation, and the remapping of the relation of public to private in another mode. The critique of the political apparatus of dehumanization results in the loosening of ideological confinement, especially with regard to the terms of social exchange, as well as in the loosening of restraints of physical movement of an increasingly libidinalized body. To be sure, "subjectivity" as an evocation of perception, memory, or fantasy is a classical effect. What is under construction in the contemporary period is the inauguration of the "self" as a new, marked place for the individual in the social network. The Western ideology of the individual ("subjectivity") and its filmic trope, the "cinematic apparatus," is, however, an inadequate summary of this effort. Likewise, the imposition of Western feminist readings of sexual difference and of homosexual narcissism to map the social terrain of post–Cultural Revolution cinema, whatever its value in the Western context, misses the immanent terms of Chinese cinema's cultural critique: its analysis and display of the overdetermined figure of the woman in the socialist discourse on reform both as an agency of state control and as the ideological linchpin for the regulation of socialist society. It is evident that the cultural logic of gender in post–Cultural Revolution cinema, in the formation of its deconstructive project, transcends the simple and literal binarism ("sexual difference") of the white Western feminisms. What is at stake in the new Chinese cinema is not an epistemological category of "subjectivity" but its ethical foundations.

In the People's Republic, the mutation of aesthetic and ideological cinematic forms is the consequence of an effort by a range of filmmakers to conceive anew the relation of aesthetics and politics, to create narrative structures capable of reassessing the past and interrogating the present with respect to the possibility of new economic options, and to rethink the status of the individual apart from the technologies of control. New cinema of the People's Republic negotiates an aesthetic form that puts cinematic narrative and the imaginative worlds that it projects in a position between the historical models of the past and an introspective understanding of the experience of the Cultural Revolution. The aesthetic doctrine of Mao Zedong's Yan'an Talks and that of the Cultural Revolution's model operas have been submitted to the revisions of a new film practice.

In Taiwan and Hong Kong, the mutation of cinema's narrative form, its corresponding representation of society, and its address to the audience indicate the contradictory relations of these regions both to mainland China and to the ongoing processes and consequences of Western-style modernization. The aesthetic forms of these regions are complex, syncretic totalities composed of traditional Chinese social and cultural arrangements overlaid with a social formation of a capitalist order characteristic of "advanced" Western consumer societies. That is, they link composite cultural identities to contemporary modes of filmic representation.

Two fundamental aesthetic poles mark the dominant cultural tendencies enacted across the films of this new period in both Taiwan and Hong Kong – the traditional (nostalgic) and the modern (the cynical, the discontinuous). In Taiwan, the traditional mode might be identified with the works of Hou Hsiao-hsien (Hou Xiaoxian), and in Hong Kong, with *Homecoming* [*Sishui liunian*, 1984] by Yim Ho (Yan Hao). In each there is a strong sense of the continuity of Chinese culture and history rooted in an agrarian sensibility. Hou's work, as William Tay points out, is a sustained meditation on the social evolution of Taiwan and the personal and familial meaning of the progressive urbanization of the island. In this work, we see the memory of the loss of the mainland fade, figured by the disruption of affective or marital ties. This loss is then replaced by a second kind of emptiness, a more modern one marked by the dissolution of value and affect under the impact of industrialization to the point where even the young are disoriented. This historical recounting of double loss, told in a mode of sustained patience, is haunted by a melancholic nostalgia. In *Homecoming,* this temporal structure of separation is literally spatialized in the border crossing that contrasts the lives of two close friends, one living on the mainland, the other in Hong Kong, and so represents two forms of cultural life as different historical formations. In this sense, the retrospective narrative structure is spatialized, juxtaposing and then evaluating the concrete social grounds of two psychological attitudes, insisting on their difference but also on the continuity and communication between persons of what was once a single nation.

The contemporary, one might almost say "modernist," mode of Taiwan and Hong Kong cinemas adapts the art film format to the underlying and fundamental cultural trope of the period – cultural and psychological dislocation. Remarkably, this trope is intensified in the more popular Hong Kong genres. In films of this type, set well after the advance of consumer capitalism, traditional Chinese patriarchal social structure and its associated ethical culture have been nearly liquidated. The familial order has been replaced or put in abeyance by a new, largely masculine culture of corporate brotherhood (the syndicate) whose paramount expression in works like *Long Arm of the Law* [*Shenggang qibing,* 1984] is spectacular violence. In Hong Kong cinema, the popular action mode is perhaps the most directly "political." *Long Arm of the Law* opposes the forces of the Hong Kong police to the savage attack of a mainland gang (of robbers) and explores the opportunism, deceit, and even betrayal within Hong Kong's "military" culture. Likewise, as Li Cheuk-to insists, the victimization depicted in *The Boat People* [*Touben nuhai,* 1982] allegorizes the abandonment of Saigon by paralleling it with Britain's return of Hong Kong to the People's Republic. The spectacular paroxysms of violence produced by this overt clash of territorial interests might be read not only as the displacement of the popular rage over an imminent invasion, but also as the bearer of an ideological refusal, the displacement of political critique altogether into the taut rhythms of sensational action effects.

The Hong Kong art cinema of the late 1980s registers this cultural paralysis and anxiety through its narrative indecision over the past's relation to the present. This is evident both from the inscription of contemporary references in historical materials and from the deconstruction and suppression of clear markers of temporality. This cynical epistemology that foregrounds the panache of style as a set of explicitly aesthetic effects implies a reading of contemporary Chinese history, namely the eclipse, as Leo Lee underlines, of the promise of the future. The emphasis on the formal character of the surface effects, whether spectacularization in the popular mode or aestheticization in the elite mode, serves as a rhetoric of confinement, diminishing any truly reflexive turn and covering over a cultural critique. The "political unconscious" of the Hong Kong cinema of the late 1980s consists of the equivocation and compromise of Hong Kong between its contradictory nationalist and colonialist interests – and specifically indicates its helplessness before the task of initiating a cultural resolution. Cynicism is the dominant trope of this impasse.

Narratively speaking, the temporal mode of Hong Kong cinema is not retrospective, but future anterior – a syncretic culture caught in the complexity of an impending return that threatens to be a future undoing of its past achievement. The aesthetics of Hong Kong cinema are produced not by the efforts of neutralization or erasure of politics as in certain sectors of cinema in the People's Republic, but by the figuring of containment of its sovereignty by external powers and its displacement of cultural critique. The failure of the filmmakers to examine the basis of the fantastic wealth produced in the Colony and the attending dissolution of traditional ethical culture (giving way to a substitute, second-order ethic, that of "professionalism") is covered over by the urgent political problem – Hong Kong's 1997 return to mainland China. This irresolvable problem of contention with overpowering political forces corresponds to an ethical paralysis and an aesthetic stylization.

In Taiwan cinema, the significance of dislocation is another matter. Its central emblem is the aleatory form of metropolitan simultaneity and contingency. In this aesthetic mode, the separation (escape) from China, regarded as a political question, is neither simply displaced nor repressed. In Hou's films, the separation is treated as a memorable loss, recoverable in a sentiment that verges on melodrama. In contrast, as Fredric Jameson argues in "Remapping Taipei," *Terrorizer* [*Kongbu fenzi*, 1986] adopts a European form – a sustained formal reflexivity for the playing out of a plot that juxtaposes and commingles writer's block, marital dissolution, juvenile delinquency, professional disappointment, prostitution, and murder. In sum, it gives us a kind of modernist picture of total dissolution of the traditional social and ethical complex. The professional world, evidently linked to the larger world of international business, has its own functioning order, remote yet intertwined with the life on the street and in the apartments. Cultural dislocation is figured and acted out as marital discord and delinquency. It is not that the traditional ethical order has been displaced. Rather it has been violated and quite possibly liquidated. The traditional moral network of hierarchical obligations and lateral reciprocity by which the individual takes up a place within the larger social Chinese order – that is, the extended sense of family or clan – has dissolved in this metropolitan setting. Social relations, the sense of totality, lie shattered. This social assault on the individual is registered most evidently in the strata of the population where contemporary acculturation takes place. As the patriarchal order, the support for the old economic system, dissolves, the figure of the mother serves increasingly as the medium by which social change is registered and responsibility situated. The daughter is the vehicle for the depiction of change in the structure of affective life. The authorial cynicism that regulates the telling of the story is less judgmental or condemning than it is a diagnostic of the contemporary professional sensibility staged in the film. What previously were represented by moral categories have been transvalued into affective states and movements and transposed into investments in architectural forms and spaces.

Terrorizer's historical perspective on this social world is a thoroughly synchronic one – the past is absent and the present strongly marked by the signifiers of the contemporary, imported world. Evocative designations of strangely empty, urban spaces, psychic estrangement, and presentation of professional anomie in a fashionable mode indicate reference to the sensibility behind Antonioni's films of the 1950s and 1960s. The analogy with this European style of emotive abstraction is only partial, however, in that the Italian setting of the 1950s was clearly a transformation of the aesthetics of the city constructed by Italian neorealism. In *Terrorizer* the historical picture of the economic transformation of Taiwan is compressed and schematized. In form and style, the film is quite self-consciously Western, presenting itself as an "art film." As in Hong Kong cinema, its style subordinates the reflexive form, deleting the possibility of social critique and historical analysis. The film, in other words, becomes part of the consumer culture that produced it while relaying its underlying contradictions.

Chinese film in the "new period" (roughly from 1979 to 1987) converges around a significant cultural "problematic" that defines a common historical and cultural moment. This problematic, however, is neither unitary nor simple. It consists, we might say, in the cultural transformation that attends the dismantling of Maoism and the reassertion of an alternative, mixed socialist mode of economy in the People's Republic. The Maoist program showed itself in the microstructure of everyday life, in the workplace, in the changing configuration and status of the family, and in the status of the self in its divided alliance between the work unit, the lineage, the Party, and the nation. Within the territorial subunits of the region, the responses to this economic and cultural de-Maoification vary. In Hong Kong, for example, the "new movement" in film concludes in 1984 with the intervention of a political event – the British–Chinese agreement to reintegrate Hong Kong into China, that is, decolonization. In Taiwan and Hong Kong a related set of social transformations within traditional patriarchal structure were under way, but these evolved under the circumstances of distinctive forms of neocolonial capitalism closely tied to the larger world system. Thus, the reorganization or mutation of the traditional Chinese family and its ethical support, and its articulation with economic and political objectives or consequences, proceeded differently in its larger cultural implications through the region.

In the post-1949 period, the cinema occupied a specific place aesthetically and politically in relation to the matter of identity, both within and of the subunits of the region. However, one common development across Chinese culture in the People's Republic, Taiwan, and Hong Kong in the 1980s was the emergence of a view (if not the fact) of film as an autonomous art with distinctive aesthetic properties and the assertion (if not the reality) of film's independence from the requirements of a given political line whether from the Left or from the Right. In the "new period" it was the task of Chinese film theory in the People's Republic especially to put forward new theses about the character of film realism, matters of filmic ontology, and the basis of a distinctive film language. The reading of André Bazin, the postwar French theoretician of filmic realism, for example, served within debates over film to protect "reality" from its subordination to state and party politics. In its insistence on film's aesthetic autonomy and on the value of filmic realism, film theory in the People's Republic can be understood as supporting the depoliticization of the Maoist legacy. These debates in the field of theory coincided with the return to Taiwan and Hong Kong of Chinese film directors like Edward Yang (Yang Dechang) and Allen Fong (Fang Yuping) who had attended film schools in the United States and helped to create the support for what might be called the Chinese "art film." Traditional ethics had provided the moral foundation of the system of the arts, but theory's claim for filmic autonomy fractured the presumption of a coherent and integrated system of belief that linked aesthetics with politics and ethics. The debate over the relation of form and ideology is an epiphenomenon and symptom of the deeper fracture lines running across and through the culture, one that turns, as it did for the May Fourth intellectuals, on the question of the form and value of Western-style modernization within traditional Chinese culture.

The common feature of Chinese film in this new period of historical transformation is the emergence of a distinctive stylistic and ideological antinomy that serves as an emblem of the deeper dispute over the terms of reproduction, reform, or rejection of traditional culture. The emergence of the forms of an "art film" in the People's Republic is traceable jointly to innovative work by unorthodox younger filmmakers made possible in small, outlying studios still supported by a socialist budget system and to the availability of major examples of European filmmaking from the 1960s for viewing and discussion. The substantial moderation of the Guomindang cultural policy and the diversification of production circumstances at the nongovernment studios allowed for a parallel change in Taiwan. Chinese art cinema is, therefore, an "event" against the background of the "dominant cinema" – a highly variable critical category across the region. In the People's Republic, for example, the term "dominant" indicates a socialist mode of explicit ideological legitimation that in the post–Cultural Revolution context serves the process of readjustment, reform, and even struggle, worked out in a version of classical Hollywood style. Thus, the dominant cinema in the People's Republic seeks a reinvestment of socialist ideology in modernized social and economic circumstances. In Taiwan dominant cinema carries forward the Guomindang belief in a China under Republican principles. Works in this mode adopt a North American style of storytelling with the presumption of a theatrical model of the actors' performances. Its narrative forms and stylistic treatment provide the evident link between past and present.

The aesthetic "event" of the 1980s throughout the region was the appearance of a distinctive mode of filmmaking that might in a limited sense be called "independent," one different both from what in the West is called the "avant-garde" and from mainstream entertainment fare. In the People's Republic it was called the "Fifth Generation." In Taiwan and Hong Kong it was designated "new cinema." This mode adopts a new film language of pictorial design, syntax, and narrative structure to project a re-visioning of Chinese cultural traditions. As social forms, these films are generally identified with the contemporary metropolitan experience (although the astounding and influential *Yellow Earth,* for example, a product of the experience of rustification, is not), separate themselves from traditional and official political culture, and explore in an introspective, or explicitly self-referential, mode the author's relation to the culture, often by taking up a position at the fringe. Autobiography and cultural critique often converge in figures of cultural estrangement or physical dislocation. The sensibility behind a number of the most important works of the new Chinese cinemas explores the condition of cultural paralysis or deterioration attendant upon a particular moment in the history of the "modernization" of East Asia. At this moment, the fact of a surging consumer capitalism coincides with depoliticization that exposes, in unusually explicit ways, both the human and the aesthetic to the shock and stress of jarring historical and ideological change. The central cultural dilemma addressed by these filmmakers is the consequent despair and dystopian vision figured across a region caught between a past nearly impossible to sustain and a dispiriting commodity-oriented future, nearly impossible in traditional ways to imagine or tolerate. The outstanding works of the new period seem closely tied to the outlook and fate of the contemporary Chinese intelligentsia.

The larger import and value of this aesthetic "movement" are the constitution in film of a profound cultural contradiction between a mode of traditional social identity and either socialist or capitalist modernization. In the West, the cultural negotiation between Christianity and capitalism over the status of the individual proceeded progressively over several centuries. In East Asia, the renegotiation of the relation between the status of a person in traditional social structure and ideology and twentieth-century modes of "subjectivity" and economic organization has been radically compressed and foreshortened. Thus, new films of the 1980s are the visible site for both intellectuals and the public at large of this historical mutation and its associated cultural contradictions. Often supported only by the cultural elites, and repudiated by both the public and the political bureaucracy, certain of these films and their reception within the People's Republic, Taiwan, or Hong Kong indicate something of the changing nature of cinema within the larger cultural and public sphere. They indicate both film's elevation as an art and the precipitation within film as a mass medium of a set of aesthetic distinctions that we in the West recognize as "high" or "low." We can observe a new kind of aesthetic stratification across Chinese film. The loud complaint by film circles in the People's Republic in the late 1980s against the rise of the commercial "entertainment film" and the consequent contraction of possibilities for "art film" production is resonant testimony to the new market logic in the People's Republic at the end of this period, as well as to a change in the economic basis of film production, one that aligns the situation in the People's Republic to analogous situations in Taiwan, Hong Kong, and the United States.

Thus, the periodization of this "new" moment, its beginning and end, corresponds both to internal political change and to an economic realignment between "China" and the West. After all, it is "modernization" that inscribes, through complex relays of cultural displacement and rewriting, representations of social change and cultural identity in these films. Western interpretations of these changes, if they are to be more than projections of the Western analytic imaginary, must first be historical and cultural. Within this demanding cross-cultural frame, and between film studies and Chinese studies, the analytic and cultural problems produced by this art loom large for us and come closer.

Part I

FILM IN THE PEOPLE'S REPUBLIC

1

SPATIALITY AND SUBJECTIVITY IN XIE JIN'S FILM MELODRAMA OF THE NEW PERIOD

Ma Ning

J ust as the "new period" is considered a time of transition in Chinese politics, Xie Jin can be regarded as a transitional figure between the classical Chinese cinema and the new wave cinema of the early 1980s. In his filmmaking, Xie Jin draws heavily on the conventions of the Chinese melodramatic tradition, which generally guarantees the popularity of his films. By blending history with fiction or legend, the personal with the political, in a narrative pattern characterized by a bipolar structure that is typically Chinese, Xie Jin's films exhibit a strong social inscription and a sensitivity to the touchy political issues of the time that functioned as the catalyst for his creative activity. The deployment of a well-woven bipolar narrative structure also enables him to establish an almost endless set of contrasts in terms of setting, character traits, and actions that highlight the arbitrariness and absurdity of the ethical-political criteria used by the Party patriarchy to divide people into political insiders and outsiders. This critical edge became a source of inspiration for the younger generation of Chinese filmmakers, including the rebellious Fifth Generation, although the latter went much further than Xie Jin in their film practice and sought to break away from the melodramatic tradition his films embody. Furthermore, although Xie Jin operates within this Chinese melodramatic tradition, his attention to female subjectivity also foreshadows the emergence of women's cinema in China, discussed by Chris Berry.[1]

In this essay, I discuss the film melodramas made by Xie Jin in the new period in terms of several symbolic divisions valorized by the traditional Chinese patriarchal sociocultural order, and explore the vital role these divisions play in the construction of a viewing subject who is implicated in a set of complex social relations that make up the Chinese social formation. To this end, I pay particular attention to Xie Jin's use of spatial codes in positioning the male and female characters on screen in relation to the two dominant paradigms within which the Chinese film melodrama operates. I would argue that the coherent viewing subject constructed by Xie Jin's narrative discourse depends very much on the spatial relocation – or even dislocation – of the female characters and that this spatial relocation or dislocation must be examined in relation to the social and ideological crises the Chinese subject experienced in the new period of modern Chinese politics.

Western culture produces a hierarchy of divisions in which male–female subsumes other differences such as self–other in the equations male–phallus–order and female–lack–disorder so as to establish the supremacy of patriarchal law and individual subjectivity or identity. In contrast, the Chinese symbolic order valorizes the divisions of insider–outsider and moral–immoral, both of which can be used in various discourses to signify cultural, political, and even gender differences vital to the construction of the Chinese subject. Since the traditional Chinese sociocultural order was built on a moral edifice, ethical codes such as *ren* (benevolence, humanity) became the key signifier of the patriarchal order and the foundation of the insider–outsider, moral–immoral divisions. This is because the negative terms in those divisions signify a failure to abide by the Confucian ethical-political principles that form the basis of all Chinese institutions and are considered the hallmark of being Chinese or even human. Indeed, foreigners or people of other races are defined essentially by their refusal to act in accordance with these principles. Because the insider–outsider, moral–immoral divisions can also be equated with the human–nonhuman division, in the eyes of the Chinese the failure of foreigners to observe Confucian moral codes proves them to be nonhuman. Thus, since the nineteenth century, with the expansion of Western capitalism as a world system and its impact on traditional China, the ethnocentrism and xenophobia inherent in a culture based on these divisions have generated two typical Chinese attitudes toward foreigners: they are addressed either as "foreign devils" (*yangguizi*) to be despised or as "masters of the ocean" (*yangdaren*) to be kowtowed to and worshiped. The racist implications of the extreme hostility or friendship of the Chinese toward foreigners are obvious.

The insider–outsider, moral–immoral divisions also subsume political differences. The institutionalization of moral values was linked to the institutionalization of the means of violence. In premodern times, different political groups used whatever means available to identify opposing parties or organizations as immoral and to classify them as outsider/nonhuman. This negative categorization in turn justified the use of physical violence against the political opposition, since the benevolence (*ren*) advocated by Confucianism applied only to insider/ humans. In contemporary China, while ethical-political principles may be different from those of traditional Chinese society in their peculiar combination of Confucian and Communist elements, the ways in which politics operate are still very much the same.

In addition to political differences, the insider–outsider, moral–immoral divisions subsume those of gender. Although in traditional China sexual division and discrimination were widespread, they were not absolute criteria for the exercise of patriarchal power. Because of their social positions, Chinese women were usually defined negatively as outsiders and immoral ones. When a woman was born, she was automatically classified as an outsider since she would sooner or later be married off as an object of exchange. As well, the exclusion of women from the morally oriented educational institutions (the chief means for anyone to enter Chinese officialdom in traditional Chinese society) justified their categorization as immoral. Although, through their socialization process in the family, women were constantly instilled with the Confucian ethics of "three obediences" and "four virtues," it is ironic that in order for women to be accorded social status (and therefore humanity), they had to accept willingly the negative position assigned them. Furthermore, after the Chinese woman married into another family, she was still regarded as an outsider by her adoptive family until she had borne a son. Indeed, only when she succeeded in preparing her son for the role of family patriarch would she finally attain the position of matriarch and wield certain power over other members of the family with the tacit consent of the family patriarch. Thus, we observe a contradiction in Chinese society: a valorization of the maternal figure as a figure of power, on the one hand, and a very prejudicial treatment of women in society and culture in general, on the other.

Here we see that the insider–outsider and moral–immoral divisions correspond to another set of differences expressed in the Chinese language: human–nonhuman (used to signify racial difference) and man–a-man (used to signify class and gender differences within traditional Chinese society). These divisions, however, do not correspond to the self–other division as it is articulated in the Western cultural paradigm. One obvious explanation is that traditional Chinese culture is built on a strong repression of individual self-identity. Thus, while an insider is always a member of a family, group, community, or nation, the outsider has either an individual or a collective identity. This is clearly seen in the use of the insider–outsider division to delineate kinship relations. For instance, a vital division is made between paternal kin as the "inner family" (benjia) and maternal kin as the "outside family" (waijia). Relatives on the mother's side are marked by the word wai, such as waigong (mother's father), waipo (mother's mother), and waisun (daughter's son). In contrast, terms referring to members of the inner family do not have the word "inside" attached to them, with the exception of the term husbands use to address their wives who have married into the family (neiren, inside person).

In terms of the logic of Chinese culture, we could say that these distinctions have to do with the Chinese conception of the human subject, who is always defined in terms of his or her relationships with others. This social conception is closely related to the peculiar power structure of traditional Chinese patriarchal sociocultural order and its ethical basis. Although the traditional Chinese society was a class society, relations of domination were usually shrouded in kinship and moral terms regulated by ethical codes. What are regarded as normal social relationships are conceivable only in ethical terms. This is clearly manifest in the five basic social relationships codified by Confucianism and called *wulun:* ruler–subject, father–son, husband–wife, elder brother–younger brother, friend–friend. These relationships embody codes of loyalty, filial piety, benevolence, and honor, and each individual derives his or her personal ethical identity from them.

Although the *wulun* relationships are asymmetrical and structured as patron–client relations, they are naturalized in ethical terms. In traditional Chinese society power was exercised through relations of domination and exploitation disguised and euphemized in personal and moral terms so that they became naturalized and largely invisible, existing as what Pierre Bourdieu calls "symbolic violence."[2] The Chinese euphemism for this symbolic violence is, again, *ren* (benevolence), which here denotes an interpersonal relationship in accordance with the rule of reciprocity. A key concept in Confucianism, *ren* is the culturally sanctioned form in which what is considered normal social interaction takes place. The Chinese patriarch exercised power over his kinsmen through a structure of credit, confidence, obligation, personal loyalty, hospitality, gift-giving, gratitude, and piety – all of which were codified by Confucianism as the primary virtues of Chinese culture. For that matter, *ren* can be seen as the most economical mode of domination – that is, as the mode which best corresponds to the economy of the system.

Such was the importance of *ren* that it was considered in many Chinese discourses to be the standard of being Chinese or even human. As the famous Confucian dictum has it, *ren,* benevolence, is simply *ren,* being human. Of course, the wielding of power was not totally reciprocal in Chinese society. Physical violence was widespread, although it had always been thought by wise rulers to be only a secondary choice. Thus, in Chinese political discourse, *ren* was only the positive term in a binary pair whose negative opposite was *ban* (rule by force), which refers to the use of physical violence for coercion and domination. For wise rulers, it was only when *ren* failed that physical violence was used, and justification for the latter was based on the assumption that anyone who could not be assimilated into the symbolic system of *ren* could no longer be considered a human being, *ren,* but rather was an animal or a barbarian and should be dealt with accordingly. In everyday usage, however, *ban* did not simply mean physical violence; it also referred to nonreciprocal social interactions. For instance, in their economic dealings with customers from outside the community, Chinese businessmen would use deception and other tricks to make as large a profit as possible. Similar kinds of exploitation were widely practiced in the economic and political spheres when outsiders were involved.

Spatiality and Subjectivity in Chinese Film Melodrama

From the preceding discussion we can see that ethical codes such as *ren* function as the primary signifier of the Chinese patriarchal symbolic order and as the basis of the insider–outsider, moral–immoral divisions. These symbolic differences cannot be equated with the Western self–other division, given the strong repression of individual subjectivity in Chinese culture. The concept of *ren* conceives human subjectivity in terms of an interpersonal relationship that we have already described as that of a patron and client. In a sense, we could say that the Chinese subject is a relational subject implicated in a set of asymmetrical social relationships that make up the Chinese social formation. To be human is to be willing to accept one's social position as defined by a symbolic order that centers around *ren*. This relational conception of the Chinese subject means that a distinct self-identity, or an "I," is signifiable only in the process of symbolic exchange – making oneself dependable through the accumulation of what Bourdieu calls "symbolic capital," that is, through behavior in line with Chinese ethical values. Thus, the Chinese subject or subjectivity can be seen as an effect of the process of symbolic exchange realized in various Chinese discourses.

In the classical Chinese novel, for example, characterization is usually one-dimensional. That is, individual characters are represented by certain character traits, either positive or negative, and these characters often form pairs according to the bipolar structure of the narrative informed by the ancient yin–yang cosmological scheme. As C. T. Hsia[3] suggests, a specific character amounts to only a half-character, and it is only when different characters are combined that a single personality emerges. It seems to me that such a narrative convention is closely related to the suppression of individuality in Chinese culture. Insofar as narrative discourse also constructs a subject position, Chinese classical narrative cannot be seen simply as attempting to combine different character traits or stereotypes in order to constitute an "all-round" character with a "distinct" personality. This is because, governed by the yin–yang cosmological scheme, the narrative process relies heavily on the insider–outsider, moral–immoral divisions to create narrative conflict. The narrative function of the various one-dimensional characters is to provide a locus in which symbolic exchange can take place. Thus, interactions between characters that break the rule of reciprocity are assigned negative value and create the necessary disequilibrium or narrative conflict, while interactions that take place in accordance with the rule of reciprocity (which is the basis of the Chinese conception of being moral or human) are assigned positive value and become vital to the resolution of the narrative conflict and the introduction of a new equilibrium. The subject position of the Chinese narrative discourse is thus group-oriented and, in a sense, intersubjective.

This narrative pattern is widely adopted in Chinese film melodrama, in which the affirmation of group identity is reinforced by its peculiar cinematic structure. In his analysis of the formal system of classical Chinese cinema, Chris Berry points out that individual subjective point-of-view shots are usually subsumed by objective shots from an impersonal camera position that is not associated with any engendered character in the diegesis.[4] When such an association does occur, it functions only to signify moments of transgression, failure, and the collapse of harmony. This cinematic convention, as Berry argues, constitutes an important part of an "antiaesthetic." In addition to the use of such cinematic codes, the deployment of certain theatrical codes such as the spatial positioning of male and female characters on screen contributes to a strong suppression of individual subjectivity. By spatial positioning, I mean the use of the techniques of mis-en-scène to designate the spatial relationships among different characters, a device important to the construction of character identity and audience identification in classical Chinese cinema, and not unrelated to the stage conventions of Chinese classical theater.

Heavily influenced by the ancient Chinese yin–yang cosmology, the layout of the traditional Chinese stage is divided between yin and yang. Since the stage usually faces north, the east end of the stage is yang while the west end is yin. The male characters are positioned to the left of the female characters when facing the audience, so that the yin and yang of the actors and actresses form a balance with the yin and yang of the stage layout. From the point of view of the audience, the male characters appear to the right of the female characters. Together they form a combination of yin and yang. Thus, as in the classical Chinese novel, each character in essence amounts to only a half-character, and only when two characters converge spatially does a single personality emerge.

This stage convention is often adopted by Chinese filmmakers, especially those with a theatrical background, though the spatial positioning of the characters on screen is much more complex than on stage. It is not unusual for the right-hand side of the screen to be associated with yang/positive and the left-hand side to be yin/negative. Together, they form a balance according to Chinese cultural ideals. The male and female characters are spatially positioned either on the right-hand side of the screen or the left-hand side according to the positive or negative value of their function in the narrative and its process of symbolic exchange rather than according to mere gender differentiation, a point I shall elaborate on later. Here I would point out that such a valorization of screen space in accordance with yin–yang theory must also be considered in relation to changes in the Chinese melodramatic paradigm.

Changes in the Chinese Melodramatic Paradigm

Traditional Chinese melodramatic discourse is also informed by the yin–yang scheme. This can be clearly seen in the rather unique bipolar narrative structure of the traditional Chinese melodrama in its theatrical form, its concern with the transient nature of Chinese secular life, as well as its emphasis on didacticism. In traditional Chinese melodrama, narrative action, characterization, and setting are articulated in a series of binary oppositions. Narrative development takes place through the permutations of these terms. Consequently, the narrative interest focuses as much on human action as on nonaction (i.e., the complex familial and kinship relations in which the Chinese subject is constituted). These formal features are also present in the film melodrama of the People's Republic. Committed to implementing cultural and social change, the Chinese Communist Party and its cultural representatives have regarded melodrama as a major vehicle for disseminating and popularizing the dominant ideology of the new state as well as its policies. Traditional melodramatic conventions are thus utilized in film melodramas so that they can be enjoyed by the large, illiterate peasant populace.

However, these melodramatic conventions are usually infused with Communist ideology. Appropriating the Marxist concept of social transformation by means of class struggle, the melodramatic conflict in these films is articulated explicitly in terms of class difference. Traditional Chinese melodrama's emphasis on familial and kinship relationships and Confucian ethical codes is replaced by an emphasis on conflictual class relations, which are simplified and schematized in a Manichaean conflict between good and evil. The official version of the triumph of the Communists in China is often used as the ultimate rationale for the resolution of the conflict between good and evil. Thus, the film melodrama of the People's Republic becomes a powerful cultural means for the legitimation of the new sociopolitical order established in 1949.

As Judith Stacey has noted, this sociopolitical order is based on a combination of Confucian and Communist principles and therefore can best be described as "patriarchal socialism."[5] The social and political contradictions inherent in Chinese society under Communist rule are also reflected in the formal system of film melodrama. This is illustrated by the spatial codes according to which the female image is positioned on screen in relation to two melodramatic paradigms: the traditional one and a heavily politicized one. As I pointed out earlier, the spatial code of the right designates yang, which means masculinity/positivity/law/order, while that of the left denotes yin, which means femininity/negativity/lawlessness/disorder. The political melodramatic paradigm that evolved in the films of the People's Republic (especially in the films of the late 1960s and early 1970s) aims at reacting against and at the same time transforming these conventions. Thus, there is sometimes a reversal of the traditional spatial coding in order to signify the fundamental social transformation undertaken by the Chinese Communists in all areas of human life in what is called New China. For instance, as Gabriel notes,[6] the proletarian heroes in films made during the Cultural Revolution are usually positioned on the left in relation to the characters classified as belonging to the exploitive classes of the old China, who are usually on the right.

Gabriel's reading is confirmed by popular melodramatic film texts made before the Cultural Revolution, such as Xie Jin's *Two Stage Sisters* [*Wutai jiemei*,

1964], which offers a vivid account of changes in the life of Zhu Chunhua, a runaway child bride turned actress who suffers from sexual, economic, and political oppression in the old society and is made a cultural representative of the new sociopolitical order under Communist rule. In most dialogue scenes, Zhu Chunhua is positioned on the left-hand side of the screen. Since the narrative spans several decades, from the 1930s to the 1950s, in the first part of the film her positioning on the left signifies her social position in traditional Chinese society: the most oppressed and despised of all people, a child bride, and an opera actress. In the second part of the film, as she is influenced by Communist underground workers and becomes committed to fighting against her oppressors, her position on the left is assigned a positive value. Her life story on and off stage – her transformation from a member of the oppressed to a member of the liberating class – is reflected in the plays she enacts on stage: first, traditional operas such as *Liang Shanbo* and *Zhu Yingtai* and, then, new operas such as *Aunt Xianglin* [*Xianglin sao*] and *The White-Haired Girl* [*Baimao nü*]. The intertextuality of the film reflects changes not only in her position in Chinese society, but also in the melodramatic paradigms the film utilizes.

As a result of this unique political and ideological reappropriation and transformation of the Chinese melodramatic tradition, the individual film text is often an admixture of these two melodramatic paradigms, and gaps in the text are often covered up by positioning the female on the left. An examination of the cultural and political factors that contribute to the continued deployment of the female on the left is extremely illuminating. Culturally speaking, because the woman's position is lowest in traditional Chinese society, she has become a metonymic figure for other disadvantaged social groups. According to Communist logic, women and these other disadvantaged groups, the most oppressed in the old society, are the most revolutionary and, therefore, should be made the bearers of law and order of the New China. Thus, as the linchpin of the two different, yet interrelated melodramatic paradigms, the spatial positioning of the female often remains paradoxically unchanged. In this way, it functions as an anchor for the shifting relations of the old and the new orders and their respective representation in the melodramatic films of the People's Republic. Furthermore, the female image also signifies the fundamental social changes that the Communist revolution has brought about in contemporary Chinese society, since that image is the only reference point that can make discernible paradigmatic changes in both the melodramatic text and the social text. Ironically, the continuing spatial placement of the female on the left also embodies the female's ideological position in contemporary China: the fact that it is unchanged may indicate that women's social position has *not* changed greatly in its own terms, and that the much-publicized changes conferred upon them by the new patriarchal socialist order rely on repression and appropriation of the female image for specific political ends. Esther Yau, in her discussion of the peculiar cinematic representation of the female, emphasizes the heavy masculinization of the female in militaristic terms, which reaches hyperbolical proportions in films made during the Cultural Revolution.[7]

The Chinese film melodrama underwent further changes in what is now called the "new period," when a new leadership headed by Deng Xiaoping negated the Maoist excesses of the preceding period and initiated the modernization program. Under the imperatives of the new Party propaganda apparatus, there was a shift in the delicate intertextual relationship between the two dominant Chinese melodramatic paradigms. Informed by ancient Chinese cosmology, the traditional melodramatic paradigm was reappropriated as an integral part of a humanist discourse that critiques the excessive political repression of the Mao era and, as well, those cultural practices that formulate the melodramatic paradigm as overtly political. Typical examples are those film melodramas about the Cultural Revolution that, as I have pointed out elsewhere, reacted against the overpoliticization of the film medium in the Mao period. By deploying what I call "naturalization" and "inversion" codes, which invariably reaffirm traditional Chinese cultural and family values, these films' critique of "the political practices of the Cultural Revolution is based on a firm belief in the natural order of things and their inversion during that period."[8]

In films made during the new period, masculinized female figures are symbols of political and sexual repression, while an extremely feminized treatment of both male and female characters represents the disadvantaged parties under the old regime of Mao and becomes predominant. With changes in the Party's policy toward economic development that advocated a mixture of central planning and market economy, the latter of which was playing an increasingly active role, representation of the female in the film melodramas of the mid-1980s was burdened with the task of advocating a new economic policy that was very much an imitation of the Western capitalist model and negating past political practices. In this new propaganda task, the representation of the female drew heavily on the maternal figure in the traditional melodrama with its symbolic meanings of productivity and sacrifice.[9]

Although the Chinese melodramatic narrative facilitates the construction of a subjectivity that can be best described as intersubjectivity, it is patriarchal and contradictory by nature. In Western psychoanalytic terms, the Chinese subject can be described as incomplete, in that it often regresses to the "oral stage." Fixation at the oral stage makes the Chinese subject particularly dependent on parental figures for moral guidance and emotional support. In social terms, however, the Chinese patriarchal subject could also be described as very good at manipulating the complex and sometimes contradictory social relations in which he is implicated in order to advance personal interest. The contradictions inherent in this subject often become obvious in times of social and ideological crises, such as those we have witnessed in the new period.

The shifting social relations in China of the 1980s, and to some extent the shifting relations between China and the rest of the world, had a great impact on the Chinese subject, often resulting in identity problems that are reflected in various kinds of Chinese discourse. For instance, in the critical discourse of the new period (a discourse heavily influenced by the introduction of Western ideas), there is an unusual obsession with issues of sexuality (Who is Freud and what has he to say about sexuality?), gender differences (What should we do to create masculinity on screen?), and cultural and political differences (What does it mean to be Chinese? Why has socialism failed to produce the economic miracles enjoyed by Hong Kong and Taiwan?). These concerns are particularly reflected in Xie Jin's melodramatic films of this period.

Spatial Dislocation and Female Subjectivity in *The Legend of Tianyun Mountain*

In what follows I focus on the melodramatic films made by Xie Jin in the new period to illustrate many of the points I have made so far. In a sense, *The Legend of Tianyun Mountain* [*Tianyunshan chuanqi,* 1980], the first of these films, ushered in the new changes in Chinese politics by strongly denouncing past Party malpractices and, especially, the repressive, regressive nature of Maoism. The film tackled the sensitive issue of the vindication of the so-called rightists in the late 1970s, a vindication that partially prepared the way for the new Party leadership, headed by Deng Xiaoping. The film features three female narrative voices and points of view interwoven to construct stories about a male character who has been wrongly accused of being a rightist and counterrevolutionary in a series of political movements from the Anti-Rightist Campaign of 1957 to the Cultural Revolution. Manifested in various degrees of knowledge and communicativeness and in differences in narrative temporality and spatiality, the film's complex construction of an overarching female subjectivity utilizes insider–outsider, moral–immoral divisions to subsume political and gender differences. For that matter, the film's overarching female subjectivity is, strictly speaking, not female, for it amounts to a panoramic reconstruction of the social history of the People's Republic in its first three decades of existence. The use of three different female narrative voices can thus be seen as an attempt to subsume the viewpoints of people of different social statuses and political backgrounds who suffered during that turbulent period. Furthermore, insofar as this complex "female" subjectivity is constructed in the service of a strong critique of the excesses of Maoism in the preceding period, it is heavily informed by the dominant ideologies of the new period. Patriarchal accommodation of this female subjectivity in *The Legend of Tianyun Mountain* is evidenced by the fact that, at the cinematic level, the three female narrative voices form a hierarchy that is to some extent overdetermined by the traditional codes of Chinese familial practice as well as by political codes evolved in the Mao period.

The three female voices are those of Song Wei, Zhou Yuzhen, and Feng Qinglan. The voice of Song, wife of a senior Party official and mother of a son, is the most dominant one, since it frames the narrative – and thus the other two voices. Song's voice, however, is also ironized by Xie Jin in that it is undercut by her contradictory position in the Chinese family system: a maternal figure who has finally been recognized as an insider and has attained a certain power, yet is still under the tight control of the patriarch. For instance, in her voice-over narration in the opening scene, Song introduces herself as the newly appointed deputy director in charge of Party personnel in the immediate post-Mao period and as eager to correct the Party's past. But her authoritative voice here is already undercut by the visuals: when she sits down behind her desk (which is stacked with urgent cases to review), she casts her glance to the right, which locates us in the next shot at an empty desk belonging to her husband, who is the real boss in the Party office. She is unable to start her work because her husband is on sick leave in the south. This social dependency is accentuated in the following domestic scene, which shows that Song is totally dominated by Wu. Like other Chinese family melodramas, the film uses a wedding photo as a signifier of a cultural or political ideal toward which the characters aspire socially. Indeed, the film opens with a shot of a wedding photo on the wall in which Wu is positioned frame right and Song frame left. The camera then zooms out to reveal the setting of the room and shows Song (who initially occupies screen left and gradually moves toward the right) reading a letter from Wu in which he admonishes her to wait for his return and direction.

The voice of Zhou calling from outside the house introduces us to the second female narrative voice, which is subordinate to Song's but without the irony associated with hers. This is because, as a young daughter, Zhou still has the full potential to become an insider through marriage and to produce a son and, as the offspring of a revolutionary martyr, she also has the background necessary to be classified as a leftist. The positive value attributed to her voice is first indicated by Song's glance screen left from her room window and by Zhou's reddish clothing. In a flashback sequence embedded in this domestic scene, Zhou introduces the male protagonist of the film, Luo, an upright man wrongly accused in the Anti-Rightist Campaign, and his wife, Feng. The positive value of Zhou's voice is reinforced by the role she plays: while narrating, she is figured as a reporter taking photos of Luo. In Zhou's flashback, Feng, the third female narrative voice, first appears merely as an object of representation and she remains so until quite late in the film. Her position in the hierarchy of film narration corresponds to her position in the traditional Chinese family: she is married to someone who has been politically classified as an outsider and she has failed to produce an heir.

With Zhou's narration, a bipolar narrative structure is introduced. First of all, there is a rearticulation of public and domestic space that not only accentuates the irony already implicit in Song's narration, but also constitutes a renegotiation with the political establishment of China under Mao. In contrast to the Party office scene, where people are busy doing nothing while the absent Party boss

Wu is busy giving wrong orders in Song's narration, Zhou's flashback starts on
an open country road where Luo, down and out, is engaged in heavy manual
labor and is respected and supported by the local peasants. The contrast of
domestic scenes is even sharper due to an ironic deployment of the political
coding of Maoist cultural practice. A symbol of his power and authority, Wu's
posh residence is contrasted with the shabby village hut that shelters Luo, who
has already been shown to be regarded as a worthy leader by the peasants despite
his infamous label as a rightist. Like this political coding of the two domestic
scenes, cultural coding also foregrounds ironic contrast. In Song's narration,
although the wedding photo as a symbol of the ideal family order still dominates
the domestic space, the breakdown of this order is apparent in that Song is alone
in the house. In Zhou's flashback, the photo that organizes domestic space in the
country scene does not represent the traditional family ideal, for it is a self-
portrait of Luo in his youth before his marriage. Nonetheless, the narrative
signifies a harmonious relationship between Luo, his wife Feng, and their
adopted daughter dining together with Zhou in their hut. Within this bipolar
structure, the melodramatic conflict is intertwined in a complex play between the
two contradictory, yet complementary melodramatic paradigms discussed earlier.

Traditional melodramatic conventions abound in Song's rather colorful memory of her experience in the 1950s, a memory triggered by Zhou's account of her
meeting with Luo and Feng in the country. Here another irony associated with
her narration is highlighted. As an authoritative narrative agent, Song is somewhat masculinized, yet her objectified representation is extremely feminized.
She is portrayed as an object of desire of the two main male characters, Wu and
Luo, in a scenario that dramatizes a triangular love affair. It is interesting that,
despite their difference in age, both male characters represent the Party leadership in an exploration team to which the female characters have just been re-
cruited. However, some crucial differences between the two are already apparent. Of peasant origin, Wu is a conservative cadre and is repressive in his
dealings with the team members, maintaining sexual as well as political segrega-
tion whenever he can. Luo, who comes to replace him, is an open-minded and
learned young man who associates with the women and the intellectuals whom
Wu despises. Because of Luo's new leadership style (which makes reference to
the Liu Shaoqi faction within the Party leadership of the 1950s and early 1960s,
many of them Soviet trained), the team is able to do some productive work in
exploring the region of Tianyun Mountain for mining possibilities. In this representation of Luo, political relaxation and economic productivity are matched by a
narrative emphasis on male virility. When Luo first appears, he is mistaken for a
game hunter with a gun in hand. And it is quite natural that he soon wins the
heart of Song, the most beautiful woman on the team.

Here the bipolar narrative structure enables the film to inscribe the complex
internal conflict within the Communist Party in the late 1950s and early 1960s.

Since this political scenario is interlaced with that of a love triangle related from Song's perspective, there is a foregrounding of the sexual rivalry between the two men. Criticism of past Party excesses during the Anti-Rightist Campaign in which Wu accuses Luo of being a rightist for associating with intellectuals (who are usually associated with Western individualism) and women (whose sexuality is always regarded as a threat to the patriarchal authority and law the Party represents) is by and large explained in terms of the rivalry between the two men over a woman. What Wu cannot win through love he wins through political power. By branding Luo a rightist, he forces Song to break with Luo. And then he asks his Party boss to arrange his own marriage to her.

Such a narrative strategy is characteristic of Chinese film melodrama of the new period. Although, at the diagetic level, the film constitutes a strong criticism of past Party practices by tracing the roots of its political repression to traditional Chinese culture, this criticism is itself informed by the traditional cultural discourse at the representational level. For instance, as far as the narrative strategy is concerned, aside from foregrounding the triangular love affair, Song's narration overdramatizes traditional Chinese melodramatic conflict between personal desire and obligation to the family or the Party. This contradiction is to some extent mediated by the less visible narration associated with Feng, who is noted primarily by her absence. Her narration starts when Song begins to read her letter and an image of a timid, bespectacled, and rather homely girl is superimposed over the letter on the screen. The fact that her narration exists in the form of this voice-over confirms that, rhetorically, she has the least authority in the film narration.

Although Feng's voice is not dominant, hers is the most effective one in the text. The effect generated by her account, which is already enhanced by her physical absence, derives further strength from the film's representational level. This is because her account is an appeal for social and moral justice, and relies heavily on the moral values of the audience. Furthermore, although it is she who suffers most, this appeal is not made in her own interest but, rather, in the interest of someone else. Feng's narration is also marked by a complex play in spatial terms between the two melodramatic paradigms. Between the shots that show Song in her spacious and well-decorated lounge reading the letter with Feng's voice-over narration, there is a medium shot that shows Feng at the desk writing the letter of appeal, and her glance frame left motivates the camera to track leftward to Luo, who sits at an empty table on screen left. This shot both parallels and contrasts with Song's glance right at the beginning of the film and signifies the reversal of gender and political roles. In Song's previous flashback, Luo is a masculine figure (a hunter with a gun) and is placed right of Song and Feng in their initial encounter. Thus, the reversal of roles in Feng's narration shows the result of a process of emasculation caused by the political and sexual repression of the Mao era. In regard to Luo's political disfavor, however, this relocation of his spatial positioning also implies that he is politically correct (being a leftist) according to the political codes used to emasculate him.

Luo could be seen as a representative of the new Party leadership that assumed power in 1979. Thus, this ironic deployment of the political paradigm of Maoist cultural practice is double-edged in that it also reveals the ambiguities and contradictions characteristic of the new political order under Deng: on the one hand, strong criticism of Maoist practices and, on the other, an insistence on the Four Cardinal Principles, which use Mao Zedong's thought as the major criterion for defining counterrevolutionary activity in China.

In *The Legend of Tianyun Mountain,* the contradictions inherent in the new order are mediated by a constant process of spatial relocation or even dislocation of the female characters. This dislocation is clearly seen by the fact that in order to position Luo on screen left to show that he is a "real" leftist and the accusations against him are wrong, the female character Feng has to be positioned on screen right, although Feng in her association with Luo could not be branded a rightist. This contradiction results in a constant relocation of her spatial position in the narrative: it gives Feng a position of authority and then challenges that authority and reveals its arbitrary nature. This is evident in Feng's dialogue with a fellow worker who is secretly in love with her (Feng's narrative, like Song's, contains a love triangle, but it contrasts sharply with Song's). In this sense, Feng occupies screen right as she repeats aloud all the charges Wu has made against Luo only to point out their absurdity. Later, however, when she encounters Wu at the construction site of a reservoir dam, and is warned not to side with Luo, her spatial position changes to screen left in relation to Wu.

After the dialogue with her fellow worker and suitor, Feng enters Luo's office. In this and subsequent scenes, she and Luo constantly change screen positions. Each change on Feng's part signifies a change in Luo's political and personal life. In the office scene, Luo first appears screen right because he has not yet been removed from his post, although he has already been accused of being a rightist. When he enumerates the absurd political charges against him with great indignation, he gradually moves from right to left. When the narrative shifts its attention to Luo's affair with Song, he is shown moving to the right again. Irony abounds in this movement. He occupies the right/masculine position once again only to allow Feng to see and read Song's letter of renunciation of his "rightist" behavior and her decision under Wu's pressure to break up with him. Here, the political accusation and his emotional loss totally emasculate Luo. The scene ends with a medium close-up of Feng on the right and Luo on the left.

This significant relocation prepares for the active and, at the same time, transgressive role Feng will play against the advice of Feng's suitor and warnings from Wu. When Luo is exiled to a remote village to undertake labor reform, she pays him an unexpected visit. Her courageous act, which transgresses both political and gender norms, is also signified in spatial terms. When she calls out to Luo, who is buried in his notebook, she is shown to the right of him. Thus, her transgression in gender terms allows a temporary restoration of Luo's political status as a leftist. However, Feng voluntarily moves to screen left and allows

Luo, who has gone offscreen to get a stool for her to sit on, to assume the right-hand position. When they move into his hut, the pattern is repeated again as Feng, in her active role of establishing a sexual and political union with Luo, changes her spatial relationship to him by employing Xie Jin's codes of spatiality.

This rearticulation of the spatial codes in Feng's narration in accordance with the dominant cultural and political paradigms is significant in that it inadvertently reveals the arbitrary nature of the moral edifice on which the social and political institutions of the People's Republic are based. As I have pointed out elsewhere, moral issues in Chinese melodrama are profoundly concerned with power and politics.[10] Perhaps more than any other of Xie Jin's films, *The Legend of Tianyun Mountain* demonstrates this to an extreme extent. Wu and his associates rely heavily on the established ethical-political principles of Maoism to identify Luo's deviation and to expel him from the insider group. Feng's narration, however, negotiates these ethical-political principles in order to redefine the insider–outsider division and hence reverse the power relations between Wu and Luo as representatives of two different social and political forces. Although this negotiation amounts to a radical modification of the ethical principle, it operates nonetheless within the moral framework of the social and political institutions of the People's Republic.

As representatives of the disadvantaged in the existing Maoist power structure, both Luo and Feng resort to emotional expression to assert their moral soundness and their claim to power. Effective melodramatic mechanisms such as misrecognition and misunderstanding abound in Feng's narration, which generates an emotional instability in the viewer that needs to be redressed. The constant changes in the spatial positions of the characters function here to highlight this emotional instability as well as to punctuate the moments of pathos in the couple's encounter. Although Feng's love for Luo in his most difficult moment might convince the viewer of his innocence, this expression of love alone cannot change the situation, since Feng herself is already classified as an outsider because of her transgressive behavior. Thus, a convention of traditional Chinese melodrama, that of the Mandate of Heaven (which is the chief means for the imperial system of China to legitimate itself),[11] is evoked in her narration. In a thunderstorm scene, Wu (who has been promoted because of his active role in the Anti-Rightist Campaign) is now engaged in the Great Leap Forward – a typical example of the voluntarist and adventurist tendencies of Maoism in its heyday. Ignoring the advice of scientists and technicians because of an inherent distrust of "bourgeois intellectuals," Wu orders the completion of a reservoir dam ahead of schedule, mustering all the manpower he can command, including those involved in labor reform. A storm hits the area, destroys the hastily built dam, and floods the region – causing great property damage and loss of human lives. The natural elements in the Chinese heavenly order illustrate the illegitimacy of the political order under Wu (a figurative representative of the old

Party patriarch Mao). Wu loses not only human support for his policies, but support from the "harmonious" natural order as well.

Feng's narration also contains a sharp critique of Song, who in her blindness and weakness has aligned herself with the repressive Party patriarch. After the flood scene, the camera cuts back to a shot of Song reading the letter, obviously shaken by Feng's story. Here the narrative moves into the domestic realm again. In Feng's continuing narration, we learn that she is a very broad-minded woman who tries in vain to bring Song and her lover Luo back together by paying Song a visit and making a case for Luo. Here her narrative foregrounds another contrast with Song's previous narrative. In Song's masculinized narration, there is an extremely feminized image of Song: in this love triangle, she is shown as a weak young woman who finally succumbs to the pressure exerted by Wu in the name of the Party and the revolution. In Feng's feminized narration, Feng is masculinized. She proposes to Luo on his sickbed, puts him on a cart, and pulls the cart herself in a snowstorm to her hut, where they wed. Although Feng cannot have a child of her own, she manages to adopt the daughter of another political outsider who has drowned in the flood. As the narrative unfolds, Feng attains more and more positive value as a character and narrator, while Song's value decreases. This shift at the level of film narration is significant in that it is instrumental in constructing a position for the viewing subject in accord with the dominant ideology of the period.

"Coherent" Social Subject in Social and Ideological Crises

Although in his second film of the new period, *The Herdsman* [*Mumaren,* 1982], Xie Jin continued to explore the tensions between the two dominant melodramatic paradigms in spatial terms, the new social and political problems that beset the Deng leadership in this period forced him into new territory. The ideology of patriotism, for example, is used in *The Herdsman* to mediate various social contradictions. As well, Xie Jin adds an international touch to the insider–outsider, moral–immoral division by exploring the dilemma faced by a rehabilitated "rightist," Xiu: whether he should join his alienated father, who runs a corporation in the United States, or remain in China with his faithful peasant wife and child, who have given him great emotional and moral support in the past when he was branded a rightist (Figure 1). This dilemma is worth dramatizing because changes in social relations in China during the new period (reflected in the film by a reversal of the insider–outsider and moral–immoral divisions) result in China's changed relationship with the West. An evocation of the theme of patriotism finally resolves this dilemma.

Like *The Legend of Tianyun Mountain,* the resolution of the initial conflict in *The Herdsman* depends on Xie Jin's play with the ambiguities inherent in these divisions. Returning from abroad with a sense of loss and remorse, the father is an insider according to Chinese familial codes. However, insofar as he has

1. The herdsman and his family. Xie Jin, *The Herdsman* (1982). CHINA FILM
IMPORT AND EXPORT CORPORATION, LOS ANGELES.

foreign allegiances and intends to take his son away with him, he remains an
outsider according to Chinese political codes. This ambiguity is represented in
spatial terms in the dialogue scenes in Beijing where father and son meet for the
first time in more than thirty years. The two reaffirm their close kinship relations,
but still differ in political terms. Initially, the father is positioned on screen right,
which is consistent with both the cultural and the political codes I have identified.
In the next shot, however, father and son change screen positions, with Xu, the
son, now on screen right. In a sense, this repositioning alludes to the political
accusations against Xu; at this point, the narrative is explicitly focused on the
father's concerns for his son, whom he asks to stand up and walk a few paces to
show that he has not been crippled during the political persecution he suffered.
When they both sit down again, they resume the "normal" position – the father
right and the son left – and this position is reaffirmed as "natural" by a series of
family photos the father has brought with him.

As the narrative unfolds, the spatial relations change again. The family photos
bring back bad memories for Xu, who was deserted by his father when the latter
broke with his mother and left for the United States on the eve of Liberation. To

avoid embarrassment and to show that he has changed politically, the father is situated in a left-hand position as he quotes a popular Party slogan, "Looking Forward to a Bright Future." When the father makes clear his intention to take Xu back with him to the West, however, the spatial position changes yet again, and the political difference between the father and son is highlighted in a series of verbal exchanges that even include a discussion of Western Marxism. When, in order to persuade Xiu to come with him, the father resorts to emotional appeals and expresses his need to have a son near him in his old age, Xu is given the powerful position of screen right, in accordance with cultural codes. Here the contradiction between the implications of the cultural and political codes in spatial terms is resolved by showing the father, who is on screen left, walk out of the hotel room to the balcony outside. With this spatial change, a clear insider–outsider division is established as the son remains inside the room, adamant about his decision to stay and remain loyal to the "socialist" motherland.

Xu's loyalty can be explained in psychoanalytic terms. Like *The Legend of Tianyun Mountain* in which the deployment of a complex female subjectivity is matched by a masochistic narrative scenario, *The Herdsman* also features a masochistic scenario, but one matched by a feminized male narrative subjectivity. That is, the film foregrounds Xu's identification with the maternal, the symbol of domesticity, land of one's birth, productivity, and plenitude (Figure 2). This negative Oedipal scenario, like that in *The Legend of Tianyun Mountain*, can also be analyzed in spatial terms. Between the father–son dialogue scenes set in Beijing, there is a flashback narrated by Xu and set in the country, showing his parting with Xiuzhi, his wife, and illustrating why he decides to remain in China. This flashback scene begins with a shot of Xu, Xiuzhi, and their son traveling in a horse cart on their way to the bus station, a shot in which Xu is positioned screen right. However, as Xu boards the bus and his wife gives him money, food, and a warm, emotional goodbye, he is positioned screen left of her. This change in the spatial positioning of the male and female characters signifies the dual role played by Xiuzhi: as an obedient wife and as an authoritative and demanding mother.

In psychoanalytic terms, this contradictory representation of the female can be seen as a projection of the psychic needs of the male Chinese subject. But in this particular film, as in other melodramatic films by Xie Jin, including *The Legend of Tianyun Mountain*, it can also be seen as a projection of the political needs of the Chinese patriarchal social subject. The need for the new Party leadership to distance itself from Party practices of the past calls for strong criticism of those practices. And as pointed out earlier, this criticism depends on a reaffirmation of traditional Chinese family and cultural values. The reconstruction of an ideal Chinese family and social order, however, requires that women and members of other disadvantaged social groups willingly assume the subordinate role. Thus, in the post-Mao melodramas, masculinized female figures in dominant social positions are usually negatively represented as symbols of political (or even

2. The herdsman. Xie Jin, *The Herdsman* (1982). CHINA FILM IMPORT AND
EXPORT CORPORATION, LOS ANGELES

sexual) repression. However, the new leadership's insistence on Communist
principles as guidelines in a period during which the people's faith in Communism was fading also generated the need to reenergize those principles with the
ideology of patriotism. The valorization of the maternal figure in the Chinese
film melodrama of the new period meets this ideological demand. The ideological contradiction results in a parallel contradictory figurative articulation of the
female characters in Xie Jin's films.

The theme of patriotism also runs through his next two films: *Qiu Jin: A
Woman Revolutionary* [*Qiu Jin*, 1983] and *Wreaths at the Foot of the Mountain*
[*Gaoshanxia de huahuan*, 1984]. Like *The Herdsman*, both lend an ironic twist
to the insider–outsider, moral–immoral divisions so that a new cultural and
political identity can be established in the times of cultural, social, and ideological crisis experienced by the Chinese patriarchal social subject. Set around the
1911 Revolution, which ended the Qing dynasty and Manchu rule in China, *Qiu
Jin* is based on the biography of a woman martyr who, at the turn of the century,
broke away from her feudal family and sailed alone to Japan to study. Exposed to
Western democratic ideas, she joined the Chinese Democratic League headed by

Dr. Sun Yat-sen (Sun Zhongshan) and returned to China to engage in revolutionary activities. After a failed coup, she was arrested and executed by Qing dynasty officials. The melodrama in this film plays with defining and redefining the insider–outsider, moral–immoral divisions. Subscription to the reform and modernization program initiated by Deng is now the main criterion for establishing the status of political insider.

The narrative of *Qiu Jin* concentrates on the emotional life of a supposed outsider (woman, divorcée, expatriate, and rebel leader), but this emphasis also enables the viewer to see her as a warm human being (possessing *ren* values of friendship, generosity, honor, and patriotism), acting upon a clearly defined ethical-political principle (reformation of the established Chinese social and cultural institutions through Western learning). The emotional appeal of the melodrama has much to do with this play on the ambiguities of what constitutes an insider in cultural, political, and gender terms. Insofar as they subscribed to Confucianism and sought to preserve it, the Manchu rulers of Qing China were more Chinese than those Chinese who advocated learning from the West. But their closed-door policy also turned China into a weak nation on the verge of extinction. Indeed, this historical melodrama can be seen as a displacement of the ongoing debate on reform in China in the early 1980s. And Xie Jin's play with the insider–outsider division provided Chinese viewers with a cognitive scheme that enabled them to categorize the different factions of the new leadership under Deng – as conservatives who preferred to stick to the Maoist practices of the previous period or as radicals who advocated a total overhaul of Chinese social, political, and economic institutions.

Wreaths at the Foot of the Mountain is set during the Sino-Vietnam border war of 1979. With the readjustment of China's relationship to the West came a reversal of its relationship with former allies, including Vietnam. In this film, the enemy is never shown. What the viewer is allowed to see is the pain inflicted by the enemy in terms of loss of property and human lives. This exclusion is understandable, since any realist screen representation of the Vietnamese would make the insider–outsider, moral–immoral, and human–nonhuman divisions less tenable, especially if the outsider were a "brother in the socialist big family" and a former "comrade-in-arms." The absence of an outsider forces the film to concentrate on complex interpersonal relationships among the insiders, relationships that were very problematic in the social context of China in the late 1970s. The rift between the Party leadership and the masses was so great that a new consensus ideology had to be created to mediate the conflictual relationships between the leaders and the led. Thus, the creation of a new outsider was crucial to the dissemination of the ideology of patriotism, which is no more than a means of binding insiders together despite their class and gender differences.

As pointed out earlier, the power relationships among insiders are governed by symbolic violence – the use of ethical-political principles, especially codes of honor, generosity, and unselfishness – and hence are characterized by personal bondage and dependency. The bipolar structure of *Wreaths at the Foot of the Mountain* focuses on the soldiers and officers of a company in the Chinese People's Liberation Army, who are all of peasant origin, and the company's political instructor, who is the son of a high official (a woman) in Beijing. The spirit of self-sacrifice embodied by the soldiers and officers causes a great change in the personality of the political instructor and turns him into a worthy army officer. Unlike Xie Jin's previous films, this film, informed by the traditional Chinese cultural discourse, brings into play the traditional melodramatic paradigm. For example, a major melodramatic convention of the film is the conflict between political loyalty to the Party and the state (answering the call and going to war), and filial piety (trying to stay alive and support one's family). The peasant soldiers choose the former, while the political instructor and his mother choose the latter. The sacrifices made by the soldiers (one of them dies in order to save the political instructor's life) are overshadowed by the sacrifices made by their families: peasant mothers or grandmothers encouraged their sons to join the Communist rebel forces in the pre-Liberation years and are now sacrificing their grandsons. Here, the already disadvantaged constitute the insider group. In debt and enduring living conditions that have not improved greatly

3. Army comrades: the officer (left) and the political instructor (right). Xie Jin, *Wreaths at the Foot of the Mountain* (1984). CHINA FILM IMPORT AND EXPORT CORPORATION, LOS ANGELES

since the Liberation, it is the peasants who are made the bearers of the ethical-political principles on which the new sociopolitical order is built, rather than the other way round. Indeed, this reversal contributes greatly to the pathos of the film.

In *Hibiscus Town* [*Furongzhen*, 1986], the last of Xie Jin's films made during the new period, the deployment of a female figure as a symbol of maternity and the locus of audience identification is loaded with new ideological meaning given the culture's shift to emphasis on economic development. While *The Legend of Tianyun Mountain* highlighted past excesses of the Party patriarchy by tackling the sensitive issue of the vindication of so-called rightists in the late 1970s, which in a sense prepared the way for the new Party leadership headed by Deng, *Hibiscus Town* focuses on economic matters to show how productive the rightist Party policy could have been and will be when it is vindicated. The shift in the Party's policy toward economic development results in a representation of the female protagonist Hu Yuyin as a symbol of fertility and productivity. She, like the male characters of Luo in *The Legend of Tianyun Mountain* and Xu in *The Herdsman*, is branded a negative figure in former political campaigns. The repressive nature of Maoism in its heyday is highlighted by the fact that, as a symbol of maternity, she is politically deprived of her "naturally endowed" role in the arena of material production and human reproduction – a role, as we know, that was assigned exclusively to women and members of other disadvantaged classes (including, to some extent, the merchant class in traditional Chinese culture). At the end of the narrative, her innocence is vindicated by the logic of the dominant ideology of the new period, which valorizes both humanistic emotionalism and material productivity.

It should be noted that the female figures in *Hibiscus Town* are polarized: the virtuous maternal figure of Hu Yuyin is opposed by Li Guoxiang, a politician who remains single throughout the film and is busily engaged in political and sexual prostitution. Along with being a real outsider/immoral person because of her association with past Maoist practices, Party Secretary Li is represented in negative terms as unproductive both materially and biologically.

In *Hibiscus Town*, the spatial coding of male and female characters is as complex as that of *The Legend of Tianyun Mountain*. But I will limit my comparison to the closing sequences of these films. In *The Legend of Tianyun Mountain*, after Song is hit by her husband Wu, she divorces him and goes back to the Tianyun Mountain in the hope of meeting Luo, her former lover. When she finds Luo at Feng's grave, she hides behind a tree. Her glance screen right motivates a pan shot in which the camera's slow movement leftward matches Luo's leftward movement from his initial position on screen right. He passes Song, who is positioned perpendicular to the axis of the camera (a position that alludes to her compromised political position) and he moves further left to exit frame left. In a sense, this shot epitomizes the changes in the political position of the male protagonist Luo and the social and political forces he represents. It is obvious that screen left is still the location of positive values in the film. This is manifest in the next shot, which shows Song pining for Luo as she casts her glance leftward in his direction. Insofar as these three shots are organized from Song's point of view (which is the dominant narrative agency), the waning value of her narration is significant. It is marked by a deep sense of loss and loneliness. Song's point of view and the place of the viewing subject associated with it generate a desire to establish a firm identification with what Song loses and desires: Luo as the new Party patriarch. The last shot partially fulfills this desire: taken from the position of one of Luo's followers, it shows Luo and others overlooking the landscape of the Tianyun Mountain, envisioning a bright future when his development plan (abandoned when he was named a rightist) material-izes.

Such an optimistic ending is lacking in *Hibiscus Town*. There is a significant change in the spatial positioning of the characters. The turning point of the film is the moment when, after the arrest of her rightist husband, the pregnant female protagonist Hu collapses and the army doctors and nurses rescue her and her premature child. Out of gratitude, she names her newborn son Jun (Army). The social context alluded to in the rescue sequence is the military coup that ended the reign of the Gang of Four, the followers of Mao, immediately after his death. In the following sequence, we see that Hu is rehabilitated, and upon her request, her husband Qin is released from prison.

On his way back home, Qin encounters his former persecutor, Secretary Li, on a ferry. Throughout this sequence, as the rehabilitated Qin converses with Li, he is positioned screen right of her. The only exception occurs after an ironic exchange between the two. When Li senses Qin's sarcastic tone, she reminds him that it was she who signed the rehabilitation papers. Qin simply replies that she had to do it. In the next shot, the camera crosses the 180-degree axis so that their screen positions reverse. It is interesting that this is the only shot in the sequence in which Li is positioned screen right, and it is exactly at this moment that the chauffeur calls out to ask Li to get into her car. After this brief cut across the 180-degree axis, both Qin and Li resume their previous screen positions: Li on the left and Qin on the right.

The sequence ends when, before she steps into her car, Qin advises Li to get married and raise a family, like himself and other ordinary people, and not seek to destroy the normal, happy lives of others. Here, it seems to me, screen right is given positive value in relation to Chinese cultural codes. The fact that Li is given such a position in the single cut across the 180-degree line suggests, however, that Maoist persecutors are still in possession of political power. The danger they pose is accentuated in the closing scenes of the film. Following the ferry sequence is a moving account of Qin's reunion with Hu, which ends with a shot in which Qin occupies the frame's central position flanked by Hu, the enterprising businesswoman on his right, and by Jun, his son named after the army, on his left. The allegorical meaning of this shot is obvious.

When Hu's private family business again thrives in the new period with Qin's assistance and guidance, we see Wang (a former poor peasant who was promoted by Li to a leading position during the Cultural Revolution but who later lost that position and became mentally ill) disrupt the couple's business by hitting a gong and crying, "A new political movement will start again!" Qin advises Hu to offer Wang two bowls of the famous bean curd that is their specialty. He says to his customers and friends that there might be some truth in Wang's crazy prophecy and warns them to be on the alert. When given the bean curd, Wang snatches the cigarette Qin is smoking, takes a drag and blows the smoke in Qin's face, then hits the gong again and cries, "Another movement!" walking first toward frame left and then toward frame right. The next shot shows Wang crying and disappearing toward the far end of the street, which extends toward frame left. The shot, however, does not constitute sympathy for the pathetic Wang. His response to Qin's offer of food is nonreciprocal; the camera firmly situates him in the category of outsider/immoral one. Furthermore, this shot is presumably taken from the point of view of those who suffered from such political movements in the past, for what follows and ends the film is a series of shots of people looking and thinking: first a shot of Gu, the present Party secretary of the township, who remains single because he was disabled during the war, then one of a couple who suffered because of their association with Hu, and finally a shot of Qin flanked by Hu on the right and his son on the left.

It seems to me that the construction of the final shots of *Hibiscus Town,* like those in *The Legend of Tianyun Mountain,* situates the viewing subject in a locus of movement from an individual subjective point of view to an intersubjective point of view whose origin can be traced to the Chinese symbolic order. This position of the viewing subject is patriarchal in that it is a textualization of the hierarchical social and family relations that make up the Chinese sociopolitical order. In sum, as I have argued and illustrated through the films of Xie Jin, the melodramatic discourse's construction of a coherent patriarchal viewing subject relies heavily on the textual relocation or even dislocation of the female characters and members of other disadvantaged social groups.

NOTES

1. See Chris Berry, "China's New 'Women's Cinema,'" *Camera Obscura,* no. 18 (September 1988), pp. 8–41.

2. Pierre Bourdieu, *Outline of a Theory of Practice* (Cambridge: Cambridge University Press, 1977).

3. C. T. Hsia, *The Classical Chinese Novel* (New York: Columbia University Press, 1974).

4. Chris Berry, "Sexual Difference and the Viewing Subject in *Li Shuangshuang* and *The In-Laws,* in Chris Berry, ed., *Perspectives on Chinese Cinema* (Ithaca, N.Y.: Cornell University East Asia Papers, no. 39, 1985), pp. 32–47.

5. Judith Stacey, *Patriarchy and Socialist Revolution in China* (Berkeley and Los Angeles: University of California Press, 1983).

6. Teshome Gabriel, *The Third Cinema in the Third World* (Ann Arbor: University of Michigan Press, 1982).

7. Esther Yau, "Cultural and Economic Dislocations: Filmic Phantasies of Chinese Women in the 1980s," *Wide Angle,* 11, no. 2 (Spring 1989), pp. 6–21.

8. Ma Ning, "Notes on the New Filmmakers," in George Semsel, ed., *Chinese Film: The State of the Art in the People's Republic* (New York: Praeger, 1987), pp. 63–93.

9. Ma Ning, "Symbolic Representation and Symbolic Violence: Chinese Family Melodrama of the Early 1980s," *East–West Film Journal,* 4, no. 1 (December 1989), pp. 79–109.

10. Ibid.

11. Sun Longji, *Zhongguo wenhua de shenceng jiegou* [The Deep Structure of Chinese Culture] (Xianggang: Jixian she, 1983).

2

SOCIETY AND SUBJECTIVITY

ON THE POLITICAL ECONOMY OF CHINESE MELODRAMA

Nick Browne

A study of filmmaking in the People's Republic of China will, almost inevitably, take as its starting point the relation of the character ("the self") to the social space in which it moves. The assumption that this dramatic relation is also, at bottom, ideological is evident in contemporary Chinese cinema through the continuity with and conflict between the pre-Liberation traditions of Confucianism and the post-Liberation ideologies of socialism, a continuity and conflict that turn on the relation among the self, the family, the workplace, and the state, the fundamental terms of any image of the social totality. Starting from these premises, this essay argues that the most complex and compelling popular film form that embodies the negotiation between the traditional ethical system and the new state ideology, one that articulates the range and force of the emotional contradictions between them, is what is known in the West as "melodrama." Because this category is not part of the Chinese genre system, its use entails a shift of cultural perspective.[1]

The legacy of Western criticism of melodrama in literature and film is complex and contradictory in its theoretical formulation of the affective foundations of subjectivity. For Elsaesser, melodrama is the representation of the subjectivity of the European bourgeoisie in its struggle against the authority of a declining feudalist system.[2] That is, melodrama is a passionate meditation on the historical experience of bourgeois subjection to the economic authority of the ancien régime, an account of action and subjectivity in the social formation from the standpoint of loss and from the point of view of its victims. This representation of historical victimization as a social catastrophe is registered by narrativizing the subjective and ethical aspect of the drama within an economic interpretation of class relations and by viewing the story's individual protagonist as an overdetermined ideological figure. The shape of the story underscores a fate of suffering and of eventual social insistence on reconciliation through conformity that locates this sentimental drama and its protagonist within an ultimately oppressive social order.

The main alternative to Elsaesser's understanding of melodrama emerges from Peter Brooks's psychoanalytic account of the melodramatic imagination.[3] On this account, "melodrama" is founded on the (French) postrevolutionary attempt to institute in the Republic a morality founded on an ethical imperative centered around a new and troubled figuration of the self in its relation to the unconscious. Melodrama is a theater of social misfortune in which personal virtue is contested, hidden, misrecognized, or subverted, a form of theater that seeks within the confining and largely recalcitrant parameters of the old society to restore and recenter the ethical imperatives required of the bourgeois age. The personification of innocence and villainy constitutes the dramatization of the democratic reverberations of a newly emergent, post-traditional mode of romantic individuality. In this, melodrama is a mise-en-scène whose system of figuration is caught between restoration and reform. For Wylie Sypher, melodrama, seen from a political point of view, is the characteristic form of nineteenth-century bourgeois aesthetic thought that marks out the impasses and the paralysis of Western revolutionary programs and aspirations, informing even the theatrical metaphors and schemes of Marx's *Kapital*.[4]

For contemporary film studies, melodrama indicates a site of ideological critique centered on the representation of sexual difference.[5] Its logic as an aesthetic ideology is founded on the contradiction between a potentially transgressive feminine sexuality and a social system that seeks to delimit and contain it. As a transcription of the tragic into the domestic order, melodrama exemplifies the instability of the ideology of private life under capitalism and, from women's perspective, the domains of affect and action within the nuclear family. The dominant explication of the conflict of law and desire is founded on the psychoanalytic paradigm of the (white) bourgeois patriarchal family. The "social" itself – the workplace, politics – enters the familial configurations of subjectivity through the mediation of the father. The specifically aesthetic impasse of melodrama, and to a certain extent the limitation of its critique, consists of the form's failure to constitute the family in a clear or comprehensive relation to the larger social formation.

From a feminist perspective, melodrama is a dominant mode of mass culture and the site of the central contradictions of patriarchy. Owing to the centrality of its figuration of women's experience, it has been the chosen ground for the delineation of the affective stakes of social constraint and transgression. Hollywood melodrama's aesthetic ideology, in distinction to the strongly marked class oppositions characteristic of its European prototypes, reflects the democratizing of its cultural scope and generic meaning.

Even with certain ambiguous precedents, the translocation of the critical/aesthetic category of "melodrama" from its Western inscription to a contemporary Chinese context is hardly unproblematic. On what basis can an aesthetic ideology so embedded in the popular entertainment forms of Western culture – Christian and capitalist – be treated as significant, culturally speaking, to the form and meaning of contemporary Chinese film? Strictly speaking, the Chinese system of genre classification and its categories are incommensurable with the Western system. The comparability of critical terms like "genre" is not simply a question of formal similarity, but one related to recognizing both significant similarities and differences in literary *and* cultural contexts.[6] It is true that important conventions of both Chinese *spoken drama* and *butterfly fiction*, instances of popular, vernacular entertainment that influenced Chinese filmmaking in the early decades of the century, are arguably Western influenced.[7] Though the terms "melodrama" and "family melodrama" have been used rather widely in the 1980s in discussions of films from Hong Kong (to emphasize sacrifice for family order),[8] I am unaware of a general account of the cultural or critical genealogy of the term in relation to Chinese aesthetics.

Ma Ning's analysis of contemporary cinema of the People's Republic shows how what he calls melodrama renegotiates the relation between tradition and modernization in a narrative that introduces a justification for a new economic order, represents a transformation of power relations within the family order, and shows this change from the vantage point of an established power structure. This social order, he argues, is ultimately subordinated to the system of hierarchy and patronage that supports the political power of patriarchal socialism and its new, ideological imperatives.[9] The constitution of the family drama calls on a system of family ethics that serves in turn the project of ideological legitimation. But a depiction of the designated conflicts within the family does not, it seems to me, constitute in a sufficiently clear way the melodramatic problematic as it has been enacted in Western cultures. The "other" can be reduced to the "same" only at a price. That is, though important elements associated with Western melodrama are present in films in the People's Republic, these films do not exemplify its distinctive, constitutive features – the form's schematization of good and evil, its emotional effects, its mode of theatricality and spectacle, its mode of characterizing the individual as victim, and its mode of understanding the relation of the individual to the social as a matter of justice. At best, the term "melodrama" indicates a rough critical analogy.

I express this reservation about the relevance of Western melodrama to an accounting of Chinese film forms for several reasons: in order to motivate a move toward a more specific account of the constitution, function, and interpretation of these forms as works functioning within the culture in which they originate; to qualify the colonizing power and domination of Western critical theory for an accounting of the specificity of Chinese film and culture; and within the discipline of film studies, to work toward a new model of figuring melodramatic structure and affect in the Western context, through an alternative to its familial focus, namely through the juridical. To the extent that Western theory of melodrama has privileged the nuclear family and its psychoanalytic account of the private sphere of "sexual difference" and "subjectivity," it has lost sight of the broader social conditions of the meaning of the form. I want to proceed, in other words, on the premise that what has been called the genre of Chinese "family melodrama" is neither a true analogy nor the exclusive site for the expression of what we might call the "melodramatic mode." Cross-cultural exchange/interpretation of what is meant by "melodrama" can be elaborated by considering the form of what I will call "political melodrama" as it is dramatized in the work of the Chinese film director Xie Jin. In this way, we might treat "melodrama" as an expression of a mode of injustice whose mise-en-scène is precisely the nexus between public and private life, a mode in which gender as a mark of difference is a limited, mobile term activated by distinctive social powers and historical circumstances.

The political melodrama that I want to consider is best exemplified in Xie Jin's films focused on the figure of the rightist, the nature of his crime, punishment, and process of political rehabilitation. In the 1980s, this thematic is an authorial preoccupation in *The Herdsman* [*Mumaren*, 1982], *The Legend of Tianyun Mountain* [*Tianyunshan chuanqi*, 1980], and *Hibiscus Town* [*Furongzhen*, 1986]. Indeed, *Hibiscus Town* addresses the emotional complexity of the central ideological question of the post–Cultural Revolution era – the place accorded to individual entrepreneurship within the socialist order.

Hibiscus Town tells how a young woman laboriously and diligently builds up a small business (a bean curd restaurant), then is denounced by the local Party leader, who is jealous of her large income. She loses her business, her house, and her husband (who is persecuted to death), suffers years of ostracism, becomes sick and slides into despair, falls in love with a fellow street cleaner (an old rightist who cares for her), becomes pregnant, is illegally married, is judged and condemned again by the Party (it isolates her and imprisons her new husband), and bears the illegitimate child. At the end of the Cultural Revolution, she has her second husband, home, and business restored to her. The "text" of *Hibiscus Town* narrativizes these events through a sexual, economic, and political description of the organization of the society of a small Chinese rural town from 1963 to 1979. The film centrally dramatizes the relation between "subjectivity" (self) and society as it is organized and mediated by the Communist Party.

At the very outset of the film, the population of Hibiscus Town consists of three groups: the "people," the "bad elements," and the Party. The action proper begins with the arrival of local Party Secretary Li, a woman, under the banner of "class struggle," and the initiation of her investigation of Hu, the small restaurateur. The latter is building a new house with her business profits on land bought from a local Party official, Wang, a land-reform activist who lives elsewhere in a dilapidated section at the edge of town. Li's investigation moves forward with a public accusation of Hu's "illegal" self-enrichment (realized, it is alleged,

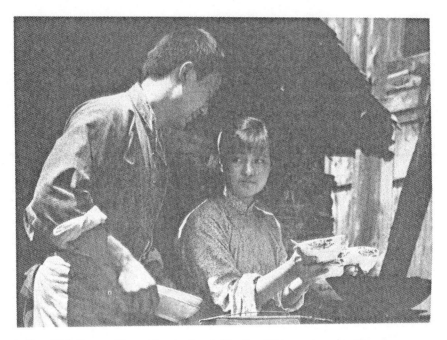

4. New Rich Peasant Hu and her husband. Xie Jin, *Hibiscus Town* (1986). CHINA FILM IMPORT AND EXPORT CORPORATION, LOS ANGELES

through favorable terms she had negotiated with the local manager of the state's granary stores). The state confiscates Hu's property, condemns her as a "bad element," "a newly rich peasant," and sets her to work cleaning the town streets. Three years later with the onset of the Cultural Revolution, Secretary Li is herself stigmatized – as a slut (she protests saying she is a leftist) – and is publicly humiliated. In 1979, with the close of the Cultural Revolution, Li returns to the town to carry on Communist politics.

In posing the question of how, fifteen years after the founding of the socialist state, hard work leading to the purchase of a house can be regarded as a crime, the film points directly to the contradictory ideology and practices of socialism in the reform years. Indeed, the film's complexity consists of the fact that the sexual, economic, and political systems that comprise this social network are almost completely imbricated and intermixed. Notwithstanding this, the film is organized around distinctive binarisms, identified and labeled as "rightist" and "leftist."

Most important, these political categories (which are also economic categories) intersect with moral categories. That is, in the film's principal reversal, the oral perspective contradicts the long-standing correspondence of "Left" with "good" and "Right" with "bad." Indeed, the film inverts the dogmatic formula of the 1950s in which the Party leaders come to the small village and liberate the people from an oppressive feudalism by dissolving the forced marriage contracts that serve as the quintessential emblem of feudal patriarchy. *Hibiscus Town* inverts this formula by showing that the Party system of social control through classification by type leads to persecution and criminalization of a marriage between two persons freely choosing each other outside the authority of the Party. In *Hibiscus Town* the agents of the Party are designated as oppressors.

The personification of the moral and sexual conflict between Right and Left is realized in a dramatic comparison between two women – New Rich Peasant Hu and Secretary Li (Figures 4 and 5). Each woman is authoritative in her own sphere of work. Hu, the younger, is married both at the beginning of the film and at the end; Li is older, more severe, and unmarried throughout. Li's political comrade and lover Wang is a boastful, self-important toady, imperious in his own sphere but wholly subordinated to her power. The film's evident inversions of traditionally subordinated power relations between women and men under-score and thematize male masochism.

In conjunction with the moral evaluation of political positions is a moral evaluation of sexual relations. In this way, the personal and sexual characteristics of the two leading women contribute to an understanding of the legitimacy – and even the rectitude – of their political status. In one central difference – not of gender but of politics – the film points up the superiority of Confucian morality

5. Party Secretary Li (left) and former Secretary Gu (right). Xie Jin, *Hibiscus Town* (1986). CHINA FILM IMPORT AND EXPORT CORPORATION, LOS ANGELES

over socialist pragmatism. That is, the ethical perspective at work in the film contends with the political system.

The narrative of *Hibiscus Town* is organized around three major clusters of events that can be summarized as crime, punishment, and restitution. Hu's trajectory through the film marks them out: the allegation of criminal self-enrichment through the sale of state property; her punishment and suffering through the loss of business, house, and husband; and the restitution and restoration of her home, a new husband, and the birth of a boy child. The film supplies a detailed and comprehensive literal accounting of the economic foundations of Hu's bean curd business that includes the cost of raw materials, gross sales, and so forth. Indeed, her product is explicitly analyzed as a commodity. The fact that the business is part of the food cycle puts the enterprise in close proximity to a biological understanding of the requirements of maintaining life. Indeed, attention to food – both its lack and its abundance, its necessity and its symbolism (as in the wedding feast) – grounds this film, linking it to one of the dominant preoccupations of the Chinese cinema and underlining its foundations in the representation of scarcity. This sequence of narrative events, then, is the figuration of a political interpretation of economic events: acquisition, loss, and return of objects of value (literal and symbolic).

Hibiscus Town shows a fundamental and strict understanding of the political economy of the social order – its modes and relations of production organizing goods, social relations, and indeed "subjectivity" within the framework of the same system. The narrative intelligibility of this Chinese text as a system of signs is predicated not only on a series of motivated consequences, but also on a system that correlates its objects with modes of subjectivity. In this sense, the political classification scheme is coextensive with the order and hierarchy of the social body, and is a means of deciding individual obligations and privileges. Social positions and subjectivity are named and determined by the political system; the Party's political criteria provide a legal justification for the assignment of persons to social ranks. The film shows in methodical, narrative detail the deprivation of life and goods by a political machine that serves at the same time as a judicial apparatus.

In the Chinese political melodrama, the political process is narrativized as a trial that occupies the thematic center in the way that the family conflict does in the family melodrama. Here the drama arises from the Chinese institution of crime and punishment worked out through socialist culture. The film represents the Party's action on the social body. But in the contemporary period, a political perspective vies with and is contested by the ethical one. In this sense Xie Jin's narration and point of view include a perspective on the world of the characters that includes a historical critique. At stake in this form of melodrama is a definition of the self and of the relation of the individual to the social as a fully public matter. Melodrama is the mode of representation of a historical experience that inscribes "subjectivity" in a position between the expectations of an ethical system (Confucianism) and the demands of a political system (socialism), a condition that typifies the Chinese dilemma of modernization.[10] The form's principal significance lies in the affective dimension of the self's relation to the social order, catalyzing two affective regimes that are acted out in the narrative as intensified performances of betrayal, disappointment, or defeat. Chinese melodrama's mode of arbitrating the relation of subjectivity/society is, in other words, a specific cultural formation.

Confucianism's traditional ethical doctrine linked the social body at all levels, modeling the responsibilities and duties of self, family, and state on an analogical "great chain of being." Socialism has undertaken to remodel these relations without abandoning them, recruiting film as a state ideological apparatus for the representation of this new, ethical system and its corresponding prescriptions on subjectivity. In this sense, Xie Jin's films work explicitly to monitor and readjust these new ideological premises to old ethical standards and – through a cultural critique of ongoing antirightist violence – to explore the limits of the political administration of socialist justice. *Hibiscus Town* lays out the political process of justice – crime and punishment – but it also subjects that process to a critique that puts politicization itself on trial from an ethical standpoint. For its audience, the film is a kind of judicial hearing with its own rules of evidence and argument. The film, both as a narrative institution and as a legal institution, mediates the relation of the audience to the abuses, disturbances, and injustices of the real, ongoing events of the Cultural Revolution.

In what way, we must ask, can the representation of the experience of Western capitalism viewed from a Christian perspective be analogous to the representation of the experience of contemporary Chinese socialism viewed from a Confucian perspective? The cultural specification of "subjectivity" and of victimization in melodrama implies, from the first, the concept of the "person." In the ethical and political writings of these two traditions, the treatment of this concept is traceable to the difference between Western "subjectivity" as the private, personal, and perspectival representation of a single mind and the Chinese definition of the person as a set of conventions, social relations, and transactions within the group (mind serving as the ground of social relatedness).[11] The Kantian foundation of ethics in individual responsibility defines the moral autonomy of the self as a matter of choice based in a universal faculty of reason beyond or above social convention. What grounds this personal ethical autonomy, legally speaking, is an acknowledgment of rights. Western individuality is treated as a freedom from social and governmental control, surveillance, and the like, and hence individual autonomy is closely associated with the sphere of privacy. In its ideal form, the law guarantees and institutionalizes these freedoms and rights.

In Chinese culture, traditional writings on Confucian individuality underscore the transitive obligations between subjective terms within a hierarchy that regards the person as a social function, a position placed within the five cardinal relations of domination and subordination that draws its meaning and its codes from hierarchically organized social practice, and not from the status of the person as an agent of free choice. This tradition of ethics based on the cooperation of person and group and institutionalized by social practice is the basis of Confucian legal and administrative theory, a theory that posits human improvement through the exemplification of virtue and correction through education. Confucian legal doctrine[12] was elaborated over several centuries in conflict with an alternative, secular "legalist" theory that called for equal treatment of all before a uniform law and an ethical system backed up by rewards and punishments. Confucian ethics, in contrast, was constituted almost entirely as a code regulating *hierarchical* social relations within and beyond the family. It was the basis of the legal theory in one fashion or another that was inherited by the Communist social administration. Legalist theory, however, with its democratic instincts and its doctrine of reform through punishment, provided in some measure one of the intellectual resources for Communist administrative reform of Confucian feudalism.

We might ask, then, about the form of individualism implied in Xie Jin's political melodrama and how it stands in relation to Chinese models of justice. Who are Xie Jin's characters? What is his mode of characterization? First, people's social and political positions are designated by titles: Secretary Li, Director Gu, etc. The society understands the importance but also the superficiality of identity through this kind of symbolic positioning – and the problem of personal identity is articulated in the film around a cinematic topos constructed by distinguishing between the space of the house and that of the street. The spatial coordinates of personal identity are "inside" and "outside," "home" and "workplace." Xie Jin's revisionist mode of socialist spatialization – of construction of the lived relation between person and environment – both deconstructs and institutes the frontier between private and public spaces and the equivalent distinction within the *mentalité* of the social subject. In this sense, the project of revising established conventions of socialist spatialization (i.e., there is *only* public space) seeks to locate the self in the spaces of both the house and the street. In *Hibiscus Town* cinematic *découpage* articulates the revision of the political valence of space.

The main interest of the film, then, lies in the problematic of the marginal characters, the social and political outsiders. What is the form of their social nonbeing? *Hibiscus Town* provides significant representations of the life of these outsiders. For a long time, one feels, they have lived in the streets. Indeed, in the long midsection of the film that traces the development of Hu and Qin's relationship, exterior social space and its representation are transformed lyrically. The bodily movement of the work of sweeping becomes the dance of the courtship ritual (Figure 6). This part of the film opens onto a strangely isolated cultural space that is roughly divided in equal parts between the street and Hu's room, between long shots of alleyways receding into the depth (largely bluish gray), which serve as the narrowed space of romantic choreography, and the smallish, rose-tinted scenes of the interior, nondescript private space in which the bed and the hearth are the most evident furnishings, the site of passion and its consummation. Outside this room, on both sides of the door, are posters announcing the place to the public as the residence of a "black couple." That is, the place of the outsiders explicitly signed as a space apart is the space of a criminalized marriage. Thus, the space of the social outsider is, in a way, indifferent to the discrimination between house and street. At the same time, there is a single space of romance, of song, and of sexual pleasure. This middle section of the film is composed through what we might think of as a romantic comedy centered around the formation of the transgressive couple (see Figure 7).

Politically speaking, however, the spatialization of this interlude is contradictory and paradoxical and stands as the film's central instance of a mode of subjectivity at the margin of official discourse. It is the space of unauthorized and indeed transgressive assertion of individual choice. It, alone, is the space abandoned to the private and is explicitly, I think, the "space of human rights" as it might be understood in the West.

6. Rightist Qin and New Rich Peasant Hu cast out during the Cultural Revolution. Xie Jin, *Hibiscus Town* (1986). CHINA FILM IMPORT AND EXPORT CORPORATION, LOS ANGELES

7. Formation of the transgressive couple, Qin and Hu. Xie Jin, *Hibiscus Town* (1986).
CHINA FILM IMPORT AND EXPORT CORPORATION, LOS ANGELES

The theme of the rights of political outcasts to marry is repeated and under-lined in Xie Jin's work in the 1980s. In *Hibiscus Town*, with Hu's announcement to Qin that she is pregnant, the couple seek permission from Party authorities to marry. The request is received by Wang with astonishment at "class enemies screwing on the sly!" – and is refused. Qin protests that even members of the "five bad elements" have the right to marry and have children. Qin's assertion of this right is assigned special status – differentiating the human as such. Mar-riage, however, requires legitimation by civil authority. Old Gu, former Party secretary, observing that no one else would dare to attend the wedding of a "black couple," performs this office. Subsequently, the couple is condemned by the Military Commission for "threatening the dictatorship of the proletariat" and the man is sent to jail. The space of romantic privatization is illusory and short-lived, and is soon rearticulated with the larger public space of the mise-en-scène of trial and punishment. The dark result, announced on the steps of a municipal building in the rain to the assembled community, underlies the Party's real power – if not over biology itself, then over the definition of the social status of human relations. It is part of Xie Jin's humanism to depict the injustice of this eclipse of the space of the human.

Two scenes underline the authority of the Party to decide the propriety of individual action: the early night scene of Secretary Li's public denunciation of New Rich Peasant Hu and the late scene pronouncing the verdict on the couple. Both have a similar formal design traceable to the explicit theatricalization of juridical politics – the official speaker is center stage and points out the accused both to incriminate and to condemn. The scene of judicial decision is presented theatrically to an assembled audience as a public lesson for didactic purposes. The mise-en-scène of human rights exists in the relation between the empty streets of political nonbeing and the private room, and the administrative display of public and formalized deprivation and castigation. The two spaces – of being and administration – are dialectically related.

The subjective state of the victims that corresponds to these public sanctions is ambiguous. Generally, Confucian punishment rests on the premise of corrective reeducation through shame rather than guilt as a *social* means for the production of conformity. Guilt, a private emotion, seems more consistent with the punitive theories of Western individualism. The film depicts the couple's refusal to accede to either punitive state. Rightist Qin, the town's artist manqué and poster maker, having had more experience at being an outcast, teaches Hu the way to bear this public sanction when he writes and then posts outside their own door the signs announcing the residence of a "black couple" to the assembled public. Qin's comic resilience, bemused distance, and elevated indifference to these self-authored critiques (an attitude carried, as well, in the movement, gesture, and carriage of his body) give form to a personal style of Chinese autonomy. It is a style of resistance to public sanction. He must bear the injustice, but it does not touch him or alter his fundamentally comic and ironic outlook on life.

This is a form of melodrama founded on the concept of the "person" apart from gender per se. The chief antagonists are both women, though one is "masculinized." In both Xie Jin's *The Legend of Tianyun Mountain* and *The Herdsman*, the political victims are men, although the women are the active figures and the ones who sacrifice themselves to maintain the men. The evident victim in *Hibiscus Town*, the one whose misfortunes are recounted, is the woman Hu, while it is the man, already stigmatized, who supports her. The dynamics of Xie Jin's victimized couples, between male and female, passive and active, are not irrevocably fixed. The woman suffers, as does the man, but neither sacrifices him- or herself for the other. Both characters adopt an ethic of survival, living when necessary like animals. Although in *Hibiscus Town* the woman is victimized, the man, the rightist, is the reference point for Xie Jin's humanist critique. The two figures are in a sense condensed in an emblem of social injustice. The Party's amnesty returns Hu's confiscated property and provides her with a legitimate husband. With his return, the family as a social unit is reformed and the bean curd business resumed. The formation of the family, with child, however, stands outside the strict terms of literal accountability. No price can be put on their suffering. In Xie Jin's hands the political melodrama concludes with the restoration of the family, embedded in a profitable, small entrepreneurial business.

The humanist ideology of the film is simultaneously transparent and complex in its relation to the processes of both socialist revolution and modernization in China in the 1980s. Contemporary Western film criticism since 1968, heavily invested in ideological critique, has not generally confronted the problem of the critique of socialist representation. Following Althusser, Western Marxism in its cultural criticism has treated ideology as a discourse of mystification justifying the capitalist order by naturalization. The spectator, on this account, is forced into an implicit agreement with the terms of the text's construction, one that precludes a critical reading. This process of ideological interpellation is literalized by an account of the functioning of cinematographic apparatus.[13] This paradigm has become an article of critical faith across a range of "progressive" perspectives. Yet what can the Western critique of bourgeois ideology and its associated critical technology achieve in application to Chinese film? And more to the point, what from a Western point of view constitutes an adequate critical model of the relation of film and ideology in the People's Republic? Socialist "ideology," it would seem, is hardly in need of demystification – it is explicit and taught as such. This fundamental difference of perspective indicates that a political reading of *Hibiscus Town* as a melodrama and as ideology should proceed in close relation to the political time and culture in which it is embedded and not simply as the transcription of a Western critical problematic.

Soviet analysts of China in the 1920s and 1930s were undecided about the terms of analyzing the potential for Marxist revolution in China because of its complicated and entrenched mix of feudalism and capitalism.[14] *Hibiscus Town*, however, appears in a postrevolutionary culture, after the Liberation. It is a given that the feudal order so evident in many mainland films (especially those in the leftist tradition of the 1930s and 1940s) has been dismantled. Indeed, in this earlier period there was another version of Chinese political melodrama in which the central antagonist that victimizes the main characters is the feudal order itself. But in the film under discussion, "class struggle" is waged by the socialist victors against the defeated remnants, practices, and personnel of the prerevolutionary period.

Melodrama centered around such persons as Hu and Qin as victims seems possible only retrospectively – *after* the socialist revolution and after the shift of policy that permitted in the 1980s what was prohibited in the 1960s. "Modernization" as it is understood in China in the 1980s necessitated a change of ideology and, in particular, the process of de-Maoification. The new socialism borrows a moral perspective from Confucianism in order to criticize the old ways and to justify a new concept of the self appropriate to the new economic order. However, the film argues that this mode of subjectivity is *not* new, but is found in the villages of the past. What is new is the ideological task of introducing the legitimacy of individual entrepreneurship.

The Cultural Revolution in the film is a negative political reference mobilized as a framework in which to present the case for a more local and particular change – the process of modernization. The relationship of the form of political melodrama to the process of modernization is as complex as its relation to revolution. This fact puts the form of Chinese socialist melodrama, and *Hibiscus Town* in particular, in relation to a certain historiography. The fictional form of the film is articulated around the contrast between past and present, by the process, told in multiple interrupting flashbacks, of Hu remembering scenes from an earlier and happier life. The narrative itself is marked out by a series of dates – 1963, 1965, 1979 – that organize the entire film and put this melodramatic form in relation to the audience's popular memory of contemporary history. The film restates the problems of the Civil War and Liberation through its figuration of the Cultural Revolution and its aftermath. In this, socialist historiography confronts the ambiguities of the post-Liberation period. Assistant Party Secretary Wang, driven crazy by events, is left wandering the streets, banging a gong and shouting his prophetic announcement of the return of another "movement." History, as seen by the film, threatens social dismemberment by repetition of the struggles that led to Liberation.

It is difficult to consider the film as fully a part of the new ideological campaigns of the 1980s. It looks backward – and in Xie Jin's account, the Party is assigned responsibility for the strife and suffering of the past. Yet the film stages an alteration of the social category of the "individual" that answers to the needs of both the past and the present. It is precisely the redefinition of human rights of citizens, that is, civil rights, that Xie Jin formulates in the film.

We have detailed the system for figuring the emotional content of the characters' experience in terms of the relation of personal subjectivity to social structure, and treated it as a matter of victimization. The film explores the scope and content of the "space" of human rights through an analysis of complicating relations between the two large systems of ethical/political thought, Confucianism and socialism, that operate in some composite form in contemporary Chinese society. In this, the film indicates the affective basis of Chinese political melodrama. Suffering is linked ultimately to the injustices of the political administration of social power. In this sense, subjectivity is part of a new political language of the post–Cultural Revolution period. It indicates an aspect of the person beyond that of the citizen. From this perspective we can see the justice of designating Xie Jin's project, as Esther Yau has aptly suggested, "rehumanization." Economic modernization, to the extent that it includes a cultural redefinition of the sphere of the personal or the private, indicates a future, yet to be realized, of both rights and desires.

The film's fundamental choice to proceed by dramatizing the central conflicts of a certain historical moment through the representation of women indicates the contradictory cultural symbolism of the figure of Chinese woman.[15] Secretary Li is a personification, no doubt, of the detested figure of Jiang Qing, Mao's wife, the leader of the Gang of Four, and the film puts the blame on her for the persecution of the couple. In this regard, the film depicts the disfiguration of the social caused by the "phallic woman." By contrast, Peasant Hu, the entrepreneur, carries the extraordinary virtues of her type. In depicting cultural and economic change through the tropological opposition of two women, Xie Jin extends the Chinese practice of representing socialist ideological change by a reduction of sexual difference to an epiphenomenon of the social formation. "Woman" is an ambiguous figure of the Chinese cinema: liberated by the Party, she has been a traditional justification for Chinese socialist domination. Xie Jin's critique of social deformation in the past neither excuses the Party nor supports a call for dismantling it. The film is situated on the cultural horizon of the 1980s in quite a different way than many of the radically conceived films of the Fifth Generation in their refiguration of the role of the political. Xie Jin remains squarely within the recognizable terrain of Han culture, and the familiar contours and problematics of a socialist vision of life, while succeeding in formulating an ethical discourse that works closely in the space between popular sentiments of disappointment or cynicism and the regime of the politically possible. For some Chinese critics and filmmakers, this form of socialist humanism and the Hollywood mode that supports it constitute a cultural monument to the past and designate the limits of sustainable cultural critique.

NOTES

1. For important contemporary statements on the question of cross-cultural method, see Esther Yau, "*Yellow Earth:* Western Analysis and a Non-Western Text," *Film Quarterly,* 41, no. 2 (1987–8), pp. 22–33, and Fredric Jameson, "Third World Literature in the Era of Multinational Capitalism," *Social Text,* no. 15 (Fall 1986), pp. 65–88, and the response, Rey Chow, "Rereading Mandarin Ducks and Butterflies: A Response to the 'Post-Modern' Condition," *Cultural Critique,* no. 5 (Winter 1986–7), pp. 69–93.

2. Thomas Elsaesser, "Tales of Sound and Fury: Observations on the Family Melodrama," in Bill Nichols, ed., *Movies and Methods,* vol. 2 (Berkeley and Los Angeles: University of California Press, 1985), pp. 166–89.

3. Peter Brooks, *The Melodramatic Imagination* (New York: Columbia University Press, 1985).

4. Wylie Sypher, "Aesthetic of Revolution: The Marxist Melodrama," in Robert Corrigan, ed., *Tragedy: Vision and Form* (Scranton, Pa.: Chandler, 1965), pp. 258–67.

5. A thorough orientation and survey of the field from this point of view is Christine Gledhill, *Home Is Where the Heart Is: Studies in Melodrama and the Woman's Film* (London: British Film Institute, 1987).

6. Andrew H. Plaks, "Towards a Critical Theory of Chinese Narrative," in Andrew H. Plaks, ed., *Chinese Narrative: Critical and Theoretical Essays* (Princeton, N.J.: Princeton University Press, 1977), pp. 309–52. For a justification of the use of the term "melodrama" in relation to Chinese fiction, see C. T. Hsia, "Hsu Chen-ya's Yü-li hun: An Essay in Literary History and Criticism," in Liu Ts'un-yan, ed., *Chinese Middlebrow Fiction from the Ch'ing and Early Republican Eras* (Hong Kong: Chinese University Press, 1984), pp. 199–240. On the relation of literature to film more generally, see Leo Ou-fan Lee, "The Tradition of Modern Chinese Cinema: Some Preliminary Exploration and Hypotheses," in Chris Berry, ed., *Perspectives on Chinese Cinema* (London: British Film Institute, 1991), pp. 6–20. For a general study of the performing arts, see Bonnie S. McDougall, ed., *Popular Chinese Literature and Performing Arts in the People's Republic of China, 1949–1979* (Berkeley and Los Angeles: University of California Press, 1984).

7. See Perry Link, *Mandarin Ducks and Butterflies: Popular Fiction in Early Twentieth-Century Chinese Cities* (Berkeley and Los Angeles: University of California Press, 1981).

8. See the remarkable documentation in Li Cheuk-to, ed., *Cantonese Melodrama: 1950–1969*, 10th Hong Kong International Film Festival (Hong Kong: The Urban Council, 1986).

9. Ma Ning, "Symbolic Representation and Symbolic Violence: Chinese Family Melodrama of the Early 80's," *East–West Film Journal*, 4, no. 1 (1989), pp. 79–112. In his Ph.D. dissertation, "Culture and Politics in Chinese Film Melodrama: Traditional Sacred, Moral Economy and the Xie Jin Mode," Monash University, 1992, Ma Ning argues that, "although Chinese film melodrama in its development in this century was subject to Western influences, it also embodies a culturally specific mode of imagination related to Chinese metaphysical, ethical, aesthetic and political traditions." It is the site in which the moral economy of traditional Chinese culture (an economy rooted in traditional Chinese cosmology and ethics) asserts itself in the area of mass cultural production. Ma argues for the specifically Chinese way of ideological domination.

10. The interaction between these two ideologies is the main theme of Judith Stacey's *Patriarchy and Socialist Revolution in China* (Berkeley and Los Angeles: University of California Press, 1983).

11. The traditions are discussed at length in Donald Munro, *Individualism and Holism: Studies in Confucian and Taoist Values* (Ann Arbor: University of Michigan, Center for Chinese Studies, 1985).

12. The classic study is T'ung-tsu Ch'ü, *Law and Society in Traditional China* (Paris: Mouton, 1961). See also M. H. Van Der Valk, *Conservatism in Modern Chinese Family Law* (Leiden: Brill, 1956). For a penetrating account of the status of rights within the liberal framework, see Mark Kelman, *A Guide to Critical Legal Studies* (Cambridge, Mass.: Harvard University Press, 1987).

13. Jean Louis Baudry, "The Ideological Effects of the Basic Cinematographic Apparatus," in Bill Nichols, ed., *Movies and Methods*, vol. 2 (Berkeley and Los Angeles: University of California Press, 1985), pp. 531–42.

14. Arif Dirlik, *Revolution and History: Origins of Marxist Historiography in China, 1919–1937* (Berkeley and Los Angeles: University of California Press, 1978).

15. For recent analyses of Chinese women by women, see Esther Yau, "Cultural and Economic Dislocations: Filmic Phantasies of Chinese Women in the 1980's," *Wide An-*

gle, 11, no. 2 (Spring 1989), pp. 6–21; idem, "Is China the End of Hermeneutics? Or, Political and Cultural Usage of Non-Han Women in Mainland Chinese films," *Discourse,* 11, no. 2 (Spring–Summer, 1989), pp. 115–36; and E. Ann Kaplan, "Problematizing Cross-Cultural Analysis: The Case of Women in Recent Chinese Cinema," *Wide Angle,* 2, no. 2 (1989), pp. 40–50. On nonwhite women more generally, see Teresa de Lauretis, "Displacing Hegemonic Discourses: Reflections on Feminist Theory in the 1980's," *Inscriptions* (Santa Cruz, Calif.), no. 3–4 (1988), pp. 127–44.

3

HUANG JIANXIN AND THE NOTION OF POSTSOCIALISM

Paul G. Pickowicz

I t is easy merely to assert that Huang Jianxin was perhaps the most politically daring young director to appear in China in the troubled 1980s. The difficulty in assessing his work arises when one tries to locate Huang's highly innovative trilogy of films, *The Black Cannon Incident* [*Heipao shijian*, 1986], *Dislocation* [*Cuowei*, 1987; also known as *The Stand-in*], and *Transmigration* [*Lunhui*, 1989; also known as *Samsara*], in any conventional conceptual framework. In a general sense, Huang's work belongs to the vaguely defined category of Fifth Generation films made between 1983 and 1989. However, he was really the only important director in the elite group consisting of Chen Kaige, Tian Zhuangzhuang, Zhang Yimou, Wu Ziniu, and a few others who dealt exclusively and explicitly with the profound problems of the contemporary socialist city. One hardly needs to be reminded that it was precisely in this sector of Chinese society that the massive popular protests of the spring and summer of 1989 originated. Thus, more than the works of any other Chinese filmmaker, Huang Jianxin's anticipated that extraordinary turmoil.

In December 1988, a time of considerable cultural openness in socialist China, I attended a prerelease screening of a rough cut of *Transmigration* at the Film Archive of China. This screening was attended primarily by film specialists and critics in Beijing such as Li Tuo and Zheng Dongtian, who were eager to get their first look at a work that was rumored to be highly controversial. Huang Jianxin flew in from his base at the pace-setting Xian Film Studio to take part in the lively discussion that followed the screening. A sense of excitement pervaded the room because *Guangming ribao*, an official news daily aimed at intellectuals, had just reported that censors in the Ministry of Radio, Film, and Television had discussed *Transmigration* in a two-hour session that, for the first time since the establishment of the People's Republic in 1949, was open to journalists. The censors, it was said, had decided that the movie could be released uncut to Chinese theaters.[1] By contrast, *The Black Cannon Incident,* Huang's first film, had been cut in about thirteen places before release was approved in 1986.

After viewing the rough cut of *Transmigration,* it was easy to understand what the furor was all about. It, like Huang Jianxin's earlier films, left me with the same sense of astonishment that I had experienced at underground screenings in Beijing in 1983 of Andrzej Wajda's stunning films, *Man of Marble* (1977) and *Man of Steel* (1980). The films of both Huang and Wajda were produced in socialist societies, and yet they are not traditional socialist works of art. Indeed, their unmistakable subject is the *failure* of socialism in places like China and Poland. Their purpose is not to salvage socialism by advocating reform, but rather to demonstrate that traditional socialist societies are afflicted with various and deeply rooted terminal infirmities. Thus, well before the popular uprisings and gory massacres of spring 1989 in Beijing, Chengdu, and elsewhere that testified in blood to the failures of the Chinese Communist Party, I had begun to struggle with the issue of how to characterize the films of Huang Jianxin. They did not seem to fit into any of the most obvious analytical categories. I was forced to ask, what conceptual framework does one use to understand works of art that are made in socialist societies, yet document a popular and massive loss of faith in socialism?

It is virtually impossible to regard Huang Jianxin's films as socialist or proletarian in the sense that these concepts have been used by official ideologists in China since 1949. From 1949 to the early 1980s, socialist or proletarian culture has always meant culture that anticipates and contributes in an explicit way to the development of a socialist society. It is, above all, a *positive* culture, a culture that expresses faith in socialism. In its crudest, Stalinist form, such culture limits itself to singing the praises of the Party and state and attacking domestic and international class enemies who seek to block the socialist transformation. But socialist art in China, especially in the mid-1950s, early 1960s, and 1980s, has also included a reformist wing. This latter type of art also expresses faith in socialism, but it acknowledges that there are problems with the traditional socialist system itself.[2] The purpose of exposing such problems is to solve them and thus to perfect the socialist system. Xie Jin's films are perhaps the best examples of reformist works that fall squarely within this tradition of socialist artistic practice.[3] Ironically, even though these reformist films seek to save the socialist system, they are consistently singled out for harsh criticism by intolerant old-school cultural Stalinists like Deng Liqun and Hu Qiaomu, who regard them as a threat.[4]

If Huang Jianxin's films do not belong to any official tradition of socialist or proletarian culture in China, then perhaps they might be discussed productively within the framework of modernism. (I am using the term "modernism" in two senses here. In a general way it refers to the "modern," or postfeudal, bourgeois culture that developed in capitalist societies in eighteenth- and nineteenth-century Europe. In a second and more specific sense it refers to avant-garde "modernist" culture that arose in the West in the late nineteenth and early twentieth centuries.) My view, however, is that while modernism is more suggestive than the stale traditional socialist or proletarian categories, it does not provide a very useful conceptual framework for discussing what I regard as the dominant tendencies in mainland Chinese culture in the 1980s. As Fredric Jameson and others have shown,[5] the modernist framework helps us understand the development of urban culture and consciousness in such industrializing societies as Taiwan and Hong Kong in the 1970s and 1980s, but I think it is incapable of accounting for what is most distinctive about post-Mao cultural and political conditions in the decidedly socialist People's Republic.

For one thing, "modern" and "modernist" cultures are both associated with the sort of capitalist socioeconomic context that developed first in Western Europe and North America and later in places like Japan, Taiwan, and Hong Kong. As Leo Ou-fan Lee has pointed out, not only was modern culture developing rapidly in urban China in the late nineteenth century, but the embryo of a distinctively "modernist" culture was emerging in the late 1920s and early 1930s, when China was in the early throes of a modern or capitalist industrial transformation and when avant-garde Chinese intellectuals like Shi Zhecun were in touch with modernist cultural currents in Western Europe.[6] However, it is crucial to underscore that this phase was abruptly terminated (with far-reaching consequences), in culture as well as in industry, in 1949 and was followed by forty years of traditional socialist development, which included the full implementation of the Stalinist cultural model. Thus, while it is true that a few writers, poets, and visual artists, such as Li Tuo, Feng Jicai, and Bei Dao, exhibited a modernist consciousness and actively promoted the emergence of a modernist culture in the early years of the post-Mao period, it would be quite misleading to suggest that modernism was the primary culture tendency of the 1980s.[7] In my view, we misuse the modernist framework and confuse the real issues when we try to employ it to explain recent cultural phenomena in a society that is perceived to be socialist by its citizens and that has undergone nearly half a century of traditional socialist development.

The problem of using a modernist framework is compounded when we recall that, borrowing directly from the Stalinist cultural tradition, the Chinese Communist Party has always used the term "modernism" in a pejorative sense.[8] When the Party introduced the idea of socialist "modernization" in the late 1970s, culture and politics were deliberately left off the list of the four sectors that needed "modernizing." The old-school wing of the Party, represented by both Deng Xiaoping and Li Peng, may have been hostile to many aspects of Maoism, but it was abundantly satisfied with the familiar socialist cultural and political models of the late 1950s. Thus, theorists and critics in the 1980s who wanted to refer to "modern" or "modernist" culture in nonpejorative ways had difficulty because this terminology had been so thoroughly delegitimized in the past. The term "modern culture" conjured up images of bourgeois, capitalist culture. "Modernist culture" brought to mind images of a degenerate, self-indulgent culture, the sort of development attacked so vociferously by such Eastern European Marxists as Plekhanov and Lukács.[9] In a place where modernism has been presented for so long in the form of a crude caricature that portrays the cultures of the West as decadent and declining, what chance does the modernist framework have of addressing the contemporary cultural problems of socialism (or the films of someone like Huang Jianxin) in a productive way?

What, then, about a postmodern framework? It is certainly sensible to argue that China should not be regarded as a totally isolated or unique cultural environment. Even though China is a traditional socialist society, it now functions in a global context dominated by the economies and cultures of postindustrial giants. In this sense, China is part of the postmodern cultural world. As Masao Miyoshi has observed, contemporary international technology and global management permit the seemingly instant lateral transfer of countless fragments of contemporary global culture, including postmodern culture, to China and other preindustrial or industrializing nations.[10] It comes as no surprise, therefore, that young Chinese intellectuals know much about postmodernism and, on occasion, seek to introduce it into their work. This is especially apparent in the efforts of Chinese artists to "deconstruct" Maoist mythology. But these fragments do not add up to the emergence of an overarching postmodern cultural mode in places like China. It seems to me that the postmodern cultural condition, however one defines it, prevails in places like the United States and Japan that long ago underwent industrialization. The postmodern framework refers primarily to postindustrial contexts.[11] Postmodernism, that is, presupposes advanced capitalism.

Chinese culture in the 1980s contained the vestiges of late imperial culture, the remnants of the modern or bourgeois culture of the Republican era, the residue of traditional socialist culture, and elements of both modernism and postmodernism. But in my view, the main tendencies of contemporary Chinese cultural development (and the films of Huang Jianxin) cannot be characterized as late imperial, bourgeois, traditional socialist, modernist, or postmodern. Each of these models fails to capture the distinctiveness and complexity of Chinese urban life in the 1980s and early 1990s. To call the films of Huang Jianxin traditional socialist works is to confuse them with what they reject; to call them bourgeois (or anti-Communist, as Party elders are inclined to do), modernist, or postmodern is to confuse them with something they are not. What is required is a new way of thinking about the art of people like Huang Jianxin, a fresh way of approaching the type of cultural identity and consciousness that prevails in urban China today.

I would like to suggest that we consider using a framework that might be called *postsocialist*. Arif Dirlik and others have already begun to use the notion of postsocialism to characterize the thought of post-Mao Party elites.[12] I use the concept in a very different way. In this essay, postsocialism refers neither to the abstract realms of theory and ideology nor to the world of Party elites and official culture.[13] That is, I seek not to evaluate the contemporary Chinese world as it looks from the top down, but to understand the way it looks from the bottom up. My definition of postsocialism deals with the domain of popular perception.[14] Indeed, it seems to me that the idea of a distinctively postsocialist condition is best used to refer to the type of popular cultural diversity, cultural ambiguity, and cultural confusion that became so pronounced in China in the 1980s. Those who live in a postsocialist environment are inclined to look upon socialism not as a theory (relatively few people in China know or care much about socialist theory), but as an actual social system that has established a particular economic, political, and cultural record over the past fifty years and has affected daily life in various concrete ways.[15] The postsocialist condition, as former Party members Liu Binyan and Fang Lizhi can probably testify, is not one in which the theory of socialism has been considered and rejected by ordinary people; rather, in postsocialist societies, it is the conduct of the Communist Party that has alienated people of all social classes, including the industrial proletariat, and given socialism a bad name. Dirlik implies that in the realm of theory there is much that is appealing about socialism, but this facile observation is irrelevant to the questions posed by Huang Jianxin's films. The powerful popular perception in postsocialist China is that the socialist system is bankrupt.

An advantage of acknowledging that ordinary urbanites in China have a distinctively postsocialist identity (an identity that strongly influences their ways of thinking and behaving) is that in doing so we are not treating China as an isolated cultural entity with an entirely unique set of problems. A postsocialist cultural identity is precisely what links China to such societies as Poland, the former Soviet Union, Hungary, eastern Germany, and the former Czechoslovakia, all of which underwent long periods of difficult Marxist–Leninist rule. Eastern Europeans, for example, would have no difficulty understanding *The Black Cannon Incident.* Indeed, these experiential links between Eastern Europe and China were acknowledged in late 1989 when demonstrators in socialist Prague carried candles to show support for their counterparts who were ruthlessly cut down in Beijing in June 1989 and when Lech Walesa appeared at the Robert F. Kennedy Human Rights Award ceremony to honor Fang Lizhi, the 1989 award winner. Needless to say, the postsocialist condition will assume different forms in each country, but what is shared is the broad context of public awareness of the failure of the traditional socialist system and the absence of a socialist identity among ordinary people who live in or have lived in traditional socialist societies. It is characteristic of the postsocialist mode that most Party members do not possess a socialist cultural identity. In late summer 1989, before the sudden collapse of the unpopular socialist regime, a Hungarian film director made the following remark about how Party functionaries who formerly espoused puritanical values now lusted after Armani suits and Gucci loafers: "Party members now have a son involved in a joint business venture with a foreign firm, a daughter with a boutique, and

Daddy can still be the Communist factory boss. This is the new leadership of the country."[16]

Postsocialism, it seems to me, refers in large part to a negative, dystopian cultural condition that prevails in late socialist societies. People may not know exactly what kind of society they want, but they know what they do not want. They do not want what life has taught them to regard as socialism. The postsocialist condition exists in societies that have been organized for decades according to what the ruling Communist parties and ordinary citizens alike view as socialist principles. But early popular faith in socialism, if it ever existed, has long since vanished. It has vanished because the Party's performance in the economic, political, and cultural fields has discredited the socialist vision. It is not that ordinary people (following the lead of Dirlik) view the system that oppresses them as false socialism and therefore that they long for "real" socialism: in an experiential sense, people regard the socialist system under which they live as the real thing. In some postsocialist societies, the Communist Party still wields almost monopolistic power in the government, military, and public security sectors and may continue to do so for some time to come. As of 1993, I include China, Cuba, Vietnam, and North Korea in this category. But, paradoxically, in such places there is an almost universal belief, shared by many, if not most, Party members, that what is known as socialism has failed and has no prospect of solving fundamental problems. In such societies socialist economic, political, social, and cultural forms remain deeply entrenched. Even loyal reform elements in the Party cannot root them out. In these postsocialist settings, discredited and failed socialist forms have a life of their own. As I have suggested, the postsocialist condition also prevails in places like Poland, Hungary, eastern Germany, the former Czechoslovakia, the former Soviet Union, Bulgaria, Romania, and Mongolia, where Communist Party power has been entirely eliminated. It does not matter who is in power; one will find a distinctively postsocialist condition and postsocialist behavior in any place where popular faith in socialism has vanished, but the economic, political, and cultural legacies of the traditional socialist era continue to have a profound influence on daily social life.

It is hard to say exactly when the postsocialist period began in China. It would be wrong, however, to suggest that the phenomenon of postsocialism appeared only after the death of Mao or that it is simply a cultural by-product of the reform decade. If the popular disillusionment with a system that has been experienced as socialist is a reform-decade phenomenon, then it is possible to hold the reform leadership fully responsible for the popular loss of faith in socialism. Such an analysis might constitute a vindication of Maoism.[17] In reality, however, the massive disillusionment with socialism among true believers and ideological agnostics and the onset of an alienated postsocialist mode of thought and behavior began midway through the Cultural Revolution (and perhaps earlier in the countryside). It found expression in the huge Tiananmen demonstrations of April 1976 (before the death of Mao) and is linked to the Democracy Wall movement of 1978 and 1979, as well as to the various popular protests of the 1980s. The shocking massacre of citizens in June 1989 did not initiate the age of postsocialism in China; the massacre was a brutal response to a current that had been forming at least since the publication of the famous Li Yizhe poster in 1973 and the release of Chen Ruoxi's short stories in 1974 and after.

Although this essay (and Huang Jianxin's trilogy) focuses exclusively on the metropolis, the postsocialist mode is not simply an urban phenomenon. There may be substantial gaps between urban and rural culture (and one suspects that these gaps also existed in the Maoist era), but a postsocialist mode of thought and behavior is one thing that urbanites share with country dwellers. The international press missed the point on this issue when it stated that the Deng Xiaoping regime survived the summer 1989 crisis because it seemed to enjoy the support of "contented" peasants. I do not mean to deny the existence of deeply rooted antidemocratic traditions in rural China, but one needs to question the assumption that peasants are satisfied. As Perry Link has pointed out, the distance between peasants and intellectuals does not imply peasant support for the state.[18] If the peasantry seemed happy in the early 1980s, it was precisely because so much of what constituted the socialist system in the countryside had been dismantled by the state. The rich popular folklore and oral culture that flourish in the Chinese countryside contain much that is postsocialist in thrust.[19]

The Black Cannon Incident: Postsocialism as Indictment

The postsocialist sense of profound disillusionment with the traditional socialist system pervades Huang Jianxin's first film, *The Black Cannon Incident*, completed in late 1985 and discussed with enthusiasm in leading film circles in early 1986. Unlike the reform films of Xie Jin, which encourage a cathartic and therapeutic purging of pent-up frustrations and which always identify righteous and heroic figures within the Party who will save the socialist system, *The Black Cannon Incident* conveys an overwhelming feeling of hopelessness and alienation from beginning to end. The citizens of postsocialist Czechoslovakia were generous to the discredited socialist state when, in late 1989, they began to set all public clocks at five minutes to twelve, suggesting thereby that the old regime still had a few moments left to do something constructive. At the end of *The Black Cannon Incident*, the public clock is set at twelve. The pessimism conveyed by this film is heightened because its subject is not China at some point in its troubled Stalinist or Maoist past; rather it is China in the midst of the much-publicized era of reform and openness, a time when everyone was supposed to be confident and hopeful. Huang's unwillingness to suggest how the socialist system might be saved gives rise to the feeling that it cannot be saved. If there are sources of hope, Huang gives us no information about where they might reside.

The focal point of Huang's analysis of China in the mid-1980s is the pathetic intellectual Zhao Shuxin, a late-twentieth-century version of Lu Xun's infamous

Ah Q, a socialist Ah Q, for whom Huang Jianxin seems to have almost no compassion or respect. Zhao's mind has been circumscribed, but as the critic Li Zhongyue has stated, like many other Chinese intellectuals, he also engages in self-constricting (*ziwo yasuo*).[20] Even Zhao's name, "Shuxin," is revealing. At one level it suggests a scholarly man who is highly moral, but at a more ironic level it suggests that his morality is related to his loyal submission to ethical norms dictated by others. He is moral only in the sense that he behaves in accord with codes set down by those who wield power. Zhao would be a more sympathetic victim of the system if his persecution stemmed from defiance of socialist norms, but in *The Black Cannon Incident* his persecution has nothing to do with defiance. His behavior is consistently conformist (Figure 8). Indeed, *The Black Cannon Incident* is painful to watch, far more painful than the sentimental melodramas of Xie Jin, because Zhao Shuxin is stripped time and again of his human dignity before our very eyes, and each time he submits without protest. He has long since been reduced to the "docile slave" referred to in the writings of the prominent Marxist theoretician Su Shaozhi.[21]

The post-Mao world of China in reform is exposed in Huang Jianxin's postsocialist work as an Orwellian realm of dictatorship and arbitrary justice. Zhao is never accused of criminal activity, is never informed that he is being investigated, and is never allowed to defend himself. And when the investigation leads to nothing, he receives no apology. A Party secretary simply states that there would have been no trouble at all if Zhao had just bought a new chess piece instead of sending a cable to retrieve his missing "black cannon." In other words, the nightmare is Zhao's fault and Zhao ought to thank the Party for finally clearing his name. The most powerful line in the film is the last one, in which the spineless Zhao declares that he has learned an important lesson: "I'm not going to play chess any more." This socialist Ah Q always assumes that, if he is being punished, he must have done something wrong to deserve it, and he should be grateful to those who are in charge of maintaining discipline and national security.

The postsocialist critique of contemporary Chinese society conveyed in *The Black Cannon Incident* involves more than political issues; it also touches on critical economic problems. Throughout the 1980s the regime of Deng Xiaoping made it abundantly clear that its quarrel with Maoism was related to economic rather than political matters. Deng Xiaoping has never given any indication that he has lost faith in the single-party Leninist dictatorship established by Mao Zedong, Liu Shaoqi, Zhou Enlai, and himself in the 1950s. Thus, he would like modern economic development to occur without the Party having to revise the Leninist–Stalinist social and political system in a fundamental way. What *The Black Cannon Incident* suggests is that the Leninist political system is so deeply entrenched that it is not capable of making even the cosmetic changes that would allow a significant degree of modern economic progress to occur. Compared with conditions that prevailed during the Cultural Revolution, China seemed "open" to the outside world in the 1980s. But, Huang shows, China is still essentially

8. Humiliated time and again by the Party, antihero Zhao Shuxin (left) accepts his fate without protest. Huang Jianxin, *The Black Cannon Incident* (1986). CHINA FILM IMPORT AND EXPORT CORPORATION, LOS ANGELES

closed. "Openness" is a cruel public relations hoax. This film suggests that the state simply wants to expropriate the advanced industrial technology required to complete a major industrial project. It is only under these circumstances that the presence of Hans, the German engineer, is tolerated. Although there is a veneer of "friendship," Hans is never accepted in China. Indeed, he is regarded by those who wield power as a representative of the international bourgeoisie and, thus, as a latent class enemy. The old-style Leninist investigation of Zhao Shuxin and the suspiciousness of his relationship with the German engineer are far more important to the life of the entrenched power system than is the successful completion of the modern industrial project. In fact, it is better to put the whole multimillion-dollar project at risk than to suspend the investigation of Zhao. The Party leaders are not really concerned about economic modernization; toward the end of the film they are shown to be entirely preoccupied with the problem of assigning blame (Figure 9). Everything will be fine if, somehow, the destruction of the priceless modern equipment can be blamed on the German. It does not occur to anyone, including Zhao, to question the priorities of the Leninist political system, a system which, to borrow the words of Xie Fei, requires that nonspecialists exercise leadership over specialists (*waihang lingdao neihang*).[22]

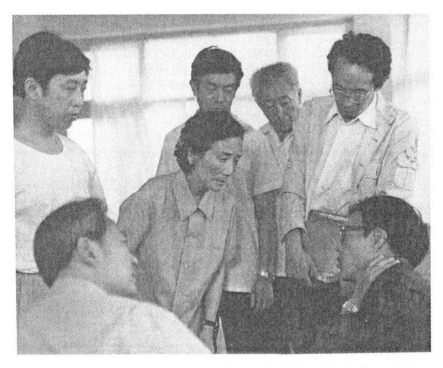

9. A panic-stricken Party Committee learns from antihero Zhao Shuxin (lower right) that the local economic disaster cannot be blamed on a foreign engineer. Huang Jianxin, *The Black Cannon Incident* (1986). CHINA FILM IMPORT AND EXPORT CORPORATION, LOS ANGELES

Film critics in China expressed great admiration for *The Black Cannon Incident*, but even in the relatively "open" political atmosphere of early 1986, they were obviously not at liberty to elaborate at length on exactly why they liked it. In January 1986 two conferences were convened in Beijing on *The Black Cannon Incident*, one organized by the editors of *Film Art* [*Dianying yishu*] and the other held at the China Film Art Research Center. Huang Jianxin told one of the gatherings that only in the most superficial sense was the film about "leftist thought," a well-known euphemism for Maoist excesses. Far more important was the treatment of the "many things" that lurked below the surface of post-Mao society.[23] Nevertheless, many commentators couched their praise of the film in the familiar and harmless political rhetoric of the post-1978 reform movement. Li Zhongyue and Chen Xihe, for example, anticipating the critique of socialist China contained in the 1988 television documentary entitled *River Elegy* [*Heshang*],[24] asserted that Huang was exposing evils that were two thousand years old, the vestiges of "feudalism" and the "small peasant" mentality, evils that had resurfaced in the Cultural Revolution.[25] Zhong Chenxiang, commenting in a similar vein, said that Huang was making a contribution by calling for the "modernization of self" (*zishen de xiandaihua*) and the "modernization of concepts" (*guannian de xiandaihua*).[26] This vague and inoffensive language does not do justice to Huang Jianxin, because it fails to accept his challenge to look below the surface of the film.

Other critics did everything they could under the circumstances to demonstrate that *The Black Cannon Incident* was something strikingly new. Huang's purpose, they implied, was not to show support for the Four Modernizations or to heap additional abuse on the convenient Cultural Revolution scapegoat. As a film that did nothing to reassure people that economic and political reforms would be implemented, *The Black Cannon Incident* functioned more as an indictment of the traditional Leninist political system than as an endorsement of Deng Xiaoping's economic reform program. According to the insightful critic Li Tuo, *The Black Cannon Incident* can be seen as a film that deals with "the attitude taken in socialist countries or socialist systems toward the issue of individual personality."[27] That is to say, the film deals with the rights of the individual in socialist societies. Kong Du, a scholar at the Beijing Film Institute, argued in a similar way.[28] *The Black Cannon Incident,* he said, does not really deal with the surface problems of the "modernization" drive. At a "deeper structural level" (*jiegou shenceng*) it addresses the more fundamental issues of "human dignity" (*ren de zunyan*) and the "value of human beings" (*ren de jiazhi*). In matters related to human dignity (a concept that Kong Du implies transcends national boundaries), the humiliation heaped on helpless and innocent people like Zhao Shuxin ought to be regarded as abnormal. But the tragedy of life in present-day China is that such humiliation has been imposed for so long it is regarded as normal and rational (*heli*). By submerging his analysis of inhuman conditions below the surface of the conventional narrative (*zhengju*), Kong stated, Huang Jianxin was one of the first people to challenge the "ultrastable structure" of Chinese filmmaking since 1949 (*chao wending jiegou*). However, even those critics who saw clearly that *The Black Cannon Incident* was in a class by itself failed to comment on the far-reaching implications of Huang's analysis. Like Kong Du, veteran critic Shao Mujun, a victim of antirightist campaigns of the 1950s, simply noted that the film deals with "the problem of the value of human life" in a way that reveals "long-term weaknesses" in the socialist legal system.[29] Xie Fei hinted that this "small" story permits one to see the "big" picture (*xiaozhong jianda*) and asked rhetorically whether China would ever be able to modernize as long as its intellectuals were like Zhao Shuxin, but he did not elaborate on these points.[30]

None of these writers dealt at length with the grim significance of Huang Jianxin's concept of circularity. Huang himself has pointed out that the wooden chess piece leaves Zhao Shuxin's hands at the beginning of the film as a meaningless object.[31] However, by the time it comes full circle and is returned to him

at the end of the narrative, it has become enormously significant. But its significance has to do with the fact that nothing of importance has been learned from
this absurd case. The entrenched system, exposed as sterile and incapable of
reforming itself, continues to function at the end of the film in the same way it
functioned at the outset. This point is reinforced in the closing scene when the
pitiful Zhao Shuxin, mockingly described by He Yanming as a "model"
(*yangban*) socialist intellectual, encounters small boys (i.e., China's hope for
the future) playing in a park with bricks lined up like dominoes. These Zhao
Shuxins of the future giggle with delight as the upright dominoes fall, like
programmed robots, without resistance, once the first one is pushed. After all the
bricks have fallen, the boys hasten to set them up again. The traditional socialist
system thus reproduces itself and the familiar game can be started again as if
nothing were wrong.

Dislocation: Postsocialism as Theater of the Absurd

Like *The Black Cannon Incident,* the second installment of Huang Jianxin's
postsocialist trilogy, *Dislocation,* was made at the Xian Film Studio, an institution that, under the bold leadership of Wu Tianming, seems to have specialized
in the production of postsocialist artworks. And like *The Black Cannon Incident,*
Dislocation uses a bitter, "black humor" (*heise youmo*), which Huang says is
inspired by such Western films as *Catch-22* (Mike Nichols, 1970) to deal with
conditions that are inherently "absurd" (*huangdan*).[32] Actually, Chen Xihe is
closer to the truth when he insists that Huang Jianxin's humor is "red humor"
(*hongse youmo*).[33] The concept of "red humor" resonates more fully with the
idea of a uniquely postsocialist art that comments specifically, and often vi-
ciously, on what James Watson calls the "rigors of life under socialism."[34]

   One of the important characteristics of socialist theory is that it includes a
built-in utopian vision of the future. That is to say, the point of socialist revolution is to hasten the inevitable arrival of a promised land of freedom, justice, and
abundance. In socialist states, citizens are taught that, compared with capitalist
society, the fully developed socialist realm of the future will be a utopia. The
communist society that eventually replaces socialist society will be even better.
Yet in spite of this visionary quality of socialist theory, since 1949 artists in
China have produced very few works of science fiction that try to imagine what
this promised land will be like. Thus, as a work of "science fiction," Huang
Jianxin's *Dislocation* was the first film of the post–Cultural Revolution era to
explore this unfamiliar genre. There is nothing utopian, however, about Huang's
postsocialist vision. Indeed, he seems to be saying that the socialist utopia
will never arrive. The Chinese future that one sees on screen is a decidedly
dystopian nightmare that has nothing in common with the socialist promise of an
ideal society.[35] Needless to say, it was not Huang's intention to take a serious
look at the future. By mocking the future, he mocks (and subverts) the present

order of things. Nonetheless, it is significant that he is the first Chinese filmmaker to suggest that China's socialist future will, in all likelihood, be a technologically dazzling version of the oppressive present-day China depicted in *The Black Cannon Incident*. In this sense, *Dislocation* elaborates in a consistent and logical way on themes that are introduced in the first film of the trilogy. There is a clear chronological progression of thematic development in Huang's work. *The Black Cannon Incident* indicts the traditional socialist system; *Dislocation* deals with the abortive attempt of one individual to rebel against conformity and slavish obedience.

The socialist antihero of *The Black Cannon Incident*, Zhao Shuxin, is reintroduced in *Dislocation*, this time as the main actor in a series of dream (or, rather, nightmare) sequences. The time is the distant future and the place is China. At first glance, the setting bears little resemblance to the China we know so well. Miraculously, it is a land of great modernity and abundance. The city in which the action takes place is full of futuristic buildings; homes and offices are equipped with a glittering array of futuristic machines and appliances. But, alas, things are too good to be true. The incredible technological revolution that has taken place has done nothing to improve the human condition. The dust and grime may be gone in this faceless and sterile world of the future, but so too are the people. The streets and shopping centers are practically deserted. China now consists almost entirely of bureaucrats and Party functionaries, whose meeting tables are adorned with black bunting, a grim decor of death. There are myriad towering glass structures, but one never sees the people who presumably inhabit them. Zhao Shuxin, the quintessential socialist team player, has been rewarded for his unquestioning loyalty to the system. He is now a department chief (*juzhang*) in an unspecified engineering ministry. Despite the dazzling "modernity" of this China of the future, the political system seems to function precisely as it did in the old socialist China of *The Black Cannon Incident*. It is abundantly clear that no political reforms were ever carried out in the past. Directives (*zhongyang wenjian*) issued by the Party center literally rain down on faceless and uncaring bureaucrats who attend endless rounds of meaningless meetings. Frustrated by the mind-bending bureaucracy of the system, Zhao decides to rebel by building a robot that looks and acts as he does and by programming the machine to attend meetings in his place (Figure 10). For reasons that are left unexplained, China has the dubious distinction of being unusually advanced in the field of robotics. Foreign scientists rush to China to learn how to make mechanical men who obey every order they are given.

The problem emerges, however, when Zhao's robot twin has rebellious ideas of its own and, consequently, cannot be totally controlled by its master. In an effort to reform the system, Zhao has unwittingly created a monster. The robot becomes addicted to meetings and gets corrupted by bureaucratic life. Not only does the robot enjoy Soviet movies; it also drinks, smokes, and eats to excess. Before long it even tries to seduce Zhao's girlfriend (Figure 11). In the end, the robot attempts to take over Zhao's position. Realizing that his plan is doomed to failure, Zhao tells the robot, "You think too much. That's dangerous. I didn't design you to have your own ideas. You're meant to obey my will. If you don't I'll have to destroy you." Zhao's attempt to liberate his own distinctively human creative powers (by allowing a robot to do a robot's work) fails miserably. Furthermore, the robot's rebelliousness is reactionary rather than revolutionary; its actions will lead not to a humanization, but to a dehumanization, of the system. Zhao is left with only two options, both of which are depressing: he can allow the corrupt monster to run wild, thus worsening an already intolerable situation, or return to the lifeless but predictable ways of the traditional socialist order.

In a superficial sense, *Dislocation* condemns the evil of bureaucratism that plagues all traditional socialist societies. Its defenders (and the censors who approved its release) could reasonably argue that bureaucratism is actually alien to the idea of socialism. If bureaucratism is regarded as a manifestation of "leftist thinking" (false socialism) or as a vestige of China's presocialist past, as something external to socialism that is corrupting the socialist system, then *Dislocation,* especially when it is viewed in isolation from the first film of the trilogy,

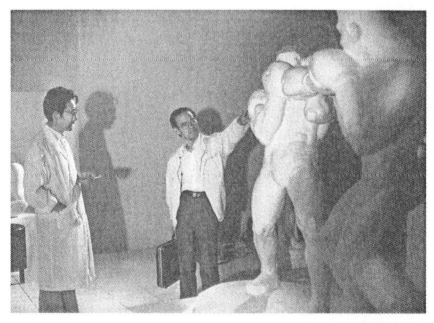

10. Frustrated bureaucrat Zhao Shuxin (center) decides to build a robot that will attend endless rounds of meetings in his place. Huang Jianxin, *Dislocation* (1987). CHINA FILM IMPORT AND EXPORT CORPORATION, LOS ANGELES

11. Zhao Shuxin's robot look-alike, hopelessly corrupted by the system, soon learns to enjoy political meetings, liquor, cigarettes, and women. Huang Jianxin, *Dislocation* (1987). CHINA FILM IMPORT AND EXPORT CORPORATION, LOS ANGELES

can be interpreted as a reform work that is consistent with Party ideology and supports the Four Modernizations drive. I would argue, however, that *Disloca- tion* cannot be viewed apart from *The Black Cannon Incident*. It is not a reform film at all, but a work that expresses a profound disillusionment with what ordinary people in China (and throughout the former Soviet Union and Eastern Europe) perceive as the socialist system. The problem of bureaucratism is not treated here as a remnant of "leftist thinking." Nor is it criticized as something external or foreign to the traditional socialist system; it is treated as a phenome- non that is fundamental to twentieth-century socialist systems. If oppressive bureaucratism is an elemental and inescapable ingredient of the traditional social- ist system, then the issue of genuine reform does not really arise. In both *The Black Cannon Incident* and *Dislocation,* bureaucratism is associated with the basic day-to-day workings of the Leninist single-party state. The idea of Party- sponsored reform is a contradiction in terms, and isolated acts of individual protest accomplish nothing. Real reform, *Dislocation* implies, would require dismantling the Leninist party and denouncing the way it has functioned in China since 1949. In *The Black Cannon Incident,* Huang Jianxin already established that the perpetuation of the Leninist system (i.e., the power of the Party) is more important to the leadership than is industrial modernization.

The discussion of *Dislocation* among film critics was seriously compromised by a sudden, unforeseen shift in the political climate in China in January 1987. Throughout December 1986, a large number of students marched through the streets of Beijing and elsewhere, making demands that amounted to a rejection of the Leninist single-party dictatorship. For several months intellectuals had been expressing the view that "the relationship between Marxism and non-Marxism should not be one between the ruler and the ruled."[36] The authorities reacted swiftly by suppressing the student movement, forcing Party General Secretary Hu Yaobang (now held responsible for the relatively open political climate that prevailed in 1986) from office and launching an old-fashioned political campaign to stamp out manifestations of "bourgeois liberalization."[37] The campaign expired by early summer because it had almost no support. Indeed, intellectuals in the film world with whom I spoke in Beijing in February 1987 were determined to subvert it. Still, the chill lasted long enough to have a negative effect on the public discussion of *Dislocation*.

In mid-January, during the most discouraging phase of the crackdown, the editors of *Dianying yishu* held a lifeless symposium in Beijing on *Dislocation*. Some of the discussants, including Huang Jianxin himself, opted to focus almost entirely on the admittedly novel and interesting formalistic and stylistic aspects of the film.[38] One gets the feeling, however, that they did so, in part, to avoid any discussion of its far-reaching political implications. Mid-January 1987 was not an opportune time to raise fundamental questions about the hopelessly rigid structure of the Leninist party-state. Although *Dislocation* dealt with many of the same large political issues treated in *The Black Cannon Incident*, the *Dianying yishu* symposium packed no political punch. Some speakers, like Jia Leilei of the Academy of Social Sciences (a stronghold of the postsocialist outlook), tried, I suspect, to protect Huang Jianxin by denying that *Dislocation* meant to suggest that Chinese society was "absurd" (*huangdan*).[39] Twelve months before, during the discussions on *The Black Cannon Incident*, many commentators, such as Huang Shixian, had agreed that it was appropriate to use a term like "absurdity" to characterize Chinese social life. In China, he asserted, reality was quite often absurd.[40] But suddenly, in January 1987, it was dangerous to suggest that Chinese society was absurd or that a cinematic theater of the absurd was an appropriate way to approach the problems of socialist society. Jia Leilei denied, therefore, that Huang Jianxin meant to say that Chinese society was absurd. If society is absurd, then life is absurd. If life is absurd, it is meaningless, and there is no reason to have any hope for the future. *Dislocation*, therefore, should not be regarded as a modernist work. Here, of course, Jia was using the term "modernist" in the pejorative sense, modernism understood as an ideology of despair.

Actually, Jia explained, *Dislocation* does not deal exclusively with China. The problems it considers are of "global significance" (*shijie yiyi*), ones that all people confront in a postmodern (*houxiandai*) or postindustrial (*hougongye*) society. Jia's friendly interpretation stripped *Dislocation,* a film that is perhaps even more subversive than *The Black Cannon Incident,* of its contemporary political significance but in doing so it served, in part, to remove Huang Jianxin from the glaring spotlight of the campaign against bourgeois liberalization, a campaign with clear anti-Western overtones. The remarks of veteran film critic Luo Yijun, in contrast, were more in tune with the thrust of the Anti–Bourgeois Liberalization Campaign.[41] Luo was more inclined to identify *Dislocation* with unhealthy "surrealist" (*chaoxianshi*) and modernist currents found in the bourgeois West. In the West, Luo proclaimed, modernist art was the product of the alienation and "solitude" (*gudu*) of intellectuals in postindustrial capitalist society. In China, however, the situation was quite different, Luo insisted. Everyone, including intellectuals, he proclaimed, had a "common ideal" (*gongtong lixiang*) and the problem of spiritual "confusion" (*kunhuo*) scarcely existed. Thus, Luo confidently concluded, "there is no fertile ground in our country for the art of the absurd and other Western modernist schools."

Transmigration: Postsocialism as Anomie

The 1987 campaign against bourgeois liberalization collapsed in the middle of the year, as the new Party general secretary, Zhao Ziyang, pressed for a fresh round of economic and political reforms. In some respects, 1988, the year in which Huang Jianxin completed *Transmigration* (also known as *Samsara*), was more "open" in a cultural and intellectual sense than any other year in the history of the People's Republic. And in some respects, *Transmigration* was Huang Jianxin's most provocative treatment of the phenomenon of postsocialist disillusionment and alienation. Adapted from a novel by the remarkably popular "new wave" writer Wang Shuo entitled *Emerging from the Sea* [*Fuqu haimian*], *Transmigration* shifts the focus of Huang Jianxin's attention away from intellectuals and bureaucrats and toward the controversial subject of directionless urban youth. Huang's new antihero, a smooth young hustler named Shi Ba, lives an empty, meaningless life. His parents are dead and he has no job.

Indeed, *Transmigration* is one of the first films to deal with the widespread problem of alienation and disaffection among urbanites who were too young to have experienced the Cultural Revolution. But Huang Jianxin's decision to explore the case of Shi Ba is of special interest because the cynical Shi Ba is no ordinary young man. He is the son of a high-ranking official (*gaogan zidi*). As such, he has benefited far more from the socialist revolution than ordinary young people. He lives a life of exceptional comfort and privilege in Beijing. His enormous apartment, for instance, is filled with state-of-the-art consumer goods and appliances. Although raised by people committed to the socialist revolution, Shi Ba has no faith in socialism or the Communist Party. His friends have similar backgrounds and hold similar views. Indeed, they openly mock the socialist state and the Party at every opportunity. In one rather amazing (and chillingly ominous) scene left unaltered by the censors at the Film Bureau, Shi Ba and two fashionable female companions stand in Tiananmen Square (the large portrait of Mao Zedong looming in the background) and ridicule the stone-faced soldiers of the People's Liberation Army who are guarding Mao's remains (Figure 12). (In a matter of months, the same spot would become a bloody battleground that pitted armed soldiers against young demonstrators.) Huang's film discussion of the corrupt sons and daughters of the ruling elite seems to conclude that it is those who know the socialist system best who are the least committed to its preservation.

One of the most interesting aspects of *Transmigration* is that it raises the question of why "the best and the brightest" among the ruling elite are so corrupt and spiritually shallow. The official answer, of course, is that the alienation of the sons and daughters of the ruling class is a new phenomenon associated with China's "opening" to the outside world in general and to the "spiritually polluting" decadent West in particular. The unstated and therefore untested assumption is that such problems did not exist in the past. The correct response to the problem of spiritual pollution is to heighten class struggle by launching periodic assaults on "bourgeois liberalization." As film critic Xia Hong pointed out some time ago, this classic approach, which in itself alienates people, amounts to "shining the flashlight of Marxism–Leninism on others, but never shining it on oneself" (*Maliezhuyi de diantong guangzhao bieren, buzhao ziji*).[42]

Even in the atmosphere of political openness that prevailed throughout 1988, Huang Jianxin was in no position to state explicitly that the single-party Leninist dictatorship had only itself to blame for the alienation of Chinese youth and that Shi Ba and his kind were literally and figuratively children of socialism. But it is highly significant that the film explicitly rejects the suggestion that alienation and corruption in China are linked to foreign influences. Indeed, Huang turns the spiritual-pollution argument on its head by illustrating two cases in which Chinese defraud unsuspecting foreigners. In the first instance we encounter the brassy Liu Hualing, a former classmate of Shi Ba's, who openly admits that she married a foreigner she did not love in order to get out of China and establish a legal residence abroad. Soon after, she divorced the man in order to be free of him and to receive regular alimony payments. In the second instance, Shi Ba, who engages regularly in quasi-legal activities, gets involved with a slick young woman who operates a vicious extortion ring. She employs pretty young women to seduce naive foreign men. Once the couple gets into bed, a male accomplice, pretending to be a public security officer, enters the room to make an "arrest." To avoid arrest, the foreigner agrees to pay a "fine" on the spot and the matter is resolved. Not only is the stereotype of wholesome, dedicated Chinese youth exploded in this film (in one especially gory scene, members of a violent street gang use a power drill to mutilate Shi Ba's knee), but Huang Jianxin also refrains, as he does in *The Black Cannon Incident*, from placing the blame for China's sorry condition on foreigners.

12. Alienated new-style youths take delight in mocking military honor guards in Tiananmen Square. Huang Jianxin, *Transmigration* (1989). CHINA FILM IMPORT AND EXPORT CORPORATION, LOS ANGELES

As in the case of Huang Jianxin's first two films, it is possible to argue that *Transmigration* is compatible with the priorities of the Four Modernizations reform drive. One might say that people like Shi Ba comprise only a small segment of Chinese youth and that the purpose of the film is to raise the issue of youth alienation so that it can be resolved. The problem with this approach is that it ignores the fact that Huang Jianxin does nothing in this or any of his films to suggest precisely how such problems might be solved. On the contrary, his films increasingly convey a profound sense of hopelessness. If *The Black Cannon Incident,* like Lu Xun's "The True Story of Ah Q," is about the need for Chinese people to awaken, and *Dislocation* is about a failed protest, then *Transmigration,* the last element of Huang's analytical progression, is, logically, about individual resignation and anomie in postsocialist society.

"Transmigration" (*lunhui*) is a Buddhist term for the cyclical process in which one's soul takes on a new body after death. Shi Ba's deep depression culminates in a shocking ritual suicide, the ultimate act of despair. His troubled and alienated soul presumably passes to his yet unborn son, who is named Shi Xiaoba (Little Ba), after his father. The son, we are told in a clinically cold postscript, is born several months later in a small black room. The message is that nothing has changed. This depressing sense that the system simply reproduces itself over and over is strikingly similar to the feeling one gets at the end of *The Black Cannon Incident* when Zhao Shuxin watches the small boys set up the brick dominoes time after time. A mechanical house ornament known as a *yongdongji,* or "perpetual motion device," is used throughout *Dislocation* to convey this same sense. It moves back and forth, lurching to the left and then to the right without ever really going anywhere; it just repeats the same pattern of movement forever. Even the music in *Transmigration* indicates that the traditional socialist system is capable only of reproducing itself. The film begins and ends with what all Chinese will recognize as the "Song of the Young Pioneers," a song that each generation must learn in school even though it is widely regarded as a meaningless relic of socialist culture in China.

It seems almost incredible now that some early Western commentary on *Transmigration* interpreted the film as a work that indirectly attacked the reform

13. Caught in the middle of another shady business deal, a paranoid Shi Ba (left) believes he is being watched by an unsavory gang member (right). Huang Jianxin, *Transmigration* (1989). CHINA FILM IMPORT AND EXPORT CORPORATION, LOS ANGELES

policies of the 1980s by showing the "underside" of the reform tide.[43] In this view, Shi Ba is a young man who cannot cope with the new competitive system, a person unable to obtain jobs or promotions based on merit. *Guangming ribao*, in a similar vein, said that *Transmigration* was an attempt to "portray the reactions of young people to the reform era."[44] It seems to me, however, that only in the most superficial sense does the film comment on the social consequences of recent economic reforms. When one views *Transmigration* as the third in a trilogy of films, all of which deal with life in the reform period, it becomes obvious that Huang Jianxin is not an opponent of the reform. He clearly supports the rejection of Maoism. But the underlying message is that the reforms are inadequate; they are not going to work. The problem with contemporary Chinese society is not that reforms have been introduced to save socialism, but rather that the reforms of Deng Xiaoping, Hu Yaobang, and Zhao Ziyang have not gone far enough. Indeed, each reform that is introduced is an admission that the traditional socialist system set up in Eastern Europe and in China after World War II is not working and cannot meet the political, economic, social, and cultural needs of the people. The reforms do not work because they are artificially superimposed on the deeply rooted Leninist system. The more that piecemeal reforms are introduced, the more it becomes evident that no one has any faith in the traditional socialist system and the more it becomes obvious that the only way reforms can make a significant impact is if the traditional system and the single-party dictatorship are dismantled as they have been in the former Soviet Union, Poland, Hungary, the former Czechoslovakia, and eastern Germany. Even then there is no guarantee of success, given that decades of socialism have left behind a mind-boggling legacy of waste, inefficiency, corruption, environmental devastation, and moral resignation. Ordinary people are ill-prepared to make a new beginning.

Thus, Huang Jianxin does not expect us to feel sorry for Shi Ba (or Zhao Shuxin). Shi Ba and his friends are not the offspring of the reform era; they are the children of the Chinese Communist Party and a socialist system that has been abusive and dictatorial for decades. Like their corrupt parents, they have no real faith in the socialist future of China. Unlike their parents, however, they are not hypocrites. They do not pay lip service to the alleged superiority of the socialist system. They do not join the Party to advance their careers and to gain more perks. They have been taught by the system to ignore the childish platitudes contained in "The Song of the Young Pioneers." They think only of themselves and how best to maximize short-term gains. Their greed and obsession with collecting material objects has little to do with flaws in the reform policies; their selfish irresponsibility derives from a process that conditions people to grab whatever they can after forty years of socialist scarcity. It is the socialist system, not the well-intentioned reform measures, that produces people who are the antithesis of Lei Feng, the plastic socialist hero who happily wasted his life for the Party and the people.

The early critical responses to *Transmigration* were quite positive. Dai Jinhua, a young faculty member at the Beijing Film Institute, praised the film's "exquisite artistry and quality production." In no sense, she argued, could Huang Jianxin be accused of celebrating the alienated and self-indulgent ways of people like the antihero Shi Ba. According to Dai, the "grimness and gruesomeness of urban life" is a reality of contemporary Chinese life that needs to be documented.[45] Even the cautious Shao Mujun, who thinks that all the films based on works of fiction by Wang Shuo contributed to an emerging "culture of vulgarity" (*pizi wenhua*) in the late 1980s, conceded that *Transmigration* "transcended" this unflattering category.[46] Predictably, critical discussion of *Transmigration*, one of the most important films made in post-Mao China, was cut short by the tragic events of June 1989. The film was no longer shown, and the bits and pieces of commentary that appeared in the press were generally negative. For example, Su Bing, writing more than a year after the initial release of *Transmigration*, severely criticized Huang Jianxin for allegedly glorifying and romanticizing Shi Ba's ritual suicide.[47] Ironically, Dai Jinhua, writing before the Beijing massacres, characterized the same scene as "brilliant."[48]

The Postsocialist Condition: Some Final Reflections

Huang Jianxin's impressive postsocialist filmmaking activities came to a sudden halt after the brutal massacres of June 1989 and the onset of the massive repression that temporarily strengthened the hand of those committed to the Leninist dictatorship. It has been suggested by some dissident Chinese intellectuals, who now reside outside China, that the strange lull in Huang's creative life had nothing to do with his political activities in April and May 1989. He was in Australia during those tumultuous weeks, and thus cannot be accused of having participated directly in antigovernment protests or street demonstrations. Some observers suggest that Huang was under a cloud for nearly five years because of the political activities of his mentor, Wu Tianming, who now lives in exile in the United States. This much is clear: Huang was not among those directors invited to attend a tightly controlled national film festival held in Beijing in late September 1989. And apparently *Transmigration*, *Dislocation*, and *The Black Cannon Incident* were not among the twenty feature films of the 1980s selected for screening at that time. Instead, titles like Tian Zhuangzhuang's *Rock 'n' Roll Youth* [*Yaogun qingnian*, 1988] were offered as films reflecting "present-day life."[49] It was not until 1993 that Huang was back at work in Xian on a new film, *Straighten Up* [*Zhan zhi luo, bie paxia*].

One wonders whether Huang's forthcoming work will continue his exploration of China's postsocialist condition. Paul Clark has suggested that the bloodletting of June 1989 may well "spell the death of domestic cinema" in China.[50] In the immediate aftermath of the massacres (during which four Beijing Film Institute students were arrested), I received frightening letters from friends who had graduated from the Beijing Film Institute in the early 1980s. One letter, dated June 16, from a well-known person who was desperate to get out of socialist China, said, "I'm certain you know all about the situation here, so there is no need for me to say a lot. There's not much time, so I'll just jot down a few things quickly. Please, whatever you do, stay in touch with me. There is no way to convey to you the sense of total hopelessness that I feel (*juewang xinqing*) under these circumstances." In a letter dated July 11, another Beijing Film Institute graduate wrote, "I often have the feeling now that I've reached a dead-end in life. My self-confidence has practically disappeared. None of the things I have wanted to do, none of my hopes, have been realized. I've tried very hard, but nothing has turned out the way I imagined. Sometimes I feel terribly discouraged and have no sense of hope (*shiwang huixin*)."

In mid-1990 Teng Jinxian, the new head of the Film Bureau under the Ministry of Radio, Film, and Television who replaced the capable Shi Fangyu in 1988, publicly announced that the party-state would now insist that the film world function once again within the traditional Stalinist framework. Teng called for a dramatic increase in the number of political propaganda films. Among other things, he said, this would require more films about "advanced workers, peasants, soldiers, and intellectuals," the sort of thing that abounded in the 1950s. Teng charged that filmmakers are guilty of "national nihilism" and "blindly worship Western film theory and artistic genres." This, of course, was a charge made time and again by Red Guards during the Cultural Revolution. Echoing remarks made by Mao Zedong in the 1940s, Teng condemned filmmakers who are interested in the subject of human nature. Such works, he intimated, dilute the class consciousness of the people and strengthen the hand of the class enemy.[51]

Huang Jianxin was perhaps the only important young director to come out of the Beijing Film Institute's direction program in the early 1980s who set all of his films in the present and, in doing so, dealt directly with many of the overriding issues taken up by the street demonstrators cut down in June 1989. This took considerable courage. Many other directors carefully avoided commenting critically on the present day. The films made in the 1980s by Huang's well-known contemporaries (Chen Kaige, Tian Zhuangzhuang, and Zhang Yimou) that have received the most critical attention are set in the presocialist Republican era or in exotic non-Han border areas. When *The Black Cannon Incident* was released in early 1986, Huang Jianxin was noticeably defensive about the charge, leveled by some film critics in China, that the filmmaking of his generation was "far removed from present reality" (*yuanli xianshi*) and "failed to bravely confront the problems of present-day reality" (*meiyou yongqi zhengshi xianshi wenti*).[52] Huang denied the charge (by pointing to *The Black Cannon Incident*), but in fact the critics were right. Now it is clear just how dangerous it is to raise questions about the fundamental nature of Leninist, single-party socialist systems and the social malaise and disaffection they engender. Thus, one wonders how in mid-1987 the *Economist* reached the odd conclusion that Huang Jianxin is "staunchly committed" to the "basic structure" of the socialist system in China.[53] Huang Jianxin's films simply do not amount to a vote of confidence in the Leninist system or the "reform" strategy. It is not that Huang does not want change; it is that he expresses serious doubts about the structure of the system and the likelihood that it can actually reform itself. To be a reformer one has to believe that the "errors" committed by the Party in the past are alien to the Leninist system, that the Party can weed out these "leftist" perversions and adopt, in a creative way, new modes of operation to deal with the realities of the present. To put it simply, a "reformer" must believe that necessary changes can be made within the framework of the "Four Cardinal Principles" of the Leninist dictatorship. One strongly suspects that Huang's views are closer to those articulated by Solidarity in Poland, Civic Forum in Czechoslovakia, and New Forum in eastern Germany on the eve of the collapse of traditional socialism in Eastern Europe. His films show that the problems of Party dictatorship (*The Black Cannon Incident*), mindless bureaucratic stagnation (*Dislocation*), and anomie (*Transmigration*) are, in essence, unrelated to the "leftist" excesses of the Cultural Revolution and other episodes of ideological extremism, as well as to the piecemeal "reforms" of the 1980s. These overarching problems are perceived as endemic to socialist states set up after 1917. Solidarity, Civic Forum, and New Forum were not reform movements; they were popular movements that recognized the need to demolish the traditional socialist system before life-enhancing changes could take place.

By using the framework of postsocialism, then, I am rejecting the notion that the devastatingly critical and artistically innovative works of people like Andrzej Wajda and Huang Jianxin must inevitably be categorized as either socialist or capitalist. Huang clearly rejects traditional socialism, but there is no evidence that he possesses a bourgeois consciousness or looks forward to a capitalist future for China. Postsocialism, the ideological counterpart of postmodernism, refers to a cultural crisis that is unique to societies that have undergone decades of Leninist–Stalinist (i.e., what I call traditional socialist) development. I realize, of course, that others may choose to place Huang's films in more conventional frameworks. One could argue, for example, that Huang's perspective is nothing more than old-fashioned cold war anticommunism, an ideology inspired by a profound confidence in the superiority of capitalism. But in my view, such an argument would be patently untenable. There is no evidence to support it.

A more interesting view (and one that is not necessarily incompatible with the concept of postsocialism) is one suggested to me by Krzysztof Wodiczko, the brilliant and highly controversial visual artist whose works had a major impact on the New York art world in the 1980s. Wodiczko, it is crucial to point out, is a nonsectarian socialist or social democratic thinker who is a strident critic of both capitalism and the sort of traditional socialist society he experienced firsthand in his native Poland. Wodiczko, who now resides in the United States, has experienced both capitalism and traditional socialism from the inside. He does not want Poland to head in a capitalist direction, but neither does he want it to revert to the inhumanity and oppressiveness of traditional socialism. Wodiczko argues that critics of socialist societies, that is, people like Huang Jianxin, can still be regarded as socialists. When they are criticizing what I call traditional socialism, he insists, they are criticizing "false" socialism, not "real" socialism. Poland, Wodiczko fervently believes, was never really socialist. Thus, it is possible for an artist or critical thinker to reject traditional or "false" socialism while looking forward to the arrival of a genuinely humane and liberating socialist era. Such an artist (and Huang Jianxin might be an example) would thus place himself or herself in the socialist category.

Wodiczko's argument, however, does not deal with the fact that traditional socialist regimes have, by their many failures, discredited in the public mind all forms of socialism. Thus, it is exceedingly difficult (if not impossible) for "real" socialists in such postsocialist settings to build a social base of support for a "real" socialist revolution. Nonetheless, Wodiczko's argument is correct at a theoretical level and is largely consistent with Herbert Marcuse's notion that the role of authentic art is to subvert the "dominant consciousness" and "break the monopoly of established reality" in order to define what is real.[54] Here Marcuse was referring to what he regarded as outstanding art in industrial and postindustrial societies, but he was also aware of the crushing inhumanity of life in socialist China. While it is true that Huang Jianxin's work (and especially *Transmigration*) is pessimistic, Marcuse reminds us that the pessimism of genuine art "is not counterrevolutionary."[55] "In the transforming mimesis," he argued, "the image of liberation is fractured by reality. If art were to promise that at the end good would triumph over evil, such a promise would be refuted by the historical truth. In reality it is evil which triumphs. . . . Authentic works of art are aware of this; they reject the promise made too easily; they refuse the unburdened happy end."[56] Marcuse's dynamic conception of art as a "dissenting force" can very easily be applied to art in traditional socialist societies. Indeed, this is precisely what Wodiczko has in mind. The result is socialist art that rejects Marxism–Leninism–Stalinism. It may well be that Huang Jianxin's work is socialist in this sense.

By arguing that Huang's contemporary and urban films are best understood through the analytical lens of postsocialism, I do not mean to suggest that the only films we can regard as postsocialist are those that are set in the present day and that deal directly with the contemporary predicaments of Chinese socialism. Many of the works of Chen Kaige, Tian Zhuangzhuang, and Zhang Yimou that are set in presocialist times or in non-Han border regions are also illuminated by the concept of postsocialism. They "subvert" (in the sense that Marcuse used the term) the oppressive traditional socialist system by deconstructing the mythology of Chinese socialism (demolishing, for instance, the romantic and heroic image of the Chinese peasantry that has been so central to Chinese socialism since the late 1930s) and rejecting the wooden class-struggle paradigm that served as the structural foundation for almost all works of art in the 1949–79 period. It is important to point out, however, that Huang's work (and the work of the deconstructionists just mentioned) has little in common with the remarkably popular films of Xie Jin. It is extremely difficult to locate Xie Jin's work in the postsocialist paradigm. Xie Jin believes in the Leninist party, has faith in the basic structure of the traditional socialist system, and, judging by films like *The Legend of Tianyun Mountain* [*Tianyunshan chuanqi*, 1980] and *Hibiscus Town* [*Furongzhen*, 1986], is confident that the Leninist party is capable of reforming itself and rooting out leftist influences. Xie Jin complains vociferously about injustices under socialism, but he believes that such injustices are foreign to the socialist system, rather than fundamental to its nature.

Although this essay has focused on the political significance of filmmaking, the glaring difference between Xie Jin, the reformer, and Huang Jianxin, the postsocialist artist, is also readily apparent in the stylistic realm. In many ways Xie Jin's films are melodramatic caricatures of real life, filled as they are with righteous socialist heroes and true believers who suffer unspeakably and are persecuted by leftist zealots or Party hacks who fail to realize that their arbitrary and undemocratic style of work is influenced by discredited leftist modes. In the end, however, socialist justice always prevails and wrongs are righted. There is plenty of human agony in Xie Jin's films, but those who have been wronged never give up the hope that an appropriate socialist solution to China's problems will be found. It is to his credit that Xie Jin's films get attacked in China, but those who attack him are frightened antireformists who believe that the reform path will undermine the thing that is most important to them – absolute Party rule.

As Ma Ning and Nick Browne have shown in Chapters 1 and 2 of this volume, melodrama is a major genre of Chinese filmmaking. It is a genre that was particularly well suited to the task of establishing a disturbingly one-dimensional socialist culture in China after 1949. It should not surprise us, then, that one of the most important characteristics of Huang Jianxin's approach to filmmaking is his total rejection of the emotional, melodramatic format. He analyzes the Chinese world with an icy detachment that allows little room for sentiment. His antiheroes are victims of socialism, but not heroes or martyrs; they are alienated from the socialist system, but they participate in the process that results in their own victimization. Xie Jin's films are meant to elicit tears (and stimulate a cathartic healing), whereas Huang Jianxin's devastating postsocialist "red humor" mocks what is most fundamental to the socialist system and produces the kind of bitter laughter that only those who have spent their lives in traditional socialist societies can fully appreciate.

In sum, the postsocialist condition that is revealed in Huang Jianxin's films is neither socialist nor capitalist. The postsocialist condition exists only in cultures that have functioned for significant periods of time as traditional socialist societies. That is, postsocialism presupposes socialism. In some postsocialist settings the Leninist party still exercises a virtual monopoly on power, while in others it has been forced to share power or has been pushed entirely from the political arena. But it is not the political situation at elite levels alone that defines the postsocialist condition. Postsocialism involves a perception among ordinary people at the bottom that socialism has failed, that it is not the solution to what ails society, but rather the very cause. The general sense is that Leninist parties that have been in power for decades are inherently incapable of reforming society. Postsocialism, in brief, involves a massive loss of faith. Some of the alienation, frustration, and anger it engenders leads to a politically healthy search for alternatives to traditional socialism, but some of that disaffection (such as the sort one sees in *Transmigration*) produces self-destructive social and psychological behavior. In postsocialist society, failed institutions remain deeply rooted and continue to have a damaging impact on social, political, economic, and cultural life even though popular alienation is widespread and nonsocialist political forces have emerged. Indeed, socialist institutions and habits are even more deeply entrenched than the ruling Leninist party.

Thus, when we try to evaluate Chinese cinema in the 1980s and the works of artists like Huang Jianxin, it might not make much sense to compare them with Chinese films made in capitalist Taiwan and Hong Kong. Over the years I have noticed that ordinary people in mainland China have little interest in and experience difficulty understanding the themes of most films made in Taiwan and Hong Kong. If there is interest in this cinema, it is because these films are perceived to be utterly exotic and otherworldly. That is to say, they have little to do with the postsocialist realities of mainland life. Similarly, ordinary people who grew up in Taiwan have difficulty relating to problems that get thrashed out in films made in mainland China. There may be a temporary interest in seeing what was once taboo, but curiosity quickly evaporates when it becomes clear that mainland films treat issues that are far removed from the problems that Taiwan residents face. In brief, forty years have created a huge cultural gap between the people of mainland China and those of Taiwan and Hong Kong, especially among young people. Indeed, it seems to me much more fruitful to compare films made in China in the 1980s with films produced in Eastern Europe both before and after the disintegration of the old socialist regimes. One is tempted to say that, after forty years of socialism, the people of mainland China have more in common with the people of the former Soviet Union, Bulgaria, and Hungary than they have with the people of Taiwan. Similarly, the people of Poland, eastern Germany, and the former Czechoslovakia would have no difficulty recognizing and understanding the issues raised by Huang Jianxin, because, like the Chinese, they have experienced socialism and now find themselves struggling in the uncharted waters of postsocialist reality.

NOTES

1. *Guangming ribao,* December 15, 1988; *South China Morning Post,* December 16, 1988.

2. Paul G. Pickowicz, "The Limits of Cultural Thaw: Chinese Cinema in the Early 1960s," in Chris Berry, ed., *Perspectives on Chinese Cinema* (Ithaca, N.Y.: Cornell University East Asia Papers, no. 39, 1985), pp. 97–148.

3. Paul G. Pickowicz, "Melodramatic Representation and the 'May Fourth' Tradition of Chinese Cinema," in Ellen Widmer and David Der-wei Wang, eds., *From May Fourth to June Fourth: Fiction and Film in Twentieth-Century China* (Cambridge, Mass.: Harvard University Press, 1993), pp. 313–26.

4. For a discussion of the reform films of Xie Jin and others see Paul G. Pickowicz, "Popular Cinema and Political Thought in Post-Mao China: Reflections on Official Pronouncements, Films, and the Film Audience," in Perry Link, Richard Madsen, and Paul G. Pickowicz, eds., *Unofficial China: Popular Culture and Thought in the People's Republic* (Boulder, Colo.: Westview Press, 1989), pp. 37–53.

5. See Fredric Jameson, Chapter 5, this volume.

6. Leo Ou-fan Lee, "In Search of Modernity: Some Reflections on a New Mode of Consciousness in Twentieth-Century Chinese History and Literature," in Paul A. Cohen and Merle Goldman, eds., *Ideas Across Cultures: Essays on Chinese Thought in Honor of Benjamin I. Schwartz* (Cambridge, Mass.: Harvard University Press, 1990).

7. See *Shanghai wenxue,* August 1982, for the views of Li Tuo, Feng Jicai, and Liu Xinwu, and see *Wenyi bao,* September 1982, for a criticism of their "modernist" views.

8. For a discussion of early Chinese Marxist encounters with Stalinist literary thought see Paul G. Pickowicz, *Marxist Literary Thought in China: The Influence of Ch'ü Ch'iu-pai* (Berkeley and Los Angeles: University of California Press, 1981), pp. 179–86.

9. Fredric Jameson, *Marxism and Form* (Princeton, N.J.: Princeton University Press, 1974), pp. 160–205.

10. Masao Miyoshi, "Against the Native Grain: The Japanese Novel and the 'Postmodern' West," in Masao Miyoshi and H. D. Harootunian, eds., *Postmodernism and Japan* (Durham, N.C.: Duke University Press, 1989), p. 143.

11. This is the sense I get from reading Brian Wallis, ed., *Art after Modernism: Rethinking Representation* (New York: New York Museum of Contemporary Art, 1988).

12. Arif Dirlik, "Post-socialism? Reflections on 'Socialism with Chinese Characteristics,'" in Arif Dirlik and Maurice Meisner, eds., *Marxism and the Chinese Experience* (Armonk, N.Y.: Sharpe, 1989), pp. 362–84. For other theoretical discussions, see Ernesto Laclau and Chantal Mouffe, *Hegemony and Socialist Strategy* (London: Verso, 1985); Norman Geras, "Post-Marxism?" *New Left Review,* 163 (May–June 1987); Nicos Mouzelis, "Marxism or Post-Marxism?" *New Left Review,* 167 (January–February 1988).

Dirlik uses the concept of postsocialism to characterize official Chinese Communist Party ideology in the post-Mao era – that is, the notion of "socialism with Chinese characteristics." He thinks of postsocialism as a coherent and elite ideology with specific traits. The ideology of Deng Xiaoping, in this interpretation, is postsocialist in the sense that it acknowledges serious deficiencies in the traditional socialist system, especially in the economic realm, and resorts to capitalist methods of economic development and management to overcome these deficiencies. At the same time, however, Deng regards capitalist society as inherently defective. Thus, postsocialism seeks to avoid a capitalist future for China. Dirlik likes the concept of postsocialism because, in matters related to theory and ideology, it gets analysts out of the intellectual quicksand of the simple socialist–capitalist dichotomy, a discourse that requires critics to identify an ideological development as essentially capitalist or essentially socialist.

At one level, Dirlik's formulation is highly subversive and would be most unwelcome to Deng Xiaoping. In effect, Dirlik, an independent and nonsectarian socialist critic of traditional Marxist–Leninist states, is saying that Deng Xiaoping's new "socialism with Chinese characteristics" is not genuine socialism. But perhaps more important, he is also saying something that would be welcomed by Deng, namely that post-Mao Communist Party ideology is not capitalist either. Dirlik's conception of a distinctively postsocialist ideological mode was mapped out before the violent crisis of spring 1989 exploded in China and well before the authority of the Communist regimes suddenly evaporated in Poland, eastern Germany, the former Czechoslovakia, Hungary, and Romania in late 1989, that is, at a time when it was still possible for sympathetic critics to hope that "real," humane socialism (as opposed to traditional Stalinist socialism or Deng Xiaoping's socialism with Chinese characteristics) might have a future in what was known as the socialist world. Dirlik's work is, in this strict sense, a rigorous effort to salvage what he regards as important life-enhancing aspects of nineteenth- and twentieth-century socialist theory by denying that Deng's program or ideology is "really" socialist.

13. For a longer discussion of Dirlik's work see Paul G. Pickowicz, "The Chinese Anarchist Critique of Marxism-Leninism," *Modern China*, 16, no. 4 (October 1990), pp. 450–67.

14. The subject of popular thought in contemporary China is treated in various ways in Link, Madsen, and Pickowicz, eds., *Unofficial China*.

15. Paul G. Pickowicz, "Post-socialism and Chinese Cultural Identity in the 1980s: A Comment on James Watson's 'The Renegotiation of Chinese Cultural Identity in the Post-Mao Era: An Anthropological Perspective,'" unpublished manuscript, University of California, San Diego.

16. *Los Angeles Times*, September 8, 1989.

17. This is essentially the position adopted by William Hinton in *The Great Reversal* (New York: Monthly Review Press, 1990).

18. Perry Link, *Evening Chats in Beijing: Probing China's Predicament* (New York: Norton, 1992), pp. 27–8. For a discussion of decollectivization and the mood of the peasantry see Paul G. Pickowicz, "Long Bow: The Movie," *American Anthropological Association Society for Visual Anthropology Newsletter*, 3, no. 3 (Fall 1987), pp. 1–5, and Edward Friedman, "Deng versus the Peasantry: Recollectivization in the Chinese Countryside," *Problems of Communism* (September–October 1990), pp. 30–43.

19. Popular culture in rural North China in the 1950s and early 1960s is discussed at length in Edward Friedman, Paul G. Pickowicz, and Mark Selden, *Chinese Village, Socialist State* (New Haven, Conn.: Yale University Press, 1991).

20. "*Heipao shijian* zongheng tan" [Perspectives on *The Black Cannon Incident*], *Dangdai dianying*, no. 3 (1986), p. 58.

21. Su Shaozhi, "The Crisis of Marxism in China," *The World & I*, no. 10 (October 1989), p. 74.

22. "Cu ren shen si de *Heipao shijian*" [*The Black Cannon Incident* Forces You to Think], *Dianying yishu*, no. 4 (1986), p. 16.

23. Ibid., p. 9.

24. Su Shaokang and Wang Luxiang, *Heshang* (Xianggang: Sanlian shudian, 1989).
25. "*Heipao shijian* zongheng tan," pp. 57–9; "Cu ren shen si de *Heipao shijian*," pp. 12–13.
26. "*Heipao shijian* zongheng tan," p. 62.
27. Ibid., p. 54.
28. Ibid., pp. 50–4.
29. "Cu ren shen si de *Heipao shijian*," p. 17.
30. Ibid., p. 16.
31. Ibid., p. 10.
32. Ibid.
33. "*Heipao shijian* zongheng tan," pp. 57–8.
34. James Watson, "The Renegotiation of Chinese Cultural Identity in the Post-Mao Era: An Anthropological Perspective," in Jeffrey N. Wasserstrom and Elizabeth J. Perry, eds., *Popular Protest and Political Culture in Modern China: Learning from 1989* (Boulder, Colo.: Westview Press, 1992), p. 78.
35. For a discussion of utopian and dystopian visions of the Chinese future, see Maurice Meisner, *Marxism, Maoism and Utopianism: Eight Essays* (Madison: University of Wisconsin Press, 1982), pp. 184–211.
36. See Jim Mann, *Beijing Jeep* (New York: Simon & Schuster, 1989), p. 260.
37. For a discussion of the historical background of recent campaigns against "bourgeois liberalization" see Paul G. Pickowicz, "The Theme of Spiritual Pollution in Chinese Films of the 1930s," *Modern China*, 17, no. 1 (January 1991), pp. 38–75.
38. "*Cuowei* cuowei?" [Is *Dislocation* Dislocated?], *Dianying yishu*, no. 6 (1987), p. 46. Instead of publishing the comments of scholars and critics, *Dangdai dianying* published remarks made by the production crew of *Dislocation*. See "Ningyuan zai tansuozhong shibai, buyuan zai baoshouzhong gouan" [It Is Better to Fail in the Process of Experimentation Than to Play It Safe by Taking No Risks], *Dangdai dianying*, no. 3 (1987), pp. 111–23.
39. "*Cuowei* cuowei?" pp. 40–1.
40. "Cu ren shen si de *Heipao shijian*," p. 12.
41. "*Cuowei* cuowei?" p. 44. For an example of Luo Yijun's cautious approach to film criticism, see his *Fengyu yinmu* [Trials and Tribulations on Screen] (Beijing: Zhongguo dianying chuban she, 1983).
42. "*Cuowei* cuowei?" p. 45.
43. *South China Morning Post* (Associated Press wire story), December 16, 1988.
44. *Guangming ribao*, December 15, 1988.
45. Dai Jinhua, "Ideology, Wang Shuo, 1988," *China Screen*, no. 4 (1989), p. 28.
46. Shao Mujun, "Why Did a Wang Shuo Cinema Craze Occur?" *China Screen*, no. 4 (1989), p. 29.
47. Su Bing, "Zisha milian de goucheng" [Obsession with Suicide], *Dangdai dianying*, no. 2 (1990), pp. 95–9.
48. Dai Jinhua, "Ideology, Wang Shuo, 1988," p. 28.
49. *Beijing Review*, 32, no. 44 (1989), p. 44.
50. Paul Clark, "June 4, 1989 and Chinese Cinema," *Asian Cinema*, 4, nos. 1–2 (1988–9), pp. 14–15.
51. Teng Jinxian, "Harmful Trends in Film Creation," *China Screen*, no. 3 (1990), p. 2.
52. "Cu ren shen si de *Heipao shijian*," p. 9. I do not mean to suggest that there were no veteran directors who approached contemporary society in a direct and critical way. Wu

Tianming and Huang Jianzhong are two obvious examples of artists who did so quite successfully.

53. "The Three Screen Faces of China," *Economist*, July 4, 1987, pp. 87–90.

54. Herbert Marcuse, *The Aesthetic Dimension: Toward a Critique of Marxist Aesthetics* (Boston: Beacon Press, 1978), p. 9.

55. Ibid., p. 14.

56. Ibid., p. 47.

4

NEITHER ONE THING NOR ANOTHER

TOWARD A STUDY OF THE VIEWING SUBJECT AND CHINESE CINEMA IN THE 1980S

Chris Berry

E mphasizing the unfinishable qualities of this essay is fundamental to what I want to communicate about Chinese film and social change in the 1980s. I have come to the conclusion that Chinese film and social change in the 1980s does not constitute an object; it is too complex, too contradictory, too dynamic, and too chaotic to be isolated and described. The impossibility of this project does not mean, however, that film and social change in the 1980s is beyond understanding. Rather, it means that what is to be understood is precisely its refusal to be one thing or another, and precisely how it refuses to be one thing or another, and I can best communicate these qualities by tracing my own failed efforts to pin it down as an object.[1]

The Classical Viewing Subject

When I first began this project, its impossibility was not apparent to me. Indeed, I had produced a paradigm for the relationship between mainland cinema and society between the 1949 Liberation and the late 1970s, and felt that I might be able to adapt and extend this work in some way to the 1980s.[2] In that earlier work, I used the term "classical Chinese cinema" to refer to the variety of socialist realist filmmaking dominant throughout the period in question and analyzed the way in which this cinema positions the viewer, with particular reference to gender.[3]

This idea of viewer positioning conceives film as discourse, and discourse as already possessing a position for the viewer. To give a very simple example, much as a reader is called upon to relate differently to the two phrases "I see you" and "He sees you," the relationship between camera position and viewer can alter the way in which a viewer relates to a shot in a film. To distinguish the viewer constructed in this way by the film from actual viewers (they are not necessarily one and the same thing), I used the term "viewing subject."[4] And by examining this viewing subject produced by the films of the 1950s, 1960s, and 1970s, I was, in a sense, analyzing the "new socialist person" the Party so frequently proclaimed the "new society" was giving birth to.

This problematic of the classical viewing subject seemed (and still seems to me) worth returning to in a consideration of film and social change in the 1980s, for a number of reasons. First, the concept of the viewing subject provides a somewhat more sophisticated way of understanding film not as merely reflecting and separate from social change, but as productive and part of social change. Furthermore, the classical mainland cinema had such longevity and dominance in the People's Republic that understanding the cinema of the 1980s demands its deployment as backdrop.

The viewing subject also promises us a way of pulling together some of the most interesting but also disparate recent critical work that has appeared on Chinese film in the 1980s and relating it back to the earlier period. Subjectivity, gender, and sexuality have all emerged as a nexus of overlapping interests, which has led to the production of a wide variety of articles over the past few years.[5] I find these writings to be among the most exciting produced on Chinese cinema at the moment, but feel that their arguments are difficult to connect because they are localized and specific, either in film coverage or in focus. For example, ideally, work on the representation of women or men should be placed in a broader context of gender systems, and work on any individual film should be placed in relation to Chinese cinema as a whole. So far this broader context is missing, but the way in which the viewer is positioned by the film promises a trajectory through this dense complex of related topics. It holds out the potential of a link between text and social formation, and with its roots in psychoanalysis as well as linguistics, it insists upon an attention to that link within a framework that considers gender, the subject, and the movement of desire.

In my earlier article, I suggested that the viewing subject produced by the classical post-1949 mainland cinema is a nonindividualized, communal subject. This subject is constructed by a specific conjuncture of Hollywood and socialist realist editing techniques and figural representation whereby the camera is relatively rarely aligned with individual characters. Furthermore, when such alignment does occur, at best it is a transitional phase in the narrative, but most frequently it signifies failure and the breakdown of the social. I also suggested that separating the viewing subject in this way from any consistent identification with individual characters signifies a privileged position from which the viewing subject can understand events as the enunciating subject, presumably the Party, sees them. Thus, power and knowledge are located not only outside the individual but also outside the ordinary people.[6]

More recent work enables me to expand this picture of the classical subject.

Initially, I was struck by the ungendered character of the Chinese classical viewing subject as contrasted with the phallocentric male subject of Hollywood cinema. However, since then, Wang Yuejin has written a remarkable, ground-breaking article on *Red Sorghum* [*Hong gaoliang*, 1987], in which he has argued that traditional Chinese ideology is structured not by the castration anxiety of the West, but by what he terms a "femininity complex." He explains that characteristics traditionally held to be feminine, such as stillness, passivity, and unquestioning obedience, are highly valorized, whether for biologically male or for female citizens. Many of the heroes of Chinese fictional discourses are, in fact, heroines, whereas masculine figures are not only aggressive and independent, but often also flawed and social outcasts.[7]

Observations similar to Wang's can also be made about classical mainland Chinese cinema; the heroes in both *Li Shuangshuang* [*Li Shuangshuang*, 1962] and *The In-Laws* [*Xiyingmen*, 1981], the films I wrote about in my earlier article, are women who act in accordance with Party policy, sacrificing their individual interest for the general good as defined by the Party. This may appear to undermine my earlier conclusion that the classical viewing subject is relatively ungendered, but in fact I believe Wang's observations complement my earlier ideas. Although women feature so frequently as heroes in classical mainland films, they are indeed not physically aligned with the camera as "relays" in the manner commonly used for male heroes in Hollywood. Rather, they are displayed as objects for emulation, divorced from the still-ungendered site of enunciation. This cinematic language echoes Wang's observations about the traditional feminine; it produces a hero who is not autonomous but who acts in accordance with a knowledge produced outside herself, and in so doing acknowledges her own interpellation and is, in return, rewarded with the status of exemplar. This is a cinematic figuring of Sun Longji's discussion of the traditional Chinese subject as the sum of relationships, and not as a subject unto itself.[8]

Continuity

This understanding of the classical viewing subject foregrounds questions of continuity, rupture, and change in regard to its origins. By rooting the classical subject in ancient, long-held conceptions of the masculine and feminine, Wang is questioning 1949 as a moment of pure rupture.[9] Instead, one of the implications of the classical subject as I have developed it in the preceding section is that, whatever other changes may have occurred, the "new socialist person" of Communist China was still constructed as subordinate to an outside force. This perspective on how people were positioned to see themselves fits well with other revisionist work on the same period of mainland Chinese history. For example, various recent works on women in China have questioned the nature of the changes wrought by the Party after 1949, seeing continuity in the continued subordination of women to the Party in the place of the imperial bureaucracy, and seeing such liberation from the family as may have occurred as being at the behest of this outside, superior force.[10]

With 1949 as a questionable moment of rupture, it is perhaps not surprising to find that the late 1970s are an equally problematic era. In general political history, there never has been a single date marking the birth of the new post–Cultural Revolution China with the same convenience that October 1, 1949, marks the founding of the People's Republic. Rather, there are a series of breakpoints in the late 1970s, among them the death of Premier Zhou Enlai in early 1976, the death of Chairman Mao later in the same year, and soon after, the arrest of the Gang of Four. Nowadays, the Third Plenary Session of the Eleventh Central Committee of the Communist Party of China, held in late 1978, which marks the end of the brief rule of Chairman Hua Guofeng and the rise of Deng Xiaoping, is frequently cited as an equally important date. Given the general difficulty of finding a single point that marks a decisive shift or break, it should come as no surprise that in the history of the Chinese cinema there is also no clear break marking the death of the classical subject and its emergence in some new form.

Indeed, just as Deng Xiaoping is now frequently noted to have maintained the existing political system while introducing all manner of social and economic reforms, the classical viewing subject who serves and perhaps even forms part of that existing political system is still a strong force in mainstream mainland cinema, alongside the various new forms of subjectivity that emerged during the 1980s. The continued existence of the classical subject marks the continued power that the Party and the state organs it controls exercise over the studios. This is clearly indicated by a remark made in 1986 by Wu Tianming, the former head of Xian Film Studio, that indicated there were three audiences he had to make films for, one of which was the government.[11]

Among these films produced for the government that sustain the classical viewing subject, hagiographies of old Communist generals and party-line melodramas are most common. Echoing the umbrella term used to cover policy in the 1980s, the latter are known as *gaige pianzi,* or "reform films." In place of the good proletarians unmasking capitalism on behalf of the Party, these films are populated by technocrats and entrepreneurs, fighting the forces of bureaucracy to modernize China and make profits, also on behalf of the Party. Like their predecessors, they are produced as objects for emulation in morality plays, and the viewing subject is constructed in a privileged, distanced relation to the characters from which the correctness of the model heroes' actions is clearly apparent.[12]

Perhaps not surprisingly, most of these dull and predictable "reform films" are little known outside China. However, the continuation of the classical viewing subject is by no means confined to these films; it can be discerned in a wide variety of other films, too. For example, both *In the Wild Mountains* [*Yeshan,* 1986] and *Hibiscus Town* [*Furongzhen,* 1986] could be cited in this regard. The bean curd seller Hu Yuyin takes on the exemplary hero role in *Hibiscus Town,* and the two very different wives, Guilan and Qiurong, share the role in *In the Wild Mountains*. Both films move away from the films of 1950s and 1960s in significant ways, but still maintain a certain continuity with them. Although Guilan's faith in the independent enterprise being promoted when *In the Wild Mountains* was being produced still signifies her as a handmaiden of the Party, the presence of the Party as the source of her actions is very much downplayed. In the case of Hu Yuyin in *Hibiscus Town*, the Party even figures as an obstacle to her progress. However, it does not take much analysis to see that this does not mean these women are figured as autonomous. Cinematically, the viewer is still positioned to see them as exemplars, acknowledged as such from an enunciatory point outside themselves. Furthermore, it can be argued that the disappearance of the Party as their guiding light simply marks their return to traditional Confucian values: all three are characterized by a primary loyalty to their husbands, for whom they quietly serve and struggle. Given Wang Yuejin's analysis of the historical links between Confucian ideology and the needs of the Communist state, this construction of Qiurong and Hu Yuyin in *In the Wild Mountains* and *Hibiscus Town* can simply be understood as a fallback position, a blind concealing the persistent effort to produce obedient citizens.

Fragmentation

Taken together, the continuity and adaptations of the type of subject positioning associated with the classical Chinese cinema, and the difficulty of marking any particular point at which it loses dominance, suggest that the idea of a paradigm shift in the 1980s is as questionable as that of revolution itself. Thus, it may be necessary to think in terms of a transitional phase, or even to follow Foucault and take up the Nietzschean model of history as genealogy – that is, as moving through a series of gradual (but not necessarily gentle) mutations from episteme to episteme, rather than radical ruptures.[13]

Certainly, the late 1970s provide plenty of evidence for the usefulness of that idea. Paul Clark has argued that this period marked a realignment of forces, which gave filmmakers themselves greater control over production. This occurred for a number of reasons: the deprivations suffered by almost everyone in the industry during the Cultural Revolution made it more difficult for the Party to operate a "divide-and-conquer" policy within the cinema; Party members were divided among themselves; and audiences were no longer so passive in expressing their opinions and desires.[14] During this same period, similar realignments on a broader sociopolitical scale led the Party to admit to a significant postrevolutionary period of "mistakes" for the first time ever. At first, during the Hua Guofeng interregnum between 1976 and 1978, these "mistakes" were seen as confined to actions of the Gang of Four and Lin Biao, and to the former group's period of dominance before and immediately after Mao's death in 1976. With the ascension of Deng Xiaoping at the end of 1978, however, the stain was allowed to spread rapidly to cover the entire decade of the Cultural Revolution (1966–76), and eventually even the Anti-Rightist Campaign of 1957 and the Great Leap Forward that followed.

Just as a "literature of the wounded" was produced about suffering during these periods of error, so films appeared that represented the same topics.[15] For the most part, these adopted existing cinematic conventions associated with the classical paradigm to represent cultural failure. In the films of the 1950s and 1960s, failure was associated with the fragmentation of the communal and corresponding cinematic techniques such as shot/reverse-shot and close-up, both of which position the viewer in close physical proximity to individual characters. In the films of the 1970s, these techniques, which were rare in the earlier films, became more common. The couple, family, or other group was broken up into individuals, and a high degree of subjectivity, often in the form of flashbacks with first-person narration, was used to render these negative periods.

Although films of this type were made as early as 1978, an example from 1981 is fairly typical. Dance Love [Wu lian] made at the Emei Film Studio in Chengdu, is a love story about a choreographer named Xiang Feng and a Yi minority dancer called Qumu Azhi. The film begins in 1978, when Xiang Feng is taking a train trip to the Yi region to visit a dance festival. In flashback, he remembers how he met Qumu Azhi in this same place twenty years before, and how they fell in love and worked together. His thoughts are rendered in voice-over, making the flashback all the more subjective. Xiang Feng thinks Qumu Azhi has been killed by the Gang of Four during the Cultural Revolution, but discovers she is still alive. When they meet again, however, she shuns him. Her flashback explains why. The film proceeds through alternating, subjective flashbacks to tell a tale of suffering and misunderstanding until mutual understanding is reestablished and the couple reunited. At this point, individual subjectivity, in this film signifying loss, disappears with the unity of the couple.

The threat to the classical system (cinematic or political) lies not in the accommodation of new elements such as these, resisted and delayed though they were at first, but in the question of their resolution. Given the particular period these films deal with, different resolutions imply different relations to the present. The Party preferred to represent the end of the Cultural Revolution as a return to the harmony of the past. This is the case in Dance Love, where it transpires that Qumu Azhi is not dead, that the separation of the couple was all a misunderstanding, and that everything can be put right. However, not all filmmakers chose the happy-ending formula. In refusing to do so, they signified their refusal to acknowledge that the individualized viewing subject in a state of loss was a temporary aberration and merely a thing of the past.

Good examples of this new type of film include The Legend of Tianyun Mountain [Tianyunshan chuanqi, 1980] and On a Narrow Street [Xiaojie, 1981]. Both films follow the multiple, highly subjective flashback technique found in Dance Love, but without its reassuring resolution. In the case of The Legend of

Tianyun Mountain, one couple is separated by the Anti-Rightist Campaign, the other by the recriminations that follow the end of the Cultural Revolution. The film constructs the entanglements between them in such a way that both couples can never return to the way they were. In one case, the man and woman die; in the other, they can never be reunited, and only a young girl remains as a sign of hope for the future. In *On a Narrow Street,* three possible endings are offered to the audience for a young couple separated by the Cultural Revolution. In one, all is restored. In another, it is impossible to restore things as they were (i.e., the girl is blinded), but there is still hope for the future. In the third, the couple have been so brutalized by their experience that everything is bleak.

This tendency to refuse the restoration of the classical subject and the construction of an exemplary hero came to a halt after the banning of *Bitter Love* [*Kulian,* 1981]. While both *The Legend of Tianyun Mountain* and *On a Narrow Street* offered some hope for the future, this film was particularly bleak, focusing on a man persecuted by the Cultural Revolution and dying before his friends can reach him with news of the fall of the Gang of Four. Before he dies, he stamps a question mark in the snow, his body forming the dot. Films about the Cultural Revolution with ambiguous endings largely disappeared after *Bitter Love* was banned, and indeed interesting deviations from the classical subject were made more difficult to get again by the short-lived Anti–Spiritual Pollution Campaign of 1983.

Impotents and Infants

Events such as the campaign against Bai Hua in 1981 and the Anti–Spiritual Pollution Campaign of 1983 indicate that even if the post–Cultural Revolution period was one of transition or mutation, it was not a simple, linear process. Rather, change was being produced unevenly out of struggle and contradiction. This process, of course, spread across the whole of Chinese society, with cinema and culture in general participating in it. Spiritual pollution, for example, was attributed to the negative influences that allegedly infiltrated China after the country opened up again after 1978. The notion of spiritual pollution, which views culture as a part of broad social patterns, reflects a highly contradictory approach to cultural and social change.

Much of this contradiction can be understood as revolving around problems of the individual and the communal. Deng Xiaoping's "reform" program placed a strong emphasis on economic devolution, whereby individual households or work units were to be held responsible for their own profits and losses in an effort to encourage efficiency and increased production. This system was introduced to the countryside at the beginning of the 1980s and to the cities in the middle of the decade. These economic reforms valorized the idea of autonomy, but as I have already noted, they were not accompanied by any similar adjustments on the sociopolitical level. Although these reforms were selective and localized, they still represent a shift from the immediate post–Cultural Revolution years. In the films from that period just discussed, individuality figures only as a failure of the social and is in no way valorized as autonomy. However, from the mid-1980s on, as the reform program began to make itself felt in the cities where the film studios were located, films that valorized the individual in various ways also began to appear. These figure the adjusted classical model that still positions the viewer in the same way but, as I discussed earlier, changes the type of character the viewer is positioned to emulate. Nonetheless, the four years of relative liberalism between the Anti–Spiritual Pollution Campaign of 1983 and the Anti–Bourgeois Liberalization Campaign of 1987 also left room for films that construct very different viewing subjects.[16]

I use the plural, "viewing subjects," here because examination of the films suggests there was no single dominant paradigm for the 1980s comparable to what I argued for the classical period, and that it would not be possible to attribute the continued appearance of the classical subject to some "lag," with the fragmentation of the immediate post–Cultural Revolution as transition. Rather, it seemed that a series of models of different subject positions, all produced within the problematic of the individual versus the communal, would be necessary. I distinguished these models on a number of grounds. Is the viewing subject constructed as collective or individual? Male, female, or nongendered? Is it positioned to perceive the diegesis (the world of the film) and the events and characters in it as providing possibilities for emulation, rejection, or neither? Is it implied in a past, present, or future relation to the diegetic? And finally, is it constructed to perceive the diegetic level as realist (and possibly realizable) or fictional?

The first model arising from this analysis is one that uses gender to shift from the communal toward the individual. It positions the viewing subject as male and desiring, rather than as neutral and pupil-like. Because the film lacks any heroic character to emulate, the viewing subject is also positioned in a negative relation to the traditional Chinese society represented in the film, which it characterizes as lacking masculinity. This is opposed to the classical model discussed by Wang Yuejin, in which lack of masculinity is not a problem at all, and indeed this cinematic moment seems in many ways to foreshadow Wang Yuejin's own discussion.

In 1985 two films set in prerevolutionary years were made about the "child-husband" phenomenon, whereby infant boys were married to pubescent girls so the husband's family could get the benefit of her labor immediately (Figures 14, 15, and 16). In both the films in question, A Good Woman [Liangjia funü, 1985] and Girl from Hunan [Xiangnü Xiaoxiao, 1986], the families have no male head or adult sons and so are particularly short of hands to work the land. The two films are fairly similar, but I will focus on Girl from Hunan both for reasons of economy and because I have had greater access to this film.[17]

In a brief discussion in her article on the representations of women in the

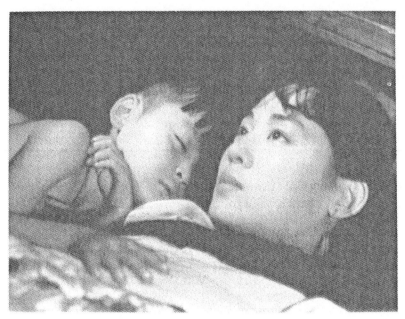

14. Husband and wife. Huang Jianzhong, *A Good Woman* (1985). CHINA FILM
IMPORT AND EXPORT CORPORATION, LOS ANGELES

15. Husband (Chunguan) and wife (Xiaoxiao). Xie Fei, *Girl from Hunan* (1986).
CHINA FILM IMPORT AND EXPORT CORPORATION, LOS ANGELES

1980s, Esther Yau draws parallels between both *A Good Woman* and *Girl from Hunan* and the films that male directors and writers were required to produce in the 1950s about the oppression of women in feudal society. She suggests that the prime difference in the 1980s films lies in their representation of ordinary peasant men, rather than the Party, as the positive harbingers of change, although in both cases change is frustrated.[18] This reading is based on narrative thematics, and is put forward as an improvement on analyses of characters that are based on typology alone. However, while I agree that this is a methodological advance, this reading is not the whole story. Rather, it can be taken further by also attending to the films' enunciation and viewer positioning.

In both films, and particularly in *Girl from Hunan,* sympathy for the fate of women in traditional society is foregrounded by the narrative and repeated dialogue to emphasize that women suffer. The picture is complicated, however, first by the fact that women are shown in the film to participate in the maintenance of this society, and second by the fact that men suffer in this society as well. Certainly, men also play a dominant role in the maintenance of the society. In the case of *Girl from Hunan,* for example, Xiaoxiao, the main character, is taken in the bridal sedan by her uncle to be married. Another example of male dominance involves a widow who is accused of adultery by the patriarchy. In this case,

16. The wedding ceremony. Xie Fei, *Girl from Hunan* (1986). CHINA FILM IMPORT AND EXPORT CORPORATION, LOS ANGELES

justice is administered by the clan headman in the name of the clan's male ancestors. More important, however, are the scenes within the household Xiao-xiao joins, which take up most of the film. Here it is her mother-in-law who is the effective head of household and who enforces and subscribes to the traditional system.

Furthermore, we also see men suffer in this system. At the end of the film, when Xiaoxiao's own little boy is of the age her husband, Chunguan, was when he was married, she takes up her mother-in-law's role. With Chunguan looking on, in a scene that reprises the wedding ceremony at the beginning of the film, she drags her own protesting little boy off to be married to a pubescent bride some ten years his senior. That Chunguan and his little stepson should be placed under the power of women in the film is particularly significant, because Chunguan has a special relationship to the enunciation of the film and therefore the viewing subject. His submission to the power of the film's women provides the foundation for positioning the viewer in a rather different relation to the represented suffering of women than the sympathetic relation one might expect.

At first, Xiaoxiao appears to enjoy the primary focus of the film. We follow her journey to the village as a bride, discover the village with her, and indeed follow her throughout almost all the film. However, although the viewer is enabled in this way to develop an understanding of Xiaoxiao's experiences and emotions as she endures her various troubles, she is not positioned as a relay or a narrative agent. Rather, Xiaoxiao is passive, focused upon, and objectified, and the viewer is distanced from her rather than called upon to identify with her. Her basically passive status is signified emphatically in the opening scenes of her journey to the village, where she is cooped up in the sedan chair, taken by her uncle to a place she has never been before, able to see little, and not even allowed to get out to relieve herself.

In some ways, Xiaoxiao's character is produced in a manner reminiscent of the construction of the classical viewing subject, in that the viewer is distanced from the character.[19] However, Xiaoxiao is portrayed not as a revolutionary heroine, but, from the opening scene, as an object of the gaze. A certain hermeneutic interest is created for the viewer because Xiaoxiao is hidden from view in her sedan. Furthermore, the desire to look upon her is represented in the diegesis through all the villagers when she arrives. Indeed, her status as a fascinating object of the gaze prepares the way for a male enunciation. What is most interesting is that this male enunciation is constructed through Chunguan, her infant husband.

Saved from guilt by the alibi of being an "innocent" child, Chunguan unwittingly aids the narrative. When he and Xiaoxiao are in the hills, it is Chunguan who suggests they go and see Huagou, the field hand. When it is raining and they take shelter in the mill, it is Chunguan who persuades Huagou to "stay and play" when he makes to leave, facilitating Xiaoxiao and Huagou's affair. Later, when Xiaoxiao is trying to induce a miscarriage, it is Chunguan who interrupts her.

And still later, after her pregnancy has led to discovery and the possibility of a death sentence, it is Chunguan who saves her by his emotional attachment to her. In other words, the boy-child plays a crucial role in the whole sadistic narrative progress to which Xiaoxiao is subjected – through transgression, punishment, recuperation, and containment.

Thus, the film positions the viewing subject to find sadistic pleasure in Xiaoxiao's fate without being held accountable for it. This is underlined by the film's epilogue, mentioned earlier. Some years later, Chunguan is witness to his little stepson going through the same thing he went through. The film closes with Chunguan wandering on a hilltop, deep in thought. Given that the film is set in the past, this scene suggests the possibility that the entire story is to be read as Chunguan's memories and reconstruction of Xiaoxiao's story, prompted by seeing his own stepson being married.

This narrative and enumerative arrangement are quite different from the typical 1950s films about the suffering of women in feudal society. First, there is no suggestion that the Party is the force that will resolve the problems of feudalism. Modernization appears in the film in the form of girl students in town, but there is no association with leftist political activities of any sort. Second, the use of the innocent child-husband as a signifier of narrative agency and enunciation effectively distances patriarchy as the source of the suffering of women in traditional society. This distancing is important if masculinity is to be signified as what is missing in this world, and if Huagou is to function effectively as a sign of ineffective and marginalized masculinity.

Aphanasis?

Around the time *A Good Woman* and *Girl from Hunan* were produced, the first few of another group of films known to us all by now as the Fifth Generation films were released. These included *One and Eight* [*Yige he bage*, 1985], *Yellow Earth* [*Huang tudi*, 1985], and *On the Hunting Ground* [*Liechang zasag*, 1985]. Interestingly, *Yellow Earth* fits the model I have just constructed from *Girl from Hunan*. Cuiqiao, the peasant girl (who eventually drowns), functions in many ways as an object of the gaze (and as an aural object) for Gu Qing, the soldier, and for the viewer (Figures 17, 18, and 19). The soldier is as responsible for getting her into trouble as Huagou the field hand was responsible for Xiaoxiao's misfortune, and equally unable to help her out of her difficulties; and the traditional peasant society itself is also populated only by little boys and old men.

Possible though such a reading is, however, it is by no means as strong as in *Girl from Hunan*. *Yellow Earth* is not constructed around desire in the same way that *Girl from Hunan* is, and this aspect of Cuiqiao's relationship with the soldier Gu Qing is entirely implicit. Furthermore, little Hanhan (Cuiqiao's brother) does not act as narrative agent in the same way as Chunguan does in *Girl from Hunan*. In all, the viewing subject is only weakly marked as masculine, and although, as

17. The peasant girl, Cuiqiao. Chen Kaige, *Yellow Earth* (1985). CHINA FILM IMPORT AND EXPORT CORPORATION, LOS ANGELES

18. From left: Cuiqiao, the peasant girl; Gu Qing, a soldier in the People's Liberation Army; Hanhan, Cuiqiao's brother; and Cuiqiao's father. Chen Kaige, *Yellow Earth* (1985). CHINA FILM IMPORT AND EXPORT CORPORATION, LOS ANGELES

19. The soldier, Gu Qing. Chen Kaige, *Yellow Earth* (1985). CHINA FILM IMPORT AND EXPORT CORPORATION, LOS ANGELES

Esther Yau has pointed out, Cuiqiao's fate can be ascribed to the two sets of rules that bind, on the one hand, her feudal father and, on the other, the Communist soldier, the problem cannot be ascribed as readily to lack of masculinity as to lack of independence itself.[20]

My ambivalence as to this reading of *Yellow Earth* relates to the ambiguity that I think nearly everyone who has written on these Fifth Generation films has noted as a marked contrast to the clear, didactic signification of the classical cinema. However, I would argue that this ambiguity in itself constitutes another model, one that by various strategies refuses either to set up a clear moral/political position for the viewer or to construct an exemplary positive or negative figure for emulation or criticism.

Esther Yau's reading of the film is probably the best-known text in this regard.[21] Among other things, she notes the deployment of the Daoist elements of the Chinese landscape painting tradition, such as its empty spaces, and argues that it is aimed at liberating Chinese cinema from the relentless signification of the classical mainland tradition. More recently, Rey Chow has taken up these ideas, but discourages any reading that might see the use of Daoist elements as an aestheticist retreat from politics. Rather, she argues that the full ambiguity of

Yellow Earth lies not only in its deployment of empty space, but also in a dynamic decentering that makes significations slip away at every attempt to grasp them.[22] For example, we learn of Cuiqiao's feelings in only an indirect way, through songs, and we witness these songs being altered in their recording by the soldier – a process that, as Chow suggests, throws into question the whole idea of recording as reliable, whether cinematic or otherwise. Thus, the general impossibility of representation undermines signification entirely.

Chow argues that this "textual elusiveness" provides the foundation for aphanasis: the fading of the subject effect. That is, every time the viewer may feel him- or herself positioned as a defined subject, a subject that can be described and named, the strategy of elusiveness undermines and dissolves this effect. Chow adds that this aphanasis is radical "in a context where politics, as the omnipresently agential, systematically wipes out the elusive." I would agree emphatically that the elusiveness constructed in *Yellow Earth* is a radical political act. I would add, however, that the text's elusiveness is strategic and that *Yellow Earth* is radical not merely because it is elusive, but because that elusiveness is politically significant in the context of its original production and reception.

The full extent of the elusiveness of *Yellow Earth* lies in the fact that it is not even clear that it is elusive. Certainly, to viewers like Chow, Yau, and indeed myself, it can be read in this way. But it is so elusive that it can also be read as transparently significatory and didactic along the lines of the classical mainland cinema. Indeed, a reading based purely on narrative and dialogue could interpret the film as a classical prerevolutionary story about the suffering of the peasantry and their need for the Communist Party. Plot elements such as the growing sympathy that the old farmer's children, Cuiqiao and Hanhan, develop for the soldier and the final scene in which Hanhan turns against the tide of superstitious worshipers praying for rain and runs toward the soldier would support this reading, as would the reappearance of Cuiqiao's voice on the soundtrack at the close of the film singing her song in praise of the Communist Party.

In the context of its production, this latter reading was necessary. Otherwise, *Yellow Earth* would not have gotten past the Film Bureau's censorship board and been released. Furthermore, the entire Chinese filmgoing public is conscious of the censorship process. Bringing this knowledge to the cinema, the Chinese viewer is unlikely to assume that the text is elusive because it wants to support the existing order, but rather to see its elusiveness as a way of inviting a critical reading. In this sense, then, *Yellow Earth* is not absolutely aphanasitic, but rather encourages the fading of the classical subject (poised to learn and emulate) and suggests its replacement by a thinking, analytical, and critical subject.

The same can be said of other early Fifth Generation texts, although few of them (an exception being *On the Hunting Ground*) employ ambiguity and elusiveness to the extent that *Yellow Earth* does. I would argue that much of the significatory elusiveness of *Yellow Earth* lies not only in its use of the empty space of quasi-landscape paintings, but also in its use of saturated signifiers. The loess plateau, a wedding scene, vast landscapes dotted with tiny figures, the raging Yellow River – these are all images that have been used over and over again in Chinese culture, and their accreted polysemy makes impossible any single, coherent interpretation.

On the Hunting Ground, in contrast, uses what for Han Chinese viewers would be empty signifiers. Set in traditional Mongol society, the film is almost a collage of everyday life, including hunting scenes, religious rites, and so forth. Other films about national minorities typically have a Han Chinese character to whom the Mongols explain the rites, but here there is no such effort.[23] As for the scenes of everyday life, although there is a thread of a plot about an outcast from society, the relevance of these scenes to the plot is difficult to establish. Again, they may seem empty of specific signification to the viewer.

As with *Yellow Earth*, however, I would argue that this elusiveness in *On the Hunting Ground* is strategic rather than absolute. For the conventionally minded, the film can be read as a semidocumentary about a national minority (albeit a rather dull one), and it seems certain that this is how it was taken by the censorship board. However, for those viewers sensitive to the possibilities the film's ambiguity opens up, other readings are encouraged. The director of *On the Hunting Ground*, Tian Zhuangzhuang, has indicated that he intended both this film and his followup film about Tibet, *Horse Thief* [*Daoma zei*, 1986], to be read as metaphors for Han Chinese society during the Cultural Revolution.[24] The oscillation between the highly ordered agricultural and domestic aspects of Mongol life and the extreme violence of the hunting ground can be read in terms of a similar oscillation between order and chaos in Han Chinese society, with the Cultural Revolution as a period of extreme chaos. As well, the theme of the group versus the individual, with the individual as an outcast, can be seen as a metaphor for aspects of Chinese society. Whether a regular Chinese viewer would read the film this specifically is open to question, but again I would suggest that the elusiveness of *On the Hunting Ground*, like that of *Yellow Earth*, is contextually (rather than textually) positioned to invite critical, analytic reading practices that demand independent thought of the viewer.

The Female Subject

During the four-year gap between the Anti–Spiritual Pollution Campaign and the Anti–Bourgeois Liberalization Campaign, a third type of viewing subject can be distinguished, and it is primarily marked as female. Like the two viewing subjects already discussed, this third type undermines and moves beyond the classical model by failing to provide a character that the viewing subject is positioned to emulate. However, unlike the other two, which position the viewer in a rather distanced and antagonistic relationship to the characters and society represented, the subject position constructed by the films known in China as "women's cinema" vacillates between a high level of identification between viewing subject and character and a distancing, questioning attitude.[25]

For the most part, Chinese women's cinema was produced by women in their thirties or forties who had gone through the Cultural Revolution during their late teens and twenties. Two of the directors are members of the Fifth Generation. *Sacrificed Youth* [*Qingchunji,* 1985] (Figure 20), *Season for Love* [*Lianai lijie,* 1986], and *Army Nurse* [*Nüer lou,* 1986] are all about women's memories of reaching adulthood during the Cultural Revolution and its impact on their later lives. However, none of the films sets these characters up as exemplary social models. Rather, the films establish a clearly marked female subjectivity and a high level of introversion in their characters, using often fragmentary and contemplative voice-over together with flashback, so that, to a Western viewer, the main characters bear comparison in some ways with the downtrodden male heroes of Hollywood film noir in the 1940s. In the Chinese women's cinema, these highly subjective characters are always unmarried in the narrative present and all are approaching the age when in Chinese society they will risk being stigmatized as spinsters. All of them have had past love affairs cut short by circumstances outside their control, be those circumstances political or familial. In *Army Nurse* and *Season for Love,* friends and family are trying to arrange marriages for them, but they ultimately determine to find their own way forward.

What is interesting about these films is that, although they clearly set up an individualized subjectivity, both individuality and subjectivity are still structured as a result of the failure of the communal, as is the case in the classical mainland

20. Zhang Nuanxin, *Sacrificed Youth* (1985).

cinema. All the major women characters in these films are separated from their families and their old, familiar lives in the cities by the Cultural Revolution, and then again from their lovers by forces beyond their control. Subjectivity and individual autonomy are forced upon them, and their loss of communal identity is a cause for mourning. Thus, there is no quasi-oedipal trajectory whereby subjectivity is seen as a triumphant achievement. Furthermore, in their faith in romance and their desire for a man, some of these women seem to express the wish to be rid of their individual autonomy, to return to some sort of communality (albeit not that of the good pupil of the Party set out in the classical mainland film). At the same time, however, in their desire to determine their own futures, these women also seem unwilling to give up their autonomy: at the very least, there is ambiguity constructed around the contradiction between the demands of the communal and the individual, with romance positioned between the two.

Some of these films are adapted from a highly introverted, subjective genre of women's writing that was under production at the same time. *Sunshine and Showers* [*Taiyang yu*, 1988], although directed by a man, is also adapted from this genre. Like the films I have been discussing, the original short story is written in the first person, from the perspective of a lonely librarian. The film adaptation eschews flashback and first-person narration, but nonetheless the type of woman it represents can be compared to that in other films of the women's cinema.[26] The librarian lives in the Shenzhen Special Economic Zone, a town on the border with Hong Kong where economic liberalization and a thriving export trade have led to the development of a quasi-capitalist society. However, although she can afford a life-style to which many young Chinese aspire and has a high level of personal independence (including her own apartment), the price she pays for this independence is loneliness and alienation. Her relationships with friends and boyfriends weaken and become more tenuous as she grows farther apart from society.

A very different instance of female subjectivity is constructed by *Three Women* [*Nürende gushi*, 1986], directed by Peng Xiaolian. (This film had not been completed when I wrote my earlier article on Chinese women's cinema.) It is a much more positive and aggressive, forward-looking film than other films of the genre in terms of the viewing subject it seeks to construct. Indeed, it almost forms a different model than the films I have been discussing. Given the way in which it positions the viewer, it should come as no surprise that it was not well received by the mostly male movie critics and censors in China and that, according to recent correspondence I have received from China, it was banned in late 1988. Unlike all the other films I have discussed, *Three Women* is not about relatively privileged urban women, but about the ordinary rural women who make up the bulk of the Chinese population. This focus is unquestionably connected to the biography of the director, who spent a third of her life in the countryside working alongside ordinary rural women during the Cultural Revolution, and even becoming the head of a women's brigade.[27] Furthermore, the film is not subjective or introspective in the manner of the other films discussed earlier. However, although *Three Women* places the viewing subject in the sort of extradiegetic third position favored by the classical mainland cinema, it still constructs the viewing subject as very definitely female.

The film follows three village women as they set off on a journey to town to sell yarn. In many ways, this is a feminist voyage of self-discovery, as the women learn to depend on each other and on other women. They learn that they are able not only to get by, but also to achieve success by themselves and independently of men. The women are shown in many scenes either where they are by themselves or where men are absent, doing and saying things they might not do or say in the presence of men. The viewer is therefore positioned as one of the group, a woman like them. Thus, the viewing subject of *Three Women* is not as individualized as in the other films and, as in the classical cinema, is not positioned physically with any character. But unlike the viewing subject in classical films, she is female. As in the classical model, the women become exemplary figures among their peers. At the end of the film, after a series of events in which the women have helped one another out, this tendency toward what we in the West would term "sisterhood" culminates upon their return to the village. One of the women is a young wife who left on her trip to town without the permission of the husband whom she had unwillingly married. After the women's triumphant return to the admiration of other women in the village, the husband and a hulking henchman come with heavy ropes to collect the errant wife. As they move toward her, her two friends go to her aid, and the frame freezes as they prepare to resist. In some ways, this is similar to the classical mainland film, which provides female heroes to emulate, promotes anti-individualism, and situates the viewing subject as pupil. In *Three Women,* however, the purpose of this didactic setup is different; rather than being oriented so as to see the benefits of obedience to the Party and its doings, women are transformed from passive subjects into a militant sisterhood in which the viewer is expected to participate.

Male Narcissism

In constructing a new and unequivocally positive relation to the characters on the screen, *Three Women* does for the female viewing subject what it might be said *Red Sorghum* [*Hong gaoliang,* 1987] does for the male. Indeed, *Red Sorghum* is marked by its strong male subjectivity, making it in this way a counterpart to some of the women's cinema films. But while none of the women's cinema films I have discussed were box office hits, *Red Sorghum* was a major success, its soundtrack songs whistled around town and played on the radio for months after the release of the film.

Wang Yuejin reads the characters of *Red Sorghum* as answering a long-felt lack of positive masculinity on the Chinese screen.[28] The hero of the film and his friends do not act out of deference to any explicit authority like the Party. Rather, their strength is autonomous and free of outside interference until the arrival on the scene of Japanese invaders. The hero, identified only as "my Grandpa" by the narrator, overthrows the traditional feudal order that restricted Chunguan in *Girl from Hunan*. He kills the old leper who has bought Jiu'er – the bride he carried to her wedding by sedan chair – and then makes off with her and makes love to her in the sorghum fields. Together with his friends, he and the leper's widow, Jiu'er, take over the remote winery owned by the leper and set up an idealized quasi-matriarchal community headed by Jiu'er. When the Japanese invaders subject the area to their rule and cut down the sorghum to make way for a road, the community rises up and resists as the sorghum grows anew. In the process of resisting the Japanese, Jiu'er dies. She is the only female character in the film, and I am tempted to read her death metaphorically. The logic of the narrative suggests that the full development of traditional masculine characteristics is necessary to fight for freedom from outside interference and that, within such a masculine world, there is no place for the feminine. It is significant that, when Jiu'er is killed by Japanese troops, she is carrying out the traditional feminine and maternal function of bringing food to the men; she dies because she gets in the way of their battle.

This reading of Jiu'er's metaphorical function complements Esther Yau's reading of the film.[29] Wang Yuejin, however, has countered it by taking into account issues of enunciation and viewer positioning. He acknowledges that Jiu'er is repeatedly kidnapped and raped in an emphatic affirmation of masculine potency, but suggests that viewer positioning complicates this purely narrative reading by positioning us with Jiu'er rather than with the men who confirm their masculinity through their domination and possession of her. The camera is placed with Jiu'er as she looks up and down at the bandit who tries to kidnap her on her wedding journey, thus turning the tables on him and objectifying him. The same camera placement constructs the "my Grandpa" figure as a desirable object when he is carrying Jiu'er to her wedding. The viewing subject is placed with Jiu'er in the sedan chair as she peeks eagerly at the sweating, barebacked figure of "my Grandpa."

I acknowledge the accuracy of this description of the two scenes and their unusualness in the Chinese cinema. However, I do not think they can be read in the same way as, for instance, the scene in *Army Nurse* where the main character remembers bandaging the soldier she loved and he is rendered as an object, naked from the waist up. Where *Army Nurse* is told in flashback through the reminiscences of a woman, *Red Sorghum* is a reconstruction of an almost mythological past through a story told by a male narrator. In this sense, the entire tale is a male fantasy/construction, not Jiu'er's, and therefore the scenes Wang Yuejin describes can be read as narcissistic in relation to the male viewing subject implied by this narrator, with Jiu'er serving as female relay to cover and disguise the transgressively homosexual component of this narcissism.

In this type of reading, the masculinity of "my Grandpa," which conforms to the characteristics of Chinese "macho" described by Wang, becomes a sort of ego-ideal for the viewing subject. Again, like *Three Women,* there is something to emulate. However, *Red Sorghum* complicates this construction, as Esther Yau has pointed out.[30] First, it is set in a sort of fantasy vision of the past, unlike *Three Women,* which could be said to represent contemporary China. Second, and most interesting in relation to the other paradigms I have discussed here, the film still displays a pull toward the maternal feminine. "My Grandpa" is not the only figure onto whom the male viewing subject can narcissistically project himself. There is also the little boy identified in the narration as "my Father." At the end of the film, after Jiu'er has been killed by the Japanese, "my Father" sings a lament for his absent mother. All the characters in the film are dead except for "my Grandpa" and "my Father," who seem to stand for two versions of masculinity, one the pure "macho" adult male, the other the impotent infant who longs for his mother in films like *Girl from Hunan. Red Sorghum* acknowledges both of these versions.

Critics writing about *Red Sorghum,* including myself, have tended to see it as unique or at the very least unusual. The film does seem to represent a breakthrough in terms of what audiences, both Chinese and foreign, have come to expect from Fifth Generation directors. Certainly, it is very different from the cerebral, even aphanasitic, subject of films like *Yellow Earth* and *On the Hunting Ground. Red Sorghum* seems less unusual, however, when it is placed in the broader context of Chinese film production as a whole. Although not as well known outside China, the kind of "macho" character figured in *Red Sorghum* was, from the early 1980s, already a feature of popular genres like *gong fu* and, to a lesser extent, crime movies (although voice-over narration is not a feature of these genres as it is of *Red Sorghum*). In the newspaper debates that followed the tremendous success in China of Sylvester Stallone's sequel to *First Blood* (1982), it became clear that macho figures, imported or Chinese, were appealing because they signified a freedom from authority. Indeed, it can be suggested that it was *Red Sorghum*'s similarity to these films that helped make it such an enormous box office hit (unlike most of the films I have discussed in this essay).

A film that vied with *Red Sorghum* for top box office honors in 1988, particularly among urban youth, was China's first detective thriller, *Desperation* [*Zuihou de fengkuang,* 1988]. There were many mainland detective movies in the earlier part of the decade, but for the most part these were whodunnits, whereas *Desperation* was more in the Charles Bronson mode, with chase scenes and frenetic editing. Also, unlike similar Hong Kong movies such as *Project A* [*A jihua,* 1983] and *Long Arm of the Law* [*Shenggang qibing,* 1984] and many Hong Kong *gong fu* movies, *Desperation* does not revolve around a group of heroes but around a single cop and a single criminal.

Like *Red Sorghum, Desperation* not only features very macho characters, but also sets the viewing subject up in a highly narcissistic relation to them. There is no voice-over or flashback to mark the viewing subject as male as there is in *Red*

Sorghum, but in *Desperation* the viewer is implicated in the dynamics of a struggle between the two men, one trying to catch the other. As in so many Hollywood films, the cop and the criminal are compared not only in characterization but also by editing. Both are displayed for the viewing subject in a different way than are the young women characters. The two men frequently appear stripped to the waist, showing off highly muscular (independently strong) bodies. They are set up as narcissistic ego-ideals for the audience, and the fact that one of them is chasing the other within the diegesis only serves to underline their connotation as objects of narcissistic male desire.

Even more interesting is the fact that, when the cop finally catches the criminal, he finds that the latter has tied dynamite around his waist. As they grapple with each other and roll down a slope, they literally explode together. What is one to make of this ending in terms of its significance for the autonomous, independent male that *Desperation, Red Sorghum,* and other films of the late 1980s move toward characterizing? Are male autonomy and independence still transgressive and impossible in a Chinese context?

Conclusion

Raising this question marked not so much the point at which I decided my project was complete, but rather the point at which I gave it up. It will already be clear to the more attentive reader that my efforts to say something coherent about 1980s mainland cinema and social change are strained. At the beginning of the section entitled "Aphanasis?" I announced the impossibility of finding a single viewing-subject paradigm adequate to describe the positioning of the viewer. I proposed that I might look for a series of more localized models. Thus far, I have produced four of these or, if we include the continued appearance of the classical model in various forms, five. However, even with the limited number of distinguishing factors detailed in the section on aphanasis, these models keep sliding into one another. *Yellow Earth* produces an aphanasitic viewing subject, but also one positioned to perceive a lack of masculinity. *Three Women* produces a female viewing subject, but one that has much in common with the classical viewing subject. *Desperation* produces a narcissistic male viewing subject, but also shares characteristics with the classical model.

In this sense, the notion of a model is little improvement on the idea of a paradigm. Thus, at best, I would conclude that the Chinese films of the 1980s do not produce a single, coherent viewing subject, nor is there a dominant paradigm. Rather, there is a matrix of distinguishing factors, among them gender, distanciation, identification, subjectivity, emulation, and rejection. These elements characterize the tension between the communal and the individual as generated by recent social change and felt by mainlanders in the 1980s. The cinema in this period participated in both the instability and dynamism of this social circumstance by moving the viewer through any number of the permutations possible in this matrix of elements. I hope that my discussion of the various "models" I have attempted to extract from the films is indicative of this instability. In fact, I would now prefer even to drop the idea of "models" and suggest that, at best, what I have observed consists of a series of moments within a dynamic situation.

However, even this yields a weak conclusion. On the one hand, the idea of matrix is already slipping away as I write, for almost immediately I find it as difficult to define precisely what elements compose this matrix and when they began to appear as I have found it to model or find paradigms for the way in which the viewing subject is positioned in the 1980s. On the other hand, I do not wish to end this essay with a last aphanasitic gesture – that is, canceling out my own work and placing it under a Derridian mark of erasure as I fade away. This would seem to me no more rigorous or acceptable than understanding the elusive qualities of the Fifth Generation films as aphanasitic.

I would prefer to end by turning the perspective around and suggesting that, although this project may be ultimately unfinishable, it is also unfinished. To put it another way, although there may be no end in sight, there is surely a visible outline of further work. For although it may be dubious to suppose that we may construct models for a decade as unstable as the 1980s, this does not mean that this decade in cinema was absolutely shifting and ambiguous. Rather, it is important to try to trace the specificity of its shifts, its twists, and its turns.

This is what I have tried to begin here, and this is what I meant earlier in the essay about tracing the specific ways in which Chinese film in the 1980s is neither one thing or the other. To emphasize that point, I have deliberately drawn the title of this article from a film not even discussed here. "Neither One Thing Nor Another" is a translation of a disparaging remark made about the hero of Huang Jianxin's prescient late 1988 production, *Transmigration* [*Lunhui*], by the hero's old classmate in a sort of Last Supper scene toward the end of the film. *Transmigration* (also known as *Samsara*) seems to me to put the viewer in a position that is still male and narcissistic, but also negative. I cannot begin to discuss this permutation of the subject position here, however; to do so would only restart the endless tracing I have decided to temporarily halt.[31]

This tracing process is important because the dynamics it details and will continue to detail have also been placed on hold. At this point, it is very difficult to know what the future of the Chinese cinema after the Tiananmen Massacre is. However, it seems to me that this displacement into an endless critical writing is one way to contribute to at least a memory (and, one would hope, some eventual continuation) of the dynamism of the 1980s.

NOTES

1. As I write this (or, rather, as I rewrite this), I am struck by the possible pertinence of the term "postsocialism." It seems to stand in the breach much as the term it echoes, "postmodernism," does; it is beyond socialism without quite being something else yet. It may be that "postsocialism" is an appropriate term for the specific qualities of being "neither one thing nor another" that pertain to mainland China in the 1980s. See Paul G. Pickowicz, Chapter 3, this volume.

2. Chris Berry, "The Viewing Subject in *Li Shuangshuang* and *The In-Laws*," in Chris Berry, ed., *Perspectives on Chinese Cinema* (Ithaca, N.Y.: Cornell East Asian Papers, no. 39, 1985; expanded 2d ed., London: British Film Institute, 1991).

3. The term "classical" is used here not as a mark of praise or a reference to antiquity, but to denote a longevity and stability of system that were not present in the Chinese cinema before 1949 and that have not been present in more recent years. In this sense, it is equivalent to the commonly used term the "classical Hollywood cinema."·

4. A longer, though still.grossly oversimplified, discussion of this concept is given in Berry, "The Viewing Subject."

5. To cite just a few key examples, Esther Yau has written on the representation of women during this decade as a series of failed fantasies in "Cultural and Economic Dislocations: Filmic Phantasies of Chinese Women in the 1980s," *Wide Angle*, 11, no. 2 (1989), pp. 6–21; on the representation of minority women in "Is China the End of Hermeneutics? Or, Political and Cultural Usage of Non-Han Women in Mainland Chinese Films," *Discourse*, 11, no. 2 (1989), pp. 115–38; and about narrative and gender in *Yellow Earth* in *"Yellow Earth:* Western Analysis and a Non-Western Text," *Film Quarterly*, 41, no. 2 (1987–8), pp. 22–33, reprinted in Berry, ed., *Perspectives on Chinese Cinema*, 2d ed. Wang Yuejin has considered the crisis in cultural identity and the viewing subject in "The Cinematic Other and the Cultural Self? De-centering the Cultural Identity on Cinema," *Wide Angle*, 11, no. 2 (1989), pp. 32–9, and issues of gender and positioning in *Red Sorghum* in "Mixing Memory and Desire," *Journal of Public Culture*, 2, no. 1 (1989), pp. 31–53, reprinted in Berry, ed., *Perspectives on Chinese Cinema*, 2d ed. Both Ann Kaplan and I have written on Chinese "women's cinema." See Kaplan, "Problematizing Cross-Cultural Analysis: The Case of Women in the Recent Chinese Cinema," *Wide Angle*, 11, no. 2 (1989), pp. 40–50, reprinted in Berry, ed., *Perspectives on Chinese Cinema*, 2d ed., and Berry, "China's 'Women's Cinema,'" *Camera Obscura*, no. 18 (1988), pp. 8–41.

6. Some of the points I make here concerning specifically cinematic discourse and the production of the classical subject are explained in greater detail in the original article.

7. Wang Yuejin, "Mixing Memory and Desire."

8. Sun Longji, *Zhongguo wenhua de shenceng jiegou* [The Deep Structure of Chinese Culture] (Xianggang: Jixian she, 1982). Translated excerpts from this book are included in Geremie Barmé and John Minford, eds., *Seeds of Fire: Chinese Voices of Conscience* (New York: Hill, 1988).

9. The deep historical roots of Wang's model raise another question: are there any homologies between this classical mainland Chinese subject and those found in Taiwan melodramas of the 1950s and 1960s or the Hong Kong films of the same period? Although I have chosen to concentrate on mainland films in this essay, this issue would certainly be worth investigating. There is a prevalence of melodramas about strong women with feckless husbands in some recent Taiwan films (*Mustard Seed* [*Youma caizi*, 1984], *Kuei Mei* [*Wo zheiyang guole yisheng*, 1984], *Sandwich Man* [*Erzide da wanou*, 1983], and *The Second Spring of Lao Mo* [*Lao Mo de dierge chuntian*, 1983]), and Hong Kong action films like *Project A* [*A jihua*, 1983] and *The Long Arm of the Law* [*Shenggang qibing*, 1984] have a tendency to center around groups rather than individuals. In Taiwan films, the same gender-based types as in the classical model predominate. The wives are self-sacrificing, faithful, and long suffering. Their husbands are little pawns in the larger world

and can rebel against their domination only through such transgressions as excessive drinking and gambling or marital violence.

10. See, e.g., Judith Stacey, *Patriarchy and Socialist Revolution in China* (Berkeley and Los Angeles: University of California Press, 1983), Kay Ann Johnson, *Family and Peasant Revolution in China* (Chicago: University of Chicago Press, 1983), and Margery Wolf, *Revolution Postponed* (Bloomington: University of Indiana Press, 1985).

11. Chris Berry, "Out of the West: The Rise of the Xi'an Film Studio," *China Screen* (1986), p. 4.

12. For further discussion and examples, see Chris Berry, "Reform and Contradiction," *Dianying shijie* [Film World] (1986), p. 7.

13. For further discussion of this model of history, see Michel Foucault, "Nietzsche, Genealogy, History," in *Language, Counter-History, Practice* (Ithaca, N.Y.: Cornell University Press, 1977), and Hayden White, "Foucault's Discourse: The Historiography of Anti-Humanism," in *The Content of the Form: Narrative Discourse and Historical Representation* (Baltimore: Johns Hopkins University Press, 1987).

14. Paul Clark, "Two Hundred Flowers on China's Screens," in Berry, ed., *Perspectives on Chinese Cinema*, pp. 40–61.

15. For discussions and examples of the "literature of the wounded," or "scar literature" as it is sometimes known, see Perry Link, ed., *Roses and Thorns: The Second Blooming of the Hundred Flowers in Chinese Fiction* (Berkeley and Los Angeles: University of California Press, 1984), Helen F. Siu and Zelda Stern, eds., *Mao's Harvest: Voices from China's New Generation* (New York: Oxford University Press), and Jeffrey C. Kinkley, *After Mao: Chinese Literature and Society, 1978–81* (Cambridge, Mass.: Harvard University Press, 1985).

16. It is interesting that this four-year gap marked a break in the biennial rhythm of crackdowns that ran through the 1980s. In 1981 there was the campaign against Bai Hua, in 1983 the Anti–Spiritual Pollution Campaign, in 1987 the Anti–Bourgeois Liberalization Campaign, and, of course, we all know what happened in 1989. Although 1985 missed out on what at least appears to be a cycle, there was an effort to start what I have referred to elsewhere as a "red light, green light" campaign, although this never really got off the ground. See Chris Berry, "Market Forces," *Continuum*, 2, no. 1 (1988–9), and "Now You See It, Now You Don't: The Arbitrary History and Unstable Future of Censorship in the People's Republic of China," *Cinemaya* 4 (Summer 1989).

17. I have written at greater length about this film in "*Girl from Hunan:* The Implication of a Lack," unpublished paper presented at the Second Asian Cinema Studies Society Conference, La Trobe University, Melbourne, July 1990.

18. Yau, "Cultural and Economic Dislocation," pp. 18–19.

19. A similar, though even more ambiguous and subtle pattern appears in the Taiwan films discussed in note 9. Like the two mainland films, *Sandwich Man, Mustard Seed,* and *Kuei Mei* are all set in the past and all feature strong women keeping the family together, working for the future, and suffering at the hands of violent, drunken, often unemployed husbands who have no positive functions and gamble away the family earnings. I was particularly struck by the scene in *Kuei Mei* in which the husband comes back after an absence to discover his wife very pregnant with what turns out to be twins. As she sits on the bed, he sits on the floor and asks her to show him her belly. When she does, he feels it and puts his head to it, asking, "It's so big – how did it get in there?" In response, his wife puts her dress down over his head, putting him "in there," too. This is almost the only scene of warmth and intimacy between the couple in the film. Like *A*

Good Woman and *Girl from Hunan*, the film suggests that traditional society provides only a quasi-infant status for the male in relation to the female – at best dependent, at worst rebellious and destructive.

However, unlike the mainland films, these films are not set in traditional feudal society, and they depict families managing to get along somehow despite the problems they endure. There is not the same sense of perversity, for in most cases the couples are at least more or less the same age, whereas in *Girl from Hunan* and *A Good Woman* we see a society composed of widows, child brides, and child husbands where the only "normal" couples are those committing what is defined by the rules of that society as adultery. Although it is impossible to prove, it is tempting to speculate that there is a connection between these age differences and different perceived relations to the past by at least some members of these two societies. The perception that society had failed to throw off the shackles of the feudal past despite revolution was a common one in the mainland during the 1980s. Taiwan, however, has undergone rapid and radical economic and social modernization over the past decades without any similar revolutionary rejection of past traditions. In the almost nostalgic films from Taiwan under discussion here, there is a sense that a great deal of suffering occurred, mostly among women, but also that a great deal has been achieved as a result of that suffering. Furthermore, in two of these films, the death of the mother figures suggests that perhaps the old society and its ways are now part of the past, as a result of the new society's success.

20. Yau, "Cultural and Economic Dislocations."

21. Ibid.

22. Rey Chow, "Silent Is the Ancient Plain: Music, Film-Making, and the Conception of Reform in China's New Cinema," *Discourse*, 12, no. 2 (Spring–Summer 1990), pp. 82–109.

23. For a discussion of the classical film's treatment of the national minorities that contrasts with this reading of *On the Hunting Ground* and *Horse Thief*, see Paul Clark, "Ethnic Minorities in Chinese Films: Cinema and the Exotic," *East–West Film Journal*, 1, no. 2 (1987), pp. 15–31.

24. Chris Berry, "Interview with Tian Zhuangzhuang," *Cinemaya*, 5 (1989); see also the translated interview by Yang Ping, "A Director Who Is Trying to Change the Audience: A Chat with Young Director Tian Zhuangzhuang," *Continuum*, 2, no. 1 (1988–9), pp. 109–113.

25. I have discussed these films in greater detail and interviewed some of their directors elsewhere: "Chinese 'Women's Cinema.'"

26. During a private conversation in Beijing in January 1988, director Zhang Zeming explained to me that he had decided to avoid first-person narration because he was under pressure to make a box office success. He had noticed that few of the recent films deploying these techniques had been particularly popular.

27. Chris Berry, "Interview with Peng Xiaolian," *Camera Obscura*, no. 18 (1988), pp. 26–31. ·

28. Wang Yuejin, "Mixing Memory and Desire."

29. Esther Yau, "Cultural and Economic Dislocations."

30. Ibid.

31. For a discussion of this film that indicates very readily how it exceeds any matrix that might be produced from the discussion of films here, see my "China's Search for Real Men," *Festival International du Cinéma Chinois de Montréal* (Montreal, 1990 catalog), pp. 48–52.

Part II

FILM IN TAIWAN AND HONG KONG

5

REMAPPING TAIPEI

Fredric Jameson

The social totality is only sensed, as it were, from the outside. We will never see it as such. It can be tracked like a crime whose clues we accumulate, not knowing that we are ourselves parts and organs of this obscenely moving and stirring zoological monstrosity. But most often, in the modern itself, its vague and nascent concept begins to awaken with the knowledge function, very much like a book whose characters do not know that they are being read: the spectator alone knows that the lovers have missed each other by only five minutes, or that Iago has lied to the hero's uncle, giving him a view of the partners' motives that will never be corrected in this life, but that has disastrous consequences. These known misunderstandings bring into being a new kind of purely aesthetic emotion, which is not exactly pity and fear but for which "irony" is a used-up word whose original acceptation can only lend to conjecture. That it is purely aesthetic, however, means that it is conceivable only in conjunction with the work of art, cannot take place in real life, and has something to do with the omniscient author who is alone supposed to observe these disjoined occurrences, unknown to each other, save when the gaze of the author, rising over miniature rooftops, puts them back together and declares them to be the material of storytelling, or literature. But the author must discover such ironies and not invent them: omniscience is like providence and not like creation. Nor does the chance seem to come often, or in every kind of social formation: the urban seems propitious to it, infinitely assembling the empty spaces of such meetings or missed encounters, while the modern (or the romantic) seems to supply the other vital ingredient, namely the sense of authorial function or of the omniscient social witness. Perhaps it also serves to seal in the monads in some airtight way, thus heightening the astonishing fact of their synchronicity.

Tom Jones and indeed the Byzantine novel itself made their living on the fact of sheer coincidence (which generally involved the mysteries of birth and genealogy); but only in the age of the modern is individual life driven so deeply into its isolated "point of view" that it is no longer capable of peeping out above the barrier. Modern relativistic plot and its fundamental category, the unity of "point of view," come into being only at the moment of late Victorian individualism, in which the monadic close of the individual self becomes a desperate case, projecting just such an abstract representational form – a kind of relativistic synchronicity in which a multiplicity of monads is imagined separately and, as it were, from above, in but the most fitful relationship with one another – as its expression and its compensation alike. The supreme plot formation of this period then undertakes impossibly and paradoxically to reunite all these isolated monads, taking the older providential form mentioned above as its distant pattern. But we may be forgiven for thinking that its spirit is the inverse of that earlier one; there, unification of the multiple destinies and strands had the effect of reassuring its subjects of the ultimate unity of the social totality, and of God's design. Here, everything that is stunning about the accidents and peripeties that draw these isolated subjects together (crossing their paths, often on the mode of showing their own individual ignorance of that momentary co-presence to space) would seem, by its very ephemerality, to have the effect of driving us all individually and privately back ever more deeply into our isolation, and of assuring us that the providence effect is little more than an aesthetic one: the bravura gesture of a Romantic or a modern, which corresponds to nothing in lived experience. I think, for example, of a wonderful book by Ann Banfield on another narrative and representational peculiarity, the so-called style indirect *libre:* her very title, *Unspeakable Sentences,*[1] conveys the argument that such sentence structure can be found only in written and printed narrative and not in any speaker's mouth. So also it is with the irony of synchronous monadic simultaneity; no human subject has ever known it as an existential experience, nor has ever witnessed it as an observing subject. To attribute it to God is as grotesque as imagining God following our innermost thoughts and muttering them out in His own form of style indirect *libre.*

Yet a return to our present context draws us up sharply and reminds us that the movie camera is also just such a nonhuman apparatus apt to produce effects and simulated "experiences" that no one can possibly have had in real individual human or existential life: even filmic "point of view" is less realistic than the other, written kind, since it shows us the viewer along with the viewed and has to include the viewing subject's body in the contents of the allegedly subjective experience, as if to mark that as seen by someone. Such artificial constructs then pose the philosophical problem of how to evaluate seemingly artificial or secondary "experiences" generated prosthetically – they are evidently real, but at the same time unauthentic or untruthful insofar as they include the suggestion that the new experience-construct is somehow natural or the same as ordinary or everyday viewing or experiencing. But this philosophical problem of film (which impossibly offers, as Cavell has argued, the world viewed without ourselves present) is no doubt already implicit in the problematic of McLuhanism; and the evaluation of a then equally new experience (writing, reading, printing) that is not natural either and that offers just such peculiar nonexistential experience-constructs as the one Ann Banfield described in her book.

The phenomenon of the providential plot, therefore, and the narrative of synchronous monadic simultaneity (henceforth, SMS) are thus compounded by the intersection with film and its philosophical problems; and those compounds are multiply compounded by the matter of modernism and postmodernism, which respecifies the SMS plot as a specifically modernist phenomenon and also, in the era of video, raises some questions as to the positioning of film itself as a medium. Historical and periodizing questions of that kind, however, require attention to the ambiguity of the term "postmodernism" itself, which must designate a whole historical period and its "structure of feeling" in the preceding sentence, but which risks here slipping inappreciably into the rather different sense of an aesthetic style or set of formal properties. The slippage is significant, since it has been argued that much of the content of what has been called, in art, architecture, and thought alike, postmodern is in reality modernist – indeed, that it is possible that a pure postmodernism is *a priori* impossible as such, but must always involve the treatment of essentially modernist residues. The return, therefore, of what looks like a Western modernist narrative paradigm (the SMS) in the work of a Third World filmmaker (in the thick of postmodernity as a global tendency, if not a global cultural and social reality) can be expected to raise new questions, which do not include the relatively idle one, debated by critics and journalists at the film's first showing in its native Taiwan, as to whether the director had sold out to essentially Westernizing methods or style.[2]

Indeed, I am tempted to say that this particular question disqualifies itself, today, by standing revealed as a specifically modernist one: in the great debates, in all the colonial countries, over nativism and Westernization, modernization versus traditional ideals and values, fighting the imperialist with his own weapons and his own science or reviving an authentic national (and cultural-national) spirit, the West connotes the modern as such in a way that it no longer can when the modernization process is tendentially far more complete and no longer particularly marked as Western. (No one asked the Ayatollah whether the use of audiocassettes marked a corrupt surrender to Western technology and values.)

I suspect, in any case, that the opposite of Westernization in such contemporary arguments cannot be China itself (even assuming that each speaker had some relatively clear conception of Chinese aesthetic values and social realities in mind), but that its empty place must rather be filled by the question of some putative Taiwanese identity that is itself as much a problem as it is a solution. In that sense, perhaps what is being objected to in the film by Edward Yang (Yang Dechang) is not so much its failure to be Chinese or Taiwanese as the relative absence from it of any ostensible worry about the nature of Taiwanese identity, or any rehearsal of its very possibility. Indeed, it does seem to be the case that *Terrorizer* (a peculiar and pointed translation of *Kongbu fenzi*, 1986) assimilates modernization, and the toll it takes on psychic subjects, more generally to urbanization than to Westernization as such. This lends its "diagnosis" a kind of globality, if not a universality, which is evidently what has made Yang's critics uncomfortable. Yet it cannot be said that Taipei (Taibei) is a modern, Western-style city in the same way that one could affirm this of Shanghai, for example. Rather it is an example of some generally late capitalist urbanization (which one hesitates, except to make the point, to call postmodern) of a now-classic proliferation of the urban fabric that one finds in the First and Third Worlds everywhere alike. But if, as I am arguing here, it no longer makes much sense to talk about such cities in terms of an opposition between Western and traditional, then it would seem to follow that the opposite term is equally problematized and that notions of national and ethnic identity (of the modernist type) are equally threatened by postmodernity. (What the television brings us in the way of civil war and nationality struggle – most notably from the former Soviet Union – is something quite different from that, which we have every interest in identifying properly as the media phenomenon of neoethnicity, a simulacrum in which it is no longer a question of *belief*, in any religious sense, but very much a question of *practices*. Ethnicity is something one is condemned to; neoethnicity is something one decides to reaffirm about oneself.)[3]

In any case, nothing is more distant from the stylistic features and formal problematic of the so-called Taiwanese new wave than the "Fifth Generation" filmmaking in the People's Republic that is contemporaneous with it. The latter indeed seems marked by properly epic ambitions, in particular reaffirming its landscapes in a fashion that is utterly different from the ways in which Hong Kong or Taiwan space is given, constructed, and experienced. A specific stylistic mannerism marks this particular ambition (this is not the moment to "decide" whether it is authentic or manipulatory, or to attempt to separate out from it what belongs to propaganda and the staging of power and what can be traced back to new and original modes of being-in-the-world). It is what may be termed a kind of aspiration to the bas-relief, the privileging of an epic midshot that associates film and frieze and scans a middle realm of landscape below the mountain peaks, eschewing the foreground plain, sweeping humans and horses along with it in an endless procession of moving figures without feet or heads, like a cinematographic scroll. This new technique of a midpanoramic perspective becomes not merely a stylistic signature for the newer mainland China cinema; it affirms its epic narrativity, by directing attention to a panning across the frieze, as in traditional painterly storytelling, at the same time that it defamiliarizes the conventional relationship of human bodies and their landscape contexts, allowing neither to be grasped independently (in old-fashioned ways) but rather in some new symbiotic relationship of volume to each other that remains to be determined. This epic shot is thus a symbolic act that promises some new utopian combination of what used to be subject and object: politically it claims to constitute some new way of appropriating tradition that is neither iconoclastic nor given over to Western individualism, with what truth one cannot say (save to register the claim as a rival form in competition with that *nostalgia film* which is currently the dominant Western or postmodern form of telling history).

Epics of this kind must necessarily include the countryside (even when the shots are limited to city space): its perceptual allegory, indeed, implies a reduction of the city to human praxis and politics, and reaffirms the immense agricultural hinterland of the peasant masses as its incontrovertible midperspective and wall in depth. Urban mainland film, however, seems to take a very different stylistic turn, as though its relations were not those that led into the Chinese land mass, but rather the discontinuous vertical openings onto the media and the Pacific Rim, that is to say, on whatever is fantasized as the West. What one notes here, in a film like *Desperation* [*Zuihou de fengkuang*, 1988], for example, a thriller directed by Zhou Xiaowen in the Xian Film Studio whose sheer physical violence takes second place to no equivalent Western product, is a peculiar process whereby the identifying marks of all specific, named cities have been systematically removed, in order to foreground the generically urban. It would be too simple and functional to impute this particular stylistic motivation (whose implementation must, as one can imagine, be very complex) to marketing strategies alone and an attention to a potentially international public; or rather it would be crucial to affirm such base, external motivation, such determination by the extra-aesthetic, in the object world that ultimately, at some wider level of analysis, always rejoin the subject in unexpected ways. In this case, surely, the problems of the market in situations of dependency always somehow rejoin the logic of the collective imaginary and the positioning of that Other to whom cultural and aesthetic production is then also implicitly addressed.

Here what seems initially clear is that the marks of the socioeconomic system must be removed: the consumer of entertainment in the overseas communities must not be distracted by politics, that is to say, by the reminders of a socialist economy in the People's Republic. The high-tech espresso bars and bullet trains of *Desperation* thus dutifully block out a world of contemporary industrial production and consumption beyond all ideological struggle. Meanwhile, by the same token, the identifying marks of the mainland cities must also be excised, since few viewers of this product will be likely to imagine that Xian, say, or Tianjin is located somewhere in the "Free World"; they must therefore not be allowed to ask themselves such questions, or to begin to identify the city in question in the first place.

It is interesting to compare such neutralization and deidentification procedures – a kind of representational laundering of the ideologically marked contents – with those I have elsewhere described[4] at work in Western (or, perhaps even more specifically, in U.S.) postmodern films in which, however, it is not the locale but rather the time period that is generalized. In *The Grifters* (1991), for example, a Stephen Frears movie version of Jim Thompson's novel about the 1950s, pains have been taken to remove the markers of 1991 contemporaneity from the Los Angeles–San Diego–Phoenix axis where the story is played out, and leaving aside all the other problems involved in transferring Thompson's plot to the Reagan–Bush era, the impulse can surely also be identified (not altogether successfully) as the attempt to create a time-free indeterminate nostalgia zone for the thriller narrative in which unpleasant reminders of contemporary social – and thereby political – issues and contradictions have been removed.[5] Thus, a postmodern aesthetic, which at its most vibrant aims at the ideal or Platonic reconstruction of some eternal 1930s or 1940s art deco Miami in a film noir beyond historical time itself, can be socially retraced to its class and ideological roots in a form of collective cultural repression (i.e., in the literal sense of an exclusion from consciousness of painful or disturbing material). The juxtaposition with a specifically Second World form of aesthetic repression (remove the marks of socialism as a system) demands reflection.

Both are in any case relatively distinct from the packaging of specifically Third World international or festival films in national, cultural, and, one is tempted to say, tourist-friendly ways. When the fact of a brand-new locale and unprecedented national provenance is stressed and marketed, as Peter Wollen has observed, what are henceforth termed "new waves" are fresh entries into the international market. I will not belabor the interesting theoretical issues of whether Taiwan is to be counted as a Third World country: if you think the label means Southern-Tier poverty, then it is clearly inappropriate, if not worse; but if it merely affirms something as structural and descriptive as the nonadherence to what is left of the socialist bloc, coupled with the constitutive distance from one of the three great capital centers of the "new world order" (Japan, Western Europe, the United States), then it may be less misleading.

In any case, the Taiwan "new wave" has tended to mark its images as specific to the island, in ways quite distinct from the mainland evocation of landscape. The city is also focused differently here (and *Terrorizer* will be an index of its richness and possibilities), for the obvious reasons that Taipei does not possess the profile or the historical resonance and associations of the great traditional mainland cities, nor is it an all-encompassing closed urban space of a virtual city-state like Hong Kong. Still, its dominance has effectively transformed the natural countryside into a kind of extended suburban space, one in which the survival of more traditional agricultural villages is nonetheless sublimated and somehow modified by their linked association in an intricate web of electric trains that lead into the capital. The image of these small suburban trains has in the camera work of films by Hou Hsiao-hsien (Hou Xiaoxian) become a virtual new wave logo, particularly in his beautiful *Dust in the Wind* [*Lianlian fengchen*, 1986], in which the empty station and the sound of the train in the distance end up articulating the narrative and standing as signs or shorthand for mutations in the Event. The shots of the commuter train here include the landscape and open to it, utterly unlike the highspeed projectiles that propel the narrative forward in *Desperation* (or in such precursors as Kurosawa's *High and Low*, 1963). The palpable interweavings of the social (no longer, in the late capitalist world system, characterizable as provincial), which are both expressed and signified by this system of recurrent imagery and then peculiarly overdetermined by such intertextuality as the casting of Hou Hsiao-hsien himself as the protagonist in Edward Yang's *Taipei Story* [*Qingmei zhuma*, 1985], the material itself (with the political opening of liberalization) moving toward such ambitious historical chronicles as Hou's *City of Sadness* [*Beiqing chengshi*, 1989] and Edward Yang's *A Brighter Summer Day* [*Guling jie shaonian sharen shijian*, 1991], make of Taiwanese new wave films a kind of linked cycle more satisfying for the viewer than any national cinema I know (save perhaps the French productions of the 1920s and 1930s).

From this cycle, *Terrorizer* stands out starkly as uncharacteristic: sharing none of the potential sentimentalism of the nativist films, its visual elegance has frequently been characterized as cold, as one would a glassy surface that repels identification. Yet *Taipei Story* combined fashion-plate visuality with pathos, and its hero – played, as I have said, by Hou Hsiao-hsien himself – was a nonintellectual, fumbling his way, in the manner of U.S. populism, through a series of odd jobs and reverses of fortune. What sets *Terrorizer* off is not the class status of its characters, who are now, as we shall see, professionals and lumpens, but the now-archaic modernity of its theme: art versus life, the novel and reality, mimesis and irony. The co-protagonist is a writer, Chou Yü-fen (Zhou Yufen), with a writer's block (Figure 21) who is freed up by an anonymous phone call denouncing her husband's adulterous affairs, at which point she sits down to write a prize-winning novella about this situation (which has no basis in fact), leaving him in the process. Under other circumstances, the process whereby the possibility of attributing guilt to the husband suddenly grants the wife independence would offer interesting material for interpretation; but Chou Yü-fen's story is only one of four distinct plot strands in this film, whose alternation, I would argue, leaves no distance for reflection of this kind, for interpretive rumination, particularly of this motivational-psychoanalytic type. What does stand out, rather, is the old-fashioned reflexivity of the theme, the residual modernism of the now-familiar mystery of the imitation of art by life and the correspondence of the novel to the aleatory realities of the real world outside. The very embodiment of the theme around the writing of literature and the pathos of the precarious role of the literary "creator" strikes a regressive note in a film of this decidedly contemporary stamp (none of the chronological laundering and neutralizations of nostalgia film here), in the age of the simulacrum and of the dominance of technological media. (In Taiwan, as elsewhere, the aesthetically ambitious now want to become great filmmakers, not great novelists.) This anachronism of literature and its once-interesting reflexive paradoxes is what – foregrounded, and as it were, quoted here, in the midst of the other plot lines we

21. The writer. Edward Yang, *Terrorizer* (1986). YANG AND HIS GANG, FILMMAKERS

shall examine in a moment – makes *Terrorizer* relatively conspicuous within contemporary Third-World production, where there are plenty of intellectuals and even writers, but perhaps somewhat less "modernism" in this Western sense.

André Gide's *Counterfeiters* (1925) is the prototype of this older classic modernist text. Its protagonist Edouard keeps a journal within the novel about the novel – called "The Counterfeiters" – which he is writing but will perhaps never finish (unlike Gide, who was then able to publish, under separate cover, the journal he himself also kept while writing and actually finishing his own novel of the same name). Edward Yang does not seem to have made a separate film about the making of *Terrorizer;* but Godard did so, after completing his film *Passion* (1981). At any rate, the archetypal scene in Gide's intricate novel (a term he reserved for a form that marked the confluence of a number of stories, plot lines, and *récits,* and used only once in his own work, for this book) is the moment in which, during a discussion of the novelist's theories about the ways in which contemporary intellectuals counterfeit social and spiritual values, another character flings a "real" coin upon the table, suggesting that the referent itself might interest him as well. But theories about counterfeiting are more interesting to this protagonist than the reality (which belongs in fact to another of the novel's multiple plot strands). Edouard is thus himself ironically dispatched along with the other hapless characters about whom he has himself ironized. More significantly, in a move that has traditionally seemed canonical for high modernism generally, the very theme of counterfeit value is thereby itself ironized and left to float in midair and midreference, passing slowly in all its optionality from the status of a social comment or critique into that of sheer aesthetic decoration and back again.

One's sense is that modernist constructs of this kind cannot be filmed. It is a proposition that could be tested against very different candidates: Jean Renoir's *Rules of the Game* [*La Règle du jeu*, 1939], for example, which has its author inside it as well (the director playing the meddling and matchmaking – "authorial" – character of Octave), along with multiple plot lines and artificial mechanisms *en abîme*. The social content in which Renoir's bravura formal operation is performed is, to be sure, very different from Gide's, turning as it does on an aristocracy of blood, culture, and merit, and posing questions about heroism and about authentic loves. But if this reflexive form constitutively includes a rift between form and content, the shift in period and social class, or in ideological preoccupation, should not make any fundamental difference. More relevant, perhaps, is the glacial distance of *Rules of the Game* from even those characters about which it seems to be sentimentalizing – a gulf seemingly too broad to be spanned by Gidean (or indeed Jamesean) irony, at least in a situation in which the terms are of two distinct modes of being. The familiar sentimental complacent relationship of viewer to character is staged by way of the visual image, whereas the judgment takes place somewhere else, in a nonvisual, nonfilmic mind. Quite distinct from this is the interpenetration of empathy and otherness enabled, indeed encouraged, by narrative language in the point-of-view ironies of high modernism.

Meanwhile, Nabokov's coy and mannered version of these games does not work on film either: Fassbinder's version of *Despair* (1979), whatever its other considerable merits, is absurdly – perhaps even pointedly – unfaithful to the novel in this respect, since in the reading we are persuaded of a virtual physical identity between the narrator and his double, which is instantly dispelled by the latter's first appearance on the screen. That very different reflexivity of Dziga Vertov's *Man with a Movie Camera* (1929), however, in which the place of the novelist and language is taken by the apparatus itself, yields a stream of visual images whose equivalent would surely not be the introspective complacencies of a Gide, but rather the *Sachlichkeit* of a Dos Passos or a Döblin (experimental objectivities whose fit with the medium of language time has itself rendered questionable).

We must conclude, then, that the media sharply diverge in their capacity for what, to use a properly Gidean term, we may call *complicity* with the fictional characters themselves, and that whatever fascination and self-identification, unconscious mimesis, mirror-stage jubilation by proxy we are capable of developing in the presence of the images of movie actors, it can have little enough to do with the games high modernist writers played on the expanding and contracting distance within the reading of the fictional sentence.

It is something that can be said, the other way round, in terms of judgment rather than of empathy, and shown on the occasion of a famous chapter in the *Counterfeiters* (Part 2, Chapter 7), in which an ostentatiously omniscient narrator now, after the fashion of the eighteenth-century novel, pretends to pass his fictional characters in review and to acknowledge their weaknesses and defects: "Edouard annoyed me more than once, and even made me indignant. . . . Lady Griffith quite impressed me in the beginning, but I quickly realized the mistake I was making. . . . Vincent interested me more. . ." etc., etc. One never quite believed it, yet it may seem in retrospect that Gide succeeded in fooling us with this ruse and in encouraging a habit of judgment in the reader by virtue of annoying us with his own. Such judgment tends to ratify a certain moral or personal commitment to these characters on the readers's part: liking them is certainly not the word for it (although Gide takes pains to make sure we dislike some of them), but a minimal willingness to compare the temperatures within this or that point of view, this or that subjectivity, is involved.

There is nothing of the sort in *Terrorizer,* whose characters are all signally lacking in any of the secret merits that might encourage our complicity. Nor are they, however, antipathetic, something that might be easier to achieve but that Yang does not really manage, even for the Eurasian girl (who on some accounts seems to have been for him the eponymous villain of the piece) (Figure 22). At least in my opinion, they are neither likeable nor dramatically evil, but rather mildly, and secretly, repulsive. The self-pity of the protagonist, Li Li-chung (Li Lichen), the doctor (and husband of the writer already mentioned), is not enhanced by his betrayal of a colleague (let alone his massive obtuseness about his wife's unhappiness). Chou Yü-fen, meanwhile, is so narcissistically unhappy (and so complacent in her subsequent moment of happiness and triumph) as to make it very easy to separate any feelings one may have about her victimization as a woman from one's judgment of her personality. Nor do the protagonists of the other plot strands fare much better: the young photographer with whom the film opens (paparazzo-like, he is trying to get some action shots of a shoot-out between drug dealers and the police; Figure 23) is surely as self-centered an idle rich youth as one would like, not quite as repulsive as the hero of *Blow-up* (1966), but only because he does not have to make a living out of it. Meanwhile, his immediate target (the fleeing Eurasian girl, nicknamed the White Chick and initially mixed up with the criminal elements in question) offers yet another version of self-centered ego indulgence and narcissistic indifference to the outside world, even leaving aside her criminal nastiness and the well-nigh impersonal ferocity with which she fights for her existence in a world of rich and stupid, corrupt johns and gulls. Her mother, floating alcoholically in her memories of the

22. The "White Chick." Edward Yang, *Terrorizer* (1986). YANG AND HIS GANG, FILMMAKERS

1950s nightlife among U.S. servicemen, is not much better, while the bureaucrats are appropriately repellent and the underworld flora and fauna unromantic and bestially uninteresting. To say that the policeman (he is the doctor's childhood friend) comes off the best is only to register the fact that we learn least about him and that, of all the things people do in this movie, act tired out, lie in a hot tub, do some drinking, and listen to a "younger brother's" complaints or boasts, are the least calculated to arouse antipathy.

To be sure, at the end of the chapter in question, Gide also tosses all his characters in the trash can: "If ever I find myself inventing another story, I will only allow into it tempered characters, whom life makes sharper, rather than blunting their edge. Laura, Douviers, La Perouse, Azais . . . what am I doing with people like this?" Yet it is that very standard of judgment that allows Gide to say so, which is lacking in Edward Yang's film, for reasons historical and social, rather than cultural or personal, reasons ultimately rooted in the differences between the modern period and our own.

In that separation of form and content I have already evoked, Gide's "novel" also formally exploits and organizes a social and personal content given in advance and somehow contingent on the vicissitudes of the writer's own life and background. Clearly enough, all the varied forms of a high modernist abstraction must in one way or another confront this contingent seam, which is the necessity for some minimal image content in the first place (the last sparse image residue of the Mallarméan vase or curtains blowing): it is an open question whether authenticity consists in acknowledging such contingency and allowing it to persist within the work as such, like a foreign body, or attempting a symbolic recuperation whereby at some higher level it again becomes "motivated" (in all the Russian formalist senses), and thus meaningful or postcontingent. In the event Gide does both, attempting to endow his homosexuality with symbolic meaning, while the fact of his social background in French Protestantism is taken mainly as a given and a contingent starting point. In *The Counterfeiters*, then, with its multivocal and collective formal vocation, Gide is obliged to draw on the French Protestant background far more extensively than in the individual *récits*, where the problem of individual destiny and individual choice fairly well ensures a "motivation" of the initial situation in terms of this or that meaning (whether "hedonistic," as in *L'Immoraliste,* or "ascetic," as in *La Porte étroite*). In retrospect, the Gide of *Les Fauxmonnayeurs* may instructively be reread as an ethnic novelist, for whom French Protestantism uniquely, in French society, has some-

23. The photographer. Edward Yang, *Terrorizer* (1986). YANG AND HIS GANG, FILMMAKERS

thing of the enclave and subcultural dynamics we associate with ethnicity in the United States. The residues of a relatively prim and pietistic moralizing in the judgments of the omniscient narrator are then overdetermined by this particular social content: in some deeper ideological sense, Gide remains a Christian novelist, whose attention is above all focused on matters of character (in the moral sense of what can manifest rectitude and steadfastness, or weakness and irresolution). From Weber all the way to David Riesman's "inner-direction," then, these matters of characterology are social in their causes as well as in their effects: if they reinforce the emergent ethos of capitalism or, later on, the spirit of the entrepreneurial moment, such moralizing categories also remain intimately bound up with a particular stage of social development from which their judgments cannot be separated.

This is clearest for categories of evil or of moral weakness and corruption. Gide can still produce a diagnosis of the social condition and identity forces for social evil in the irresponsible and corrupt Cocteau figure of Edouard's rival novelist Passavant, and even more starkly in those genuine nihilists for whom Passavant is a kind of facade and who operate by way of genuine crime ("real" counterfeiting) and an atmosphere not unlike the anarchism and terrorism indicted by Conrad in works like *The Secret Agent*. But this Manichaean and apocalyptic view of social disintegration is much less convincing in the radical Gide than in conservative and right-wing authors. Moral weakness, susceptibility to evil influences, corruptibility, the failure of nerve, or the sapping of moral fiber – these judgments are here more plausible, but seem applicable to almost everyone, from the corrupt grande bourgeoisie on the side of social order all the way to the various prototypes of youth – Edouard's second nephew Olivier is then momentarily seduced by Passavant, while the latter's older brother Vincent is irredeemably corrupted by the fashionable novelist and his partner Lady Griffith, whom Vincent murders in a tropical drama of madness and self-destruction that we glimpse only fitfully between the lines.

It is enough to juxtapose these figures with the characters of *Terrorizer* to see that in postmodern times, in the international urban society of late capitalism, such moral judgments are irrelevant or at least inoperative (to use a once-fashionable corporate word). Gidean moralism, and the monitory portraits of evil and corruption it enables, can have little to do with the maimed figures of the Taiwanese film, if only because it presupposes what the various poststructuralisms most often call the "centered subject," the old inner-directed ego of the modern period. In a postmodern universe, after the "death of the subject," or at least after the end of the "ideology of the subject" as such, it follows that nobody is evil any longer either, exactly, or at least that that is no longer the word for it: in this film, the Eurasian girl and her pimp are dangerous and violent (we witness, for example, the – not unjustified – murder of one of her clients), but given the context of urban capitalism, they are surely not much worse than anybody else. Indeed, I would argue that within the prodigious expansion of the concept of rationality in our contemporary postnatural society (taking rationality in the Habermassian sense of what one can understand or argue for), the traditional antonyms of this concept – the irrational, madness, and even evil itself – have become increasingly implausible or unfunctional. The occult revival, the taste for demonology, strikes one as a desperate or nostalgic attempt to pump life back into these moral conceptions, which remain as quaint and inappropriate in the postcontemporary period as Victorian bustles at a disco.

But already in *The Counterfeiters* crime and violence had begun to secure a somewhat different narrative function from that of moralizing judgments: in a system of parallel narrative strands, indeed, violence and crime tend to mark an "ultimately determining instance" in which the various plots come together in an explosive climax. But this is narrative rather than ontological logic, so to speak, and bears less on the ultimate meaning and interpretation of the events in question than on their visibility and their eruption as symptoms to be read. So the police investigation of counterfeiting and vice ("crimes roses") continues throughout the surface unfolding of the final sections of the novel, but the conspiracy finds its surface inscription in the related schoolboy prank whereby the student Boris shoots himself in front of his class under his grandfather's eyes.

In *Terrorizer*, meanwhile, the criminal incident – the shoot-out – stands at the starting point of the intrigue, as what accidentally links a group of destinies together: in particular, the occasion that lets the young photographer glimpse the Eurasian girl (whom he photographs). In film, however, crosscutting can just as plausibly connect these plot strands with others, with which they have not yet concretely intersected. Thus, the doctor drives to work through traffic that contains both the police vans going the other way and the ambulance that carries the wounded girl to treatment: it is a connection the camera makes for us long before the effects show up in his own life. Here at any rate violence has come to be associated with narrative rather than ethical categories, and is a matter of closure or of the interrelationship of strands and episodes rather than of judgment and evaluation.

We have not yet, however, identified the positive term in Gide's moralism, which knows an equally instructive evolution and displacement in the postmodern period. This surely has to do with youth – equally an emphasis in *Terrorizer*, although its omnipresence as a theme in media culture means that it need no longer be a marked term – and the accompanying ethical conceptions of character and characterological weakness (as well as Gide's own characteristic staging of pederasty as a pedagogical matter) make it clear that it is the residual or Goethean value of *Bildung*, or "formation," that is here foregrounded in a novel whose polyphony excludes the older *Bildungsroman* form as such. It is in the light of the residual concerns of *Bildung* alone that the Gidean attention to weakness and corrupting influences can properly be understood; the juxtaposition with *Terrorizer*, however, shows that, despite the omnipresence of the "post" category of the generation here as everywhere else in postmodern global urban culture, categories of *Bildung* or pedagogy, ideals of character formation, are peculiarly inappropriate. Education manuals like the *Cortegiano* or the *Mirror for Princes* might well be imagined for the world system of late capitalism, but they surely would bear little resemblance to the traditional models; meanwhile, the very notion of reinventing a form of Goethean *Bildung* consistent with the age of Andy Warhol or MTV is problematical to say the least. Our Wilhelm Meister is called Falsche Bewegung, and current debates about pedagogy and the humanities in the superstate give some idea, by way of their very aimlessness and utter intellectual vacuousness, of the difficulties involved in papering over the reification of consciousness in late capitalism, and indeed in reconciling the ravages left by the triumph of cynical reason and commercial media or corporate culture within any of the canonical or traditional moral and educational paradigms.

What has come to replace this kind of characterological focus is, rather, as *Terrorizer* shows, a displacement from the ethical and the pedagogical-formative toward the psychological as allegory or symptom of the mutilation of individual subjects by the system itself. It is an allegory that finds its most intense embodiment in the situations of women in this film, whose centrality can be measured against their relatively secondary position in Gide's *Counterfeiters*. There, Taure and Lady Griffith clearly mark the extremes of passive victimization and manipulative domination respectively; and in retrospect Gide's sense of the crippling effects of bourgeois marriage is as vivid and as critical as any of his more dramatic protests in the name of youth (which in any case were also accompanied by a denunciation of the bourgeois family). But as we shall see in more detail later, in *Terrorizer* it is the women's destinies – the situations of imprisonment of Chou Yü-fen and the Eurasian girl – which are paradigmatic, and that of the hapless Li Li-chung which is merely reactive. It is a historical difference that can perhaps best be marked by a shift in the object of the sociocultural critique: in both periods, that of the first classical feminism around World War I, of social democracy and the suffragette movement, of Shaw and Virginia Woolf, like that of the "second wave" of feminism from the late 1960s onward, attention to specific forms of injustice or oppression is articulated with a larger project of social change. But in the first period, which was still Gide's, it is in terms of a specifically bourgeois culture of the family and of middle-class Victorian hypocrisy and puritanism that both feminism and socialism are staged. In our own postmodern world, it is no longer a bourgeois or class-specific culture that is thereby indicted, but rather a system-specific phenomenon, the various forms that reification and commandification and the corporate standardizations of media society imprint on human subjectivity and existential experience. This is the sense in which *Terrorizer*'s characters – most particularly the film's women characters – dramatize the maiming of the subject in late capitalism or, in terms of the language of the centered subject referred to earlier, the failure of the subject to constitute itself in the first place under the new system.

Yet all this merely characterizes the variable content organized by a form about which one wants principally to know how it will then itself be historically altered by modifications in the social raw material that is its enabling pretext. For the Gidean project – the novel as a multiplicity of plot strands – presumably survives and persists in *Terrorizer*, with the difference (of degree, rather than of kind) that the urban framework is here intensified and becomes something like the primary message of the narrative form itself. Yet in its earliest forms (as in the Byzantine novel), the providential plot, based on the coincidence of multiple destinies interweaving, was not particularly urban in its spatial requirements. The following authorial complaint, by Manzoni, is indeed a standard trope of the form well up to the twentieth century:

More than once I have seen a nice, bright little boy – somewhat too bright, to tell the truth, but showing every sign of intending to turn out a good citizen – doing his best, as evening falls, to round up his little herd of guinea-pigs, which have been running free all day in the garden. He would like to get them all trotting into the pen together; but that's hopeless. One breaks away to the right, and while the small swineherd runs after him to chase him back with the others, another one – or two, or three – dash off to the left – or all over the place. After a little impatience he adapts himself to their methods, and begins by pushing inside those who happen to be nearest to the pen, and goes to fetch the others, singly, or two or three at a time, as best he can. We have to play much the same game with our characters. We managed to get Lucia under cover, and ran off after Don Rodrigo, and now we must drop him and catch up with Renzo, who is right out of sight.[6]

If the urban comes to predominate, it is because the inns and highroads in which the protagonists of the older novel meet by accident and rectify their mistaken identities necessarily require such characters to be travelers with destinies of a specific type – exiles, runaways, pursued or pursuers, so that the plot itself is always molded according to a distinct subgenre of narrative type. The city frees all this up: its chance meetings and coincidences allow for a far greater variety of character-destinies, and thereby a web of relationships that can be spread out and unfolded in a dazzling array of distinct ideological effects. Gide's novel must properly be assigned to a specific historical trans-European generic context I am tempted to identify (anachronistically) as the Edwardian SMS. To this it is instructive (besides its strong form in books like Forster's *Howards End*) to add Virginia Woolf, on the one hand, and *Ulysses,* on the other, both of which seem different when they are read as works in a preexisting formal project, namely that of uniting classical closed plot with the spatial multiplicity of the new industrial city.

Gide's novel outtrumps these in its manipulation of representational levels: where the *mise-en-abîme* of cognate narratives necessarily had to pass through the needle's eye of gossip or the orally transmitted anecdote, the eavesdropping omniscience of third parties, and the pathos of missed encounters that might have changed everything, Gide's narrative includes the journal as an innerworldly object that, opened up and read by our initial hero, Bernard (something of a false start, this young man, who solves his problems and ceases to interest the narrator), now allows the past to enter like a fourth dimension within an absolute unity of time from which the ineptitude of the psychological flashback is rigorously excluded for formal and aesthetic reasons. I would be willing to argue that we do not like to shift textual levels and are most reluctant to shift reading gears in order to scan interpolated texts and lengthy quotes inserted like a foreign body into unrelated discourse. How Gide's interpolation, which spans three chapters and some fifty pages, negotiates this particular reef is then a crucial issue, although the remarkable timing with which Gide deploys it and knows when to break it off is as much a matter of tact as anything else. That longer reading was, however, prepared by a briefer rereading of his own journal by Edouard himself, on the boat-train returning to Paris. That his own voice – that of a major, if not the principal, protagonist – prolongs the second installment of the journal read by Bernard is surely not without its relationship to the smoothness of the transition, the relatively painless immersion in the newer textual level. Emerging from it, however, is the matter of the great narrative peripeties: guilty interruptions, eavesdropping behind doors followed by dramatic entries — the stuff of melodrama that can here exceptionally be reinvented, in a nonmelodramatic way, on the occasion of multileveled textual reflexivity. Meanwhile, once the deeper conspiratorial network that unites all these destinies without the full knowledge of any single one of them is laid in place, the more conventional chance meetings, and accounts of yet further chance meetings, forecasts, projected trajectories through the city that are bound to cross other pathways we already know of, along with the finding of abandoned notes and the overhearing of secret instructions – all these well-worn devices serve to lift and rotate the gleaming polyhedron of the new form before our eyes in ways that confirm it as a unified object and exhibit the unforeseeable glitter of its unexpected facets.

It will have thereby become clear that however film expects to achieve analogous effects, it cannot do so simply by finding and matching simple filmic equivalents to these textual ones of reading and its inner analogues. The reason has already been indicated in passing, and it is not a consequence of the deficiencies of film as a medium but rather of its superiority to narrative language in any number of representational ways. Winner loses: what makes up the plenitude of the filmic image at any instant in its narrative trajectory also secures in advance, without any supplementary work, the sheer fact of transition. The novel, and language itself – whose fundamental property is lack and a deployment of essentially absent objects – has to do a great deal of energetic footwork to crosswire its plots in a plausible yet properly unexpected manner: mesmerized by the shift to a new series of filmic images, no less full and absorbing than the preceding ones, the viewer of film is only feebly tempted to raise the ever-fainter question of the motivation for such transitions. Form has to be felt as the solution to an intractable form problem. Indeed, Eisenstein's theory and practice of montage can be instructively estranged and reread not as a solution to certain existing problems of filmic narration, but as a stubborn attempt to produce the problems as such in all their aesthetic and ontological severity – problems for which his own conception of montage was then only too ready and willing to provide a henceforth satisfying "solution."

Terrorizer achieves, or reinvents, something of this by way of unique temporal overlaps that reach their climax at the end of the film, like vibrations separated from one another in time that gradually become simultaneous. The overlaps are then fastened together, one does not want to say with Lacanian tacking nails, exactly, but by recurrent leitmotivs, a term redolent of Wagner or Thomas Mann, that is also a little too modernist-traditional; let us call these, which look like images but serve as crossroads and roundhouses of various kinds, reversible signifiers. Two of these signifiers – the gas tank and the barking dog – become inscribed in the opening sequence (but like all true repetition, they do not take on their functionality, their dreary sense of only too predictable familiarity, until that second time, which for repetition as a phenomenon is really always a first). The shoot-out, as we have said, is not important in itself, but rather serves as a detonator for the other plot lines. What is more significant is that it takes place at first light, that first vacancy of the city in early morning that will gradually be filled in by characters, business, and routines of all kinds. Violent death first thing in the morning: we do not know whose body it is, except that it is the pretext for the young photographer to look for a scoop and the occasion for him to glimpse the White Chick as she climbs out a balcony window and injures her leg. At that point, as the camera now sets off to follow her flight, we reach another reversible signifier, a somehow less reified one, since it enfolds relationships rather than a static thing in a recurrent static place. This is the zebra crossing at which she collapses, but which will then accompany a shot of her legs at various stages of her recovery, framed by crutches, and then healed again and jaunty, ready to go about her predatory business.

The sirens may include the ambulance that takes her away, but they certainly include the police vans, which give us a glimpse of Taipei's morning rush hour at high tide and also intersect another plot line as their wail rises to the apartment in which the doctor, Li Li-chung, can be observed about his stretching exercises on the balcony. (In another moment, we will see him driving to work in the morning traffic, perhaps passing the police car carrying his childhood friend away from the incident, perhaps crossing the Eurasian girl's ambulance on its way to the hospital). His immediate superior has just died; he stands in line for advancement and is full of high hopes, particularly since he has taken the trouble to denounce the malpractice of his only rival (otherwise, or hitherto, a friend and colleague). He also has marital problems; his wife's writing block (of which we have spoken) makes life at home unpleasant, as she wonders whether she should go back to work at her old job in the publishing house (run by a former lover, with whom she later renews the affair), indeed, whether she should leave her husband altogether (which she does later on that day). Meanwhile, something of Li Li-chung's character is conveyed by yet another signifier, the compulsive motif of his handwashing, which he accomplishes in well-nigh surgical fashion (scrubbing all the way up the lower arm) and only gradually, with repetition, turns into a mania reenacted with every new entry into an interior space (his own apartment, that of others, hotel rooms, workplace, etc.), betokening his extraordinary inner security or "inferiority complex." The handwashing thus comes to stand for the problematic balance between public and private (career and marriage, job and home) and will eventually participate in something even more dramatic, as we shall see.

The hour of repetition meanwhile sounds for the scene of the crime when the would-be paparazzo, time weighing heavily on his hands, decides to rent and inhabit the now-empty murder apartment. Now we see the gas tank in all its splendor (this is evidently a well-known Taipei eyesore about whose dangerous emplacement in the midst of a heavily residential area there has been much public debate):[7] everything stylistically extraordinary about *Terrorizer* is already concentrated in this initial geographical move and choice of urban setting – the brilliant color of a dramatic shape that is also a depressing sign of urban squalor, a science fictional profile associated with the humdrum misery of lower-middle-class life; something like a structural inversion of magic realism is to be found here, in this utterly nonmagical and unsurrealistic photographic transformation of urban detail into solid colors whose stunning combinations are somehow chilled by the perfection of the technological apparatus and strike the viewer with that distance and coldness I have already mentioned.

Here also, the barking dog; in Taiwan, city dogs are often kept in cages, which makes for something of an auditory leitmotiv. This one binds us into a recurrent space (it will later on be visited by the novelist as a result of her "anonymous phone call"), and at least subliminally begins to sensitize us to the situation of imprisonment as such, which will undergo a remarkable phenomenological transformation in this film. Indeed, it already begins to do its work of identification and association (the interiors of dwellings are the same as prison cells) in the motive for the move itself, for another domestic quarrel, first thing in the morning, is also virtually simultaneous with the shoot-out and Li Li-chung's exercises – it is the breakup of the photographer and his girlfriend, who appreciates the photos of the Eurasian girl even less than the early morning sorties after fire engines and the like. The older apartment is sealed within blowing curtains; the boyfriend's films and stills are trashed (as in an earlier representation of the media); she throws him out and tries to commit suicide, and is then rushed to the hospital in a way that does not particularly generate sympathy for her, but raises all kinds of *nouveau roman* questions: Is it the same hospital as the one Li Li-chung himself works in? Was the White Chick treated here as well? What is the meaning of this urban simultaneity in the multinational system today, where it evidently has a rather different effect than the great village network constructed by the paths of Joyce's characters through familiar downtown sites in *Ulysses?*

As for the photographer, it should be noted that he shares with all the other characters what may be described as a time of dead transition, a temporality, not so much of waiting as of sitting it out dully: the doctor waiting for his promotion; his writer-spouse waiting for inspiration, or else to change her life completely; the White Chick waiting for her leg to heal and the cast to come off. Such characters are peculiarly condemned to a marking of time that lacks joyousness or eager anticipation, since (paradoxically in the first two cases) the outcome is not particularly appetizing, something assuredly the case for the young photographer, since he is merely waiting to do his military service. All this for him is then mere interim, a peculiar furlough from life, and his emotional life is thereby equally affected, as witness the whim of a fantasy life in the drug dealers' apartment, or even the passion for the White Chick herself, whose enormously enlarged photographic image is hung in segments on the apartment wall, in the hermetically sealed space of what is used as a darkroom, beyond the world and beyond Taipei.

At this point, then, what begins to focus our attention and our curiosity is no longer the simultaneity of the four independent plot strands (involving the doctor, the writer, the photographer, the Eurasian girl), so much as how they can eventually be expected to intersect and intertwine in that tying up of all the knots that is as much an implicit formal expectation of this practice of multiple plots as is their significantly named denouement. In *Terrorizer*, however, what may be called the event of the narrative vinculum is repeated on two levels virtually simultaneously, in a superposition that makes it realist and modernist all at once: rehearsing the great realist trope of authorial omniscience (what we see along with the author as the characters themselves remain ignorant) and then trumping it with the autoreflexivity characteristic of the modernist period and one of its obsessive thematic and formal mannerisms. The Eurasian girl in her literal confinement (the mother locks her in when she goes out at night to work) begins to make phone calls, with greater and greater abandon, picking names out of the phone book and inventing nasty stories to tell the unknown people who pick up on the other end. Presumably, for Edward Yang, this modern equivalent of the poison-pen letter (dear to the classical English detective story and a kind of symbol of what most unerringly undermines the calm of tribal or village social relations) entitles her to the eponymous characterization more than anything associated with garden-variety prostitution or murder: it marks a peculiar intensity of *ressentiment* that is surely not unrelated to her socially marginal status and to the exclusion of half-breeds from traditional Chinese society (as from most other traditional ones). In the present context, however, it is just as significant that the genes mark the presence of U.S. servicemen and U.S. empire in this hitherto Japanese colony, only recently recolonized by the mainland Kuomintang (Guomindang) (an aspect of colonization that has been extensively dramatized by Hou Hsiao-hsien, particularly in *City of Sadness*, while the U.S. residual effects have been more openly registered in Edward Yang's work, particularly in the forthcoming, and significantly titled, *A Brighter Summer Day*).

One of these venomous, but anonymous fictional shafts strikes the writer Chou Yü-fen, who then thinks she has learned about her husband's adulteries and feels herself thereby all the more empowered to go about living her own independent life: indeed, like a peculiarly reversible toxin, this liberates her from her writer's block and sets her working again. Finally, the interrupted phone call had advised her, for further information, to visit an address that is none other than the murder apartment, in which, as we know, the photographer has now taken up abode and to which the White Chick will also slowly make her way, since she still has the key and is feverish and in some desperation after the catastrophic outcome of her attempt at free-lance prostitution (undertaken when her leg is healed and she can finally escape the mother's jail sentence).

What kicks these interesting coincidences up another level into a more reflexive kind of storytelling discourse – as I have already indicated, their equivalents can be found all the way back to the Greek novel, via *Tom Jones* and any number of other classical adventure or picaresque texts – is obviously the redoubling of the narrative in written form, *en abîme,* as my references to Gide will already have begun to foretell. The reader will indeed scarcely be surprised to learn that the story Chou Yü-fen has finally been freed to write is a kind of modified alternative world in which her husband has an affair with someone not terribly unlike the White Chick herself and in which a wife, who is a writer, is thereby freed to write another story, one that in real life wins her a prize and catapults her onto the cultural page of the major newspapers, not to speak of the television screen. But this puts a very different face on narrative coincidence, which it now refashions, as from over a great distance, into patterns and shapes as abstract as the traces of mound builders' culture seen from a satellite, or the Himalayas seen from the moon: from an intention to reunite and reassemble, which can at best be attributed to Providence (when such a concept is available), the narrative intersections become reformed into demiurgic games played by the aesthetic great Other of romantic irony (aesthetics now here, for the moderns as well as the Romantics, coming to replace fate, chance, and ethics). Equally clearly, however, this quintessentially modernist turn and flavor are all the more identifiable as such because they bring an old-fashioned note into the postmodern context, which can be charming or jarring indifferently, depending on whether the ambitions of modern form bring some relief from postmodern frivolity or whether the implacable ideological stress of the modern on the aestheticality of life, and on the implicit but inescapable role of the individual genius, are now relatively intolerable. Later on, however, I will show that yet a third interpretation of *Terrorizer* can be called on to dispel the modernist appearance in its turn and reaffirm its postcontemporaneous relevance (if not exactly its postmodernity).

Even if for a moment we retain the modernist framework that Chou Yü-fen's novella establishes, it should be added that its transmission by way of the medium of film seriously problematizes the modernist effects that should accompany it, or at the very least renders them optional in what we will later on see to be a postmodern way. Nothing is more alien to this film, indeed, than the mystical-modernist overtones of the theme of inspiration from without, as when, in Cocteau's film of the same name, Orpheus copies down his poetry from enigmatic messages transmitted over the car radio like Resistance code broadcasts ("Les carrottes sont cuites, trois fois!"); nor is the book itself (in its previous incarnation we heard only a few vapid samples of nature lyricism) anything like an *Yi Jing,* which, as in Dick's *Man in the High Castle,* one consults for forecasts of individual and collective history alike. For one thing it is not clear who in the film has actually read this prize-winning production: the photographer and the girlfriend (with whom he is eventually reunited) hear about it on television and then read a summary in the newspaper. As for her most important reader (or so one would have thought), the husband does not read at all, something of an index of his general obtuseness, as the following snatch of dialogue suggests:

HOSPITAL DIRECTOR (with some suspicion)
What does your wife do exactly? What are these things she writes anyway?

LI LI-CHUNG (evasively)
Oh, I don't know. I don't read novels.

The novel thereby comes before us not as an object or an alternative world or narrative, but rather as a peculiarly disembodied effect, with all the reality and objectivity of sheer appearance: it is error made real and having taken on flesh; it is, as it were, the image-for-the-other, the simulacrum or a simulacrum, since the viewer never apprehends it directly but only by way of the judgments of the other characters (in this case the photographer, who recognizes the writer's picture as his mysterious visitor and suddenly grasps all this as the machinations of his equally mysterious Eurasian acquaintance). If, now, however, we reposition this effect within what we might as well call the Hansen–Bordwell hypothesis, writing at once takes on the status of one medium among others, competing for power and prestige with the more modern technologies of photography, sound transmission (here the telephone, although more normally the radio), and finally film itself. It should be evident that if Yang's movie camera retains the ultimate priority over all the other media, if only by virtue of the fact that they are necessarily represented within it, it nonetheless plays fair and endows each of them with a specific power not ordinarily thought to be consistent with cinemas as such.

For photography within film seems to retain what Walter Benjamin might have called an archaic aura, a dimly threatening primitive power, as when stills of the murder victims silently circulate among the police team, who thereby *see* and are present in ways denied the moviegoer even when the still is flashed on the screen for us in passing. In *Terrorizer,* to be sure, the photographer proves to be an idle rich youth with a hobby, and the emphasis is placed as much on the cash value of his various cameras as on the quality of his images (Figure 24), save for the one mesmerizing shot of the White Chick peering fearfully around a corner, unaware that she is in the process of being seen and recorded. This is then the magnified

24. The photographer with the director Edward Yang. Edward Yang, *Terrorizer* (1986). YANG AND HIS GANG, FILMMAKERS

image, three times greater than life and developed in segments of glossy prints, that will greet her eyes as she returns to the murder room: an allegory of film itself? Perhaps, but if so, only because, like the punctum in the fatal photographs of Antonioni's *Blow-up,* and unlike Rimbaud's magical flowers or Lacan's signifiers, this one does not look back at you. Here the wind that blows through the great trees in Antonioni's park only more mildly lifts and ruffles the segments of the portrait. Photography's prestige, here, is to be equal to the simulacrum and more interesting than the reality, but otherwise little more than a way of killing time.[8]

Perhaps we need to drive a wedge more dramatically between the senses, after the great synesthesias of the modern period, and to restore some of the liberating freshness and horror of the auditory image in a society that has become one immense collection of visual spectacles.[9] This is then perhaps the deeper meaning of the sequence whereby *Blow-up*'s postmodern sequels – De Palma's *Blowout* (1981) and Coppola's *The Conversation* (1974) – transfer the visible clue to the realm of sound: the unconscious, utopian longing to be awakened from the spell of images, and to be awakened by sounds as piercing as shots or whispers? The White Chick is at any rate a good deal more threatening on the phone than in her image, and the spider's web of anonymous phone calls all over the city offers a vivid figure for urban simultaneity, as well as for the misery of confinement and powerlessness: as with Stalin or Hitler in their offices, it is hard to tell supreme power from house arrest, and something of the mystery of the definitive embodiment of psychic resources in technology – what was human reality like before the telephone? before the photograph? before the mirror? – is here recovered from the forgetfulness into which the triumph of these media plunges being itself. But telephonic relief also returns us to the specific form of organization of this particular city.

As for literature, it surely fares least well of all the modes we have come to recognize as mediatic: wrong on all counts, a vehicle for narcissism and self-pity, and for the shabby pride of commercialized prizes, a shabby cultural alibi in the destiny of the most ancient of all literate civilizations on its way to television like everybody else. Significantly, here alone television rears its garish competing likenesses: in this rivalry between the arts and media (which film is in any case slated to win in advance), it is important that the small screen humiliate high culture, but not enter into too distracting a juxtaposition with film, whose brilliant capacities are so extraordinarily rehearsed. (In the era of video, someone once remarked, film recovers that aura that Benjamin had denied it in the era of its undisputed technological mastery. Is this not to say that there is something slightly old-fashioned today about the exercise of bravura cinematography, which is, in any case, as I have already observed, an icy mastery?)

All of this marks something like the content of the form; and it is important, in my opinion, to be clear about the competing interpretations that force their way through even to this level and persist in their struggle for it. The features we have just evoked, which reach their thematic climax with the novella and its relationship to a world already structured by the other media, can all be read in conjunction as a vivid contemporary replay of that modern-romantic topos of fiction and reality, the dream world, illusion and what it transfigures; indeed, *Terrorizer* would helpfully bring all that up to date and place such topics back on a postcontemporary agenda. Yet such a reading turns the film back into a set of conceptual meanings, into a vehicle for certain thoughts or reflections, or for a kind of philosophy of life – rather old-fashioned commodities in the universal sway of positivism and "cynical reason," and of the "end" of just such "ideologies." To this technocratization of philosophy, then, corresponds the transformation of the genres into the media, along with the emergence of readings such as the one sketched earlier (the deeper subject of the film consisting in its articulated rivalry with competing media). It is a *Gestalt* alternation we will observe on other levels (and in particular on that of the "form of the content"); it is perhaps most productive to use it for a degree of historical self-knowledge and to observe the plausibility with which each option comes before us respectively. The deeper "meaning" of the film, in that case, would not lie in either interpretation but in our hesitation between both.

As for the psychic content of the work, that constructed effect – that "unspeakable" narrative or filmic "sentence" – whereby a structure of synchronous monadic simultaneities seems to demand embodiment in someone's experience, if only that of God himself, is now, with the final looping of the knots, ever more suggestively passed off as this or that subjective experience. The shock we may attribute to the Eurasian girl is just such a formal "objective correlative," for it releases the multitudinous occult traditions of the *Doppelgänger* and its putative terrors – myself striding forth to meet me at midday! – at the same time it mobilizes a whole contemporary philosophy of the Look (from Sartre on down), and the way in which it endows me with an external being that is alien to me, but to which I am also condemned. The association of these motifs with narrative now has the advantage of dispelling philosophical or theosophic connotations. And not only with narrative, but with a reflexive positing of narrative in which, in writers like Gide, it is less important to produce a plot than to produce the idea of plot itself, as an object in its own right that, lacking totality, gradually disengages itself from all its local manifestations and hovers above the completed work as its visionary mirror image in the realm of objective spirit. The experience is as simple as it is unsettling: others have been seeing me without my knowing it! Others whose existences I was not even aware of have been thinking about me! At the level of urban simultaneities on which we now find ourselves, this – what are you doing with my picture? – is a virtual *cognito*, the punctual other end of all those mutually exclusive synchronicities. It is a paradox that will then, from now until the final image, continue to be turned inside out ceaselessly like Benjamin's famous socks,[10] for its sharpness is the same as Chou Yü-fen's blissful ignorance of the origins in other, unknown people of the story she believes to be autobiographical, while Li Li-chung's knowledge (the photographer puts him in the picture and shows him the photos) is as numbing a form of distraction as his other worries and as unproductive, leading to what may be called externalized, or "foreclosed,"[11] impersonal hallucinations, rather than to any shocked presentiment of unexpected worlds beyond his own.

It is to be sure about Li Li-chung's experience and about his psyche that *Terrorizer* raises the most durable questions: in this polyvocal film without a hero a certain priority seems gradually to be afforded to this one, whose destiny promises to hold the key to interpretation most reliably as the actions draw to a close. But it may be a broken promise: Li Li-chung loses out on his promotion, as we might have guessed, and as we know, he loses his wife as well. In both cases he tries aimlessly to salvage the situation with clumsy efforts that confirm our initial impression of this character as the quintessential loser – something we can tell virtually from his very first appearance, doing exercises on his balcony (although I would be hard put to say why or how). I have suggested that we can have little personal sympathy for him (a remark about which there can be nothing "personal" since it also holds for all the other characters as well), yet his destiny can awaken a certain impersonal sadness, and this identifies, I believe, the allegorical investment in the figure of Li Li-chung. He, more than any of the other characters (the traditional policeman, the Western-style modernist writer, specimens of a timeless *jeunesse dorée,* lumpens who have their equivalent in every urban center on the globe), can serve as evidence for an unconscious (and collective) meditation on dependency, that is to say, on the positioning of the national entity within the new world system of late capitalism. As a technocrat and a bureaucratized professional, indeed, Li Li-chung is well placed to offer figuration to the "national allegory"[12] of a post–Third World country that can never really join the First World (in the sense of capital export and becoming a new center of the world system, which it would do only as a structural satellite of Japan or the United States). His "brilliant career" is significantly accompanied not by dramatic and tragic failures, but by prospects that, even if successful, are not likely to modify the dreariness of his current prosperity. One does not, in other words, foresee a more gratifying continuation of this marriage, nor, if the other bureaucrats are any indication, would the coveted promotion be likely to transform him, in a thunderclap, in his very being. This – the joylessness of good fortune in the global bureaucratic system – is perhaps the new face of a dependency most often dramatized in terms of tendential improvement and the "development of underdevelopment." This is, as it were, the gentrified dimension of a postmodernity whose flip side is neopoverty and "homelessness" and a whole new attitude toward urban space also registered in this film in original ways.

From this class standpoint, indeed, in a developing or underdeveloped country, the fate of the petite bourgeoisie (in this stage, a new petite bourgeoisie or professional-managerial segment of bureaucrats and formerly independent professionals) seems to be more generally emblematic of the fate of the nation or the collectivity, at least in the popular imagination: Balzac, who wrote in a roughly comparable period of France's development, often projects his petite bourgeois figures in this way, as allegories of the national misery. It is as though the rich and successful (in our time, multinational executives) are lucky in some private and nongeneralizable way, while the poor – particularly agricultural and manual workers – are already universally exploited anyway and can scarcely be allegorical of anything save the perennity of class struggle itself. In some situations, to be sure, lumpens – like the *picaros* of the Spanish golden age – can also be allegorical of the nation, while the sadness we have attributed to the figure of Li Li-chung can be thought to include all the mixed feelings attributable to the developing Third World. He could not be allegorical of Taiwan exactly, for many other unique determinants of that special situation are omitted from his story; but his fate may at least be seen as a figural acting out of fantasies about the limits to Taiwanese development in a world system. What such an interpretation does to the potential universality of such a narrative, and in particular to its relevance to and reception by First World audiences, will be the topic of a concluding reflection.

But it would be a mistake to assimilate "national allegory" in this new postmodern sense to the traditional or stereotypical view of this structure as a supremely static and mechanical one. There is, in postcontemporary allegory, a kind of inner, self-transcending dynamic for which even the older word "reflexive" is too weak, a self-regulating transformation of such organisms under their own momentum in which initial figures are ceaselessly and dialectically modified by virtue of the very fact that in them the problem of representation is itself already thematized, and must therefore produce and reproduce itself in a variety of new guises and levels.

So here the seemingly colorless drama of Li Li-chung develops in unforeseeably dramatic ways that would seem to have little enough to do with the revelation of the story within a story, the anonymous interventions and self-reflexive modernist and conspiratorial rewritings that were the burden of his wife's narrative line. Those come only to compound the doctor's general confusion and to separate him, in his dejection, even more completely from real life. There follows what is surely one of the most astonishing scenes in recent cinema, in which Li Li-chung revisits his childhood friend the policeman and makes a remarkable announcement: beaming with joy, he explains that he has finally won his promotion, that he has also been able to come to terms with his wife's departure and to realize that he is better off without her, that he is a happy man at last – successful, at peace with himself, fulfilled. The gestural and physiognomic euphoria with which these falsehoods are conveyed transcends the usual signs of mendacity or simply lying (if only because we can see no point to the deception, so that our own confusion washes back over the effect to intensify it). It is difficult to convey the terrible joy, the radiantly false happiness, that streams in effulgence from the ghastly smile of a character who has rarely smiled before and with whom we have come to associate the furrowed brow of an essentially plodding man meeting his difficulties with uniform perplexity and without skill. The heightened expression, not registered in close-up, is projected off the screen in a way only comparable (although the content is altogether different) to that supreme *oeillade* in *Mr. Arkadin* (1955) where the zoom shot of the bearded Welles's sharp return look shows that he knows, and that he knows we know, and so forth. *Supreme* is the climactic word one wants for this kind of thing in which the event pulls itself up by its own pigtail into a higher, formally transcendent level.

As for Li Li-chung's supreme happiness, modernist readings can still be imagined for it, as in the Nietzschean-fictional suggestion that under certain circumstances the acting out of alternative, unrealized possibilities – sealed by my celebration with the brother, the ritual of festive eating and drinking, enjoyment of my new esteem, having lived up to expectations at last – might be as satisfying, perhaps more fully satisfying, than the reality. The interpretation in terms of life and art would here continue to find corroboration and plausibility, but should be complemented by a reading of what I will only for convenience sake call a relatively more postmodern type. After all, in retrospect, one of the fundamental signs of an impending change in our mode of thinking consists in the increasing dissatisfaction with what I have elsewhere called the "depth model"[13] – in this, the opposition between life and fiction modeled roughly on some notion of a reality behind or opposed to an appearance. What took the place of that appearance-and-reality model was something variously characterized in terms of textuality or in terms of practices, a conception of the succession of various surfaces, none of which was somehow metaphysically or ontologically privileged over the other. But that Li Li-chung's fictional or unreal alternative life can also be seen and read in this way is shown by a remarkable series of multiple and mutually exclusive denouements.

In another early-morning sequence, after their late-night celebration, the husband-physician awakens in the policeman's house and removes the sleeping man's revolver; assassinates the hospital director on his way to work; and then, breaking into the apartment of his wife's lover, shoots the lover in gruesome execution style. Unable to do the same to his wife, he stations himself in the crowded downtown area in which we have seen the White Chick pick up her victims, and waits for her, presumably because he has seen her photograph and has decided to hold her responsible for all his troubles. But by now we know that both of these hitherto absolutely unrelated characters are very dangerous: the final plot loop, whether involving sexual intercourse or murder, is a putative climax of great tension and instability whose narrative satisfactions, even granting the tying up of the last remaining threads, are no longer clear. But now time runs more swiftly: the policeman wakes suddenly; the pimp who classically follows the couple down the hotel corridor unexpectedly finds himself locked out of the room; the police come pounding down the hall; and at the same moment, we observe the protagonist characteristically, preparatory to anything else, wash his hands extensively one final time. But this time the motif has been activated: the liquid splashing out of the faucet coincides with the splintering of the hotel room door as the police break in. What results, however, is the splattering of blood and brain tissue over a different wall, in a different space, as Li Li-chung shoots himself in the early morning in the bathhouse of his friend's building, at which point the wife suddenly wakes up in her lover's flat, staring with wide eyes at an unidentified premonition.

It will have been obvious, from all the conventional aesthetic signals, that the preceding sequence was a fantasy or wish fulfillment of some kind. Nor do I mean to argue against the obvious either but rather to urge the return of a certain indecidability to the sequence itself, whose remarkable loop – the water faucet reappearing with all the portentous formal significance of Freudian *Nachträglichkeit* (retroactivation or "deferred action") – arrests us in its own right by its striking narrative temporality, without our being able to determine the presence of any specific content or message as such. It is rather a kind of prestidigitation in which we watch the abstract fillip of the form itself and are thereby distracted from the content, and in particular are released from the tiresome (realistic) obligation of deciding whether it is supposed to be real or to be a dream of some kind.

Indeed, this multiple ending is in my opinion very delicately balanced, carefully arranged so that such decisions can be eluded, if not avoided altogether. Its skillfulness cannot really be appreciated unless we are willing to acknowledge how tiresome the interpolation form of the flashback or the fantasy has become in recent years; they were staples of the older cinema, and knew a kind of Indian summer in the era of film noir, immediately after World War II (and immediately before the wide screen, the end of Hollywood, and the senescence of modernism itself). The framed narrative has always carried the message of fate, of sealed destinies, of events irredeemably past. The interpolated filmic (and less often, literary) daydream also probably served to reinforce the sense of imprisonment in my current situation; indeed, if Bierce's "Occurrence at Owl Creek Bridge" can be taken as the fusion and synthesis of both, their symbolic value – in the instants before a capital execution – becomes dramatically explicit. Stylized revivals of the technique – as in Gilliam's *Brazil* (1985) – would seem even more explicitly to enlist the unreal interpolated narrative segment in order to drive home the collective imprisonment of a 1984-type society. But for postcontemporary viewers, the traditional frame, which asks us to leave the present, to which predictably we will return only at the end of the film – as, for example, in *Le Jour se lève* (1939) – is evidently irritating in direct proportion to our systemic commitment to a postmodern present, while the Hollywood fantasy narrative vainly tries to substitute alternative reality satisfactions in ways that equally try our patience.

The alternate endings of *Terrorizer*, however, do not require heavy subjectification; the film is over too fast, and its polyphony, the multiplicity of protagonists, leaves it entangled with their destinies in ways impossible to sort out (our last view of the Eurasian girl, for example, which thereby continues to carry a certain informational authority). Meanwhile, if it was a fantasy, the embarrassing question arises insistently as to whose fantasy it will finally have been? The argument can indeed equally be made for the wife's having dreamed it as for the husband's having daydreamed it in passionate exhalations of revenge. (As we have seen, he is not a particularly passionate character, while the details of the White Chick's modus operandi cannot have been known to him either.) What this marks is the modernist interpretive temptation, the urge to tie up all the threads by integrating identifiable subjectivities and points of view. The "postmodern" alternative is then clearly what springs into view when subjects are abolished as meaningful categories (or if you prefer, when the hold of philosophies of the subject are significantly weakened), namely the aesthetic of textuality or of interminable segmentation, in which we are at equal distance from all successive sequences and the whole begins to offer itself as an immense set of variations or recombinations, as in the *nouveau roman* or Robbe-Grillet's accompanying filmic production. But this temptation has been carefully conjured as well: if a certain period aestheticism clung to the modernist (and Gidean) theme of the *mise-en-abîme* of the story-within-a-story, a far more contemporary but still relatively archaic 1960s aestheticism surely informs this kind of permutational free play, and it is evidently not at all the note wished for in conclusion to this film.

What we must admire, therefore, is the way in which the filmmaker has arranged for these two powerful interpretive temptations – the modern and the postmodern, subjectivity and textuality – to neutralize each other, to hold each other in one long suspension in such a way that the film can exploit and draw on the benefits of both, without having to commit itself to either as some definitive reading or formal and stylistic category. Besides his personal mastery, the possibility of this mutually reinforcing suspension may owe something to the situation of Third World cinema itself, in traditions in which neither modernist nor postmodern impulses are internally generated and both arrive in the field of production with a certain chronological simultaneity in full postwar modernization. *Terrorizer* thereby enjoys the freedom of a certain distance from both, whose advantages this essay has explored.

But in conclusion, it is worth taking this alternation and coexistence of readings and competing interpretations even further and attempting to appreciate the way everything changes if for the masculine pathos of Li Li-chung's story we substitute the rather different drama of the women figures as the film's center of gravity. To see this as a film about women's destinies – whether it can be argued to be a properly feminist film I cannot judge – is to assert a certain postmodernity about it, to the degree that the women's situations here are grasped and articulated as fundamentally spatial. The male figures – doctor and photographer alike – are wrapped up in their temporal destinies: success or failure still hangs over them like the category of the future itself. Meanwhile, as males, they are spatially more mobile and can also console themselves with public areas, whether the police station, the hospital, or the streets themselves.

But the women's spaces are essentially those of confinement; the one form of public space open to the novelist is the television screen, scarcely a space to stretch or relax in. Archetypal here, of course, is the confinement of the Eurasian girl, locked up in her mother's apartment, as though it were not bad enough to be condemned to crutches. Even more intolerable for an adolescent is the way in which, in this particular apartment, she is imprisoned in the mother's own 1950s past, a past in which the mother is herself equally imprisoned, to the tune of "Smoke Gets in Your Eyes." In any case, our significant first view of the girl had been her desperate escape from the confinement of the murder apartment, while, equally significant, her time of greatest physical mobility is a frustrating night-long bus ride back and forth across Taipei in a feverish state of exhaustion and collapse. Finally, her principal workplace, as it were, is not a public one, as with the men, but rather the quintessential anonymous hotel room, always the same, in which the selfsame drama of theft, violence, and blackmail is played out over and over again.

But this is not a unique situation in the film: the photographer's girlfriend is equally imprisoned in a place that remains his, even after he removes his pictures, blowing curtains sealing off this now-abandoned space from the street and the out-of-doors in what is a virtual minor leitmotiv.

Nor is it clear that the writer's far more sumptuous apartment is any less constricting: "My world is shrinking," she literally tells her former lover. The semitraditional rugs and furniture are wonderful occasions for catching the change of light, one of the fundamental concerns of this intensely visual and photographic film. Meanwhile, the bathroom, in which her doctor-husband washes his hands on his return from work, is suffused with a yellow glow virtually marked out as his symbolic color. We meet it again in a stunning sequence in the hospital as he mounts the stairs into a sea of yellow light; it may therefore be taken as essentially artificial, associated with modernization. But the far more open and airlit space of the rest of the apartment, associated with Chou Yü-fen – a kind of yuppie or professional space, not unrelated to the even more expensive family villa of the young photographer (with pool and maid) – is not necessarily a great deal more positive. It is a kind of dead space, filled with elegant used furniture that is there primarily to be turned into images; and from it, just as clearly as the Eurasian girl from her locked apartment, Chou Yü-fen is driven to escape.

That modernism is temporal and postmodernism spatial has often been affirmed; the spatiality of *Terrorizer* and its images is inescapable. But I would like to insist on a unique feature of the spatiality of this film, which is the insistent relationship it establishes between the individual space and the city as a whole: the women's dramas are thus spatial not only because they are somehow postmodern (although the characterization of postmodernity in terms of the new social movements in general and of feminism in particular is a widespread one), but also because they are urban, and even more because they are articulated within this particular city.

Terrorizer is indeed very much a film about urban space in general, and offers something like an anthology of enclosed apartments or even individual rooms. It is these that predominate, and they are reconfirmed by the punctuation of an occasional street scene that always tends to return us to the aerial perspective, the view from above, the glance down from the balcony, and thus implicitly the confinement to the apartment on the upper story. The zero degree of this dwelling space would then be constituted by the murder room, as it is sealed off into darkness by the photographer. This act thereby betrays the essential characteristic of all these dwelling spaces, which are to serve as cubicles that open onto the city and the street in one way or another, and are somehow incomplete and spatially parasitic upon it. Only the Eurasian girl's hotel room is somehow buried in space, beyond the city somewhere, while the underworld, redolent of the *mystères* of the classical nineteenth-century cities and melodramas, finds itself here reduced to a housing unit that gets repaired and repainted and only coincidentally rerented to someone who remembers what happened in it.

Taipei is here mapped and configured as a superimposed set of boxed dwelling spaces in which the characters are all in one way or another confined: the film thereby acknowledges what seems to distinguish it from traditional and modern Chinese cities on the mainland, as well as from the cultural and historical styles of other cities in East Asia – a rapid construction of buildings along both sides of great linear arteries that are somehow its central formal category. The apartments do not imply the formal centrality of a single building to which they belong (as belatedly and extraordinarily as in Perec's novel *La Vie mode d'emploi*, about an apartment house). Nor do they offer the kind of panorama one experiences in Jesus Díaz's film, *Lejania* – interiors into which Miami is projected by way of home movies and videotapes; a rooftop from which Havana as a whole is viewed spread out around us; and finally the real streets into which the protagonist, on the point of asphyxiation, manages to escape. But in this Second World film, the streets are still a genuinely public space of the collective social project.

The dominant First World experience of the postcontemporary city is surely that of gentrification, and of dead monuments that can no longer clearly be called public but that are no longer private either. What lies outside the gentrified zones is coming to be acknowledged as a new Third World space within the First World city. As for properly Third World urban representations, all that can be conjectured as a minimal generalization is perhaps the now-conventional form of the peasant as witness, the narrative point of view of the villager seeing the metropolis for the first time.

None of that seems to me comparable to this inscription of Taipei, which is also, as has already been observed, dialectically distinct from Hou Hsiao-hsien's images of the Taiwan countryside. A foreigner and an outsider may be permitted to conjecture that this way of looking at urban experience has something to do with the "representation of totality" of a small island that is also a non-national nation-state. The enclosed spaces in their range and variety thereby figure or embody the unevenness or inequality of the world system: from the most *traditional* kind of space, paradoxically or not, that is, the barracks apartment of the policeman (and it cannot be without significance that the protagonist, after washing his hands in so many modern and anonymous Western-style bathrooms and sinks, should kill himself in what is a very traditional-looking hot-tub-sauna type of area) all the way to the *national* space of the hospital, the *multinational* space of the publisher's office (the media, surely of a global range, now housed in a great glass high-rise), and what I am tempted to call the equally *transnational* anonymity of the hotel corridor with its identical bedrooms.

The allegorical comment being made here on Taipei itself is one that engages a kind of Third World situation we have rarely until now included in that (rather traditional) category, namely the developing Third World or the newly industrializing First World tier of the Third World or Pacific Rim (excluding Japan, to be sure). Taiwan is somehow within the world system as its citizens are in their city boxes: prosperity and constriction all at once, the loss of nature (which is observed only twice, in a park close-up and in the policeman's backyard, if one excludes the manicured pool and lawn of the student's villa), the failure of the urban to constitute itself by contrast with its counterpart. What is grand and exhilarating, light itself, the hours of the day, is here embedded in the routine of the city and locked into the pores of its stone or smeared on its glass – light also being postmodern and a mere adjunct to the making of reproducible images.

I want to conclude by stressing that, in the postmodern, the relations between universal and particular, if they persist at all, must be conceived in an utterly different way from those that obtained in previous social formations and certainly from what characterized the modern. What I have found in this work from a "semiperipheral" country is not thereby "local" or provincial in any traditional sense, but is, rather, what makes this work universal in its aesthetic value (to use an old-fashioned language). It is because in late capitalism and in its world system even the center is marginalized, and that powerful expression of the marginally uneven and the unevenly developed issuing from a recent experience of capitalism are often more intense and powerful, more expressive, and above all more deeply symptomatic and meaningful than anything the enfeebled center still finds itself able to say.

NOTES

This chapter is based on a paper, "Remapping Taipei," originally presented at the UCLA Conference on Chinese Film. The version here is from Jameson, *The Geopolitical Aesthetic: Cinema and Space in the World-System* and is reprinted with the permission of Indiana University Press.
1. Ann Banfield, *Unspeakable Sentences* (London: Routledge & Kegan Paul, 1982).
2. It is safe to say that Hou Hsiao-hsien (Hou Xiaoxian) is Taiwan's leading filmmaker today, and the first – after the liberalization of 1987, when for the first time the history of Taiwan since World War II could be discussed publicly – to launch into the construction of an ambitious historical epic, *City of Sadness* [*Beiqing chengshi*, 1989]. His social material, drawn from youth and the countryside, is quite distinct from that of Edward Yang, and the spirit of his fine works – a kind of populist pathos or sentimentalism – is also distinctive (as discussed later in this essay).
3. Renata Salecl has described such nationalisms (at work in Yugoslavian context) in terms of a most suggestive Lacanian analysis.
4. See Fredric Jameson, *Postmodernism, or, The Cultural Logic of Late Capitalism* (Durham, N.C.: Duke University Press, 1990), pp. 20–1.
5. I am indebted to Michael Denning for the observation that the Italian setting of *The Godfather, Part II* (1974) allows Coppola to avoid issues of race and drugs, which would have fatally reimposed themselves within the frame of the superstate itself.
6. Alessandro Manzoni, *The Betrothed*, trans. Bruce Penman (Harmondsworth: Penguin, 1972), pp. 223–4.
7. I am grateful to Shu-chen Chiang for her commentary on an earlier version of this essay, as well as for the indispensable information about the Taiwan setting of the film and some of its local or vernacular connotations. I have also benefited greatly from Yingjin

Zhang's "The Idyllic Country and the (Post) Modern City: Cinematic Configurations of Family in *Osmanthus Alley* and *Terrorizer*," unpublished manuscript.

8. Clearly, this treatment demands comparison with the role and function of the deaf-and-dumb photographer in *City of Sadness:* he is the youngest son, something like the excluded witness, and, with his equally excluded Japanese wife, our most privileged "point of view." For that very reason, in Hou Hsiao-hsien's film, this character would seem to provide the technical means for estrangement in its classic, Russian-formalist sense (like, e.g., the child's point of view in Ambrose Bierce's *Chicamauga*).

9. Proust's pages on the telephone are to be found in *Le Côté de Guermantes*, Part 1 (Paris: Editions de la Pleiade, 1988), vol. 2, pp. 431–6; this technological mediation is immediately followed by an ocular inspection of Marcel's dying grandmother conveyed in terms of the technology of photography (pp. 438–9). In his "Modernism and Repetition: Kafka's Literary Technologies," *Journal of the Kafka Society of America* (1990), pp. 59–63. James Rolleston draws our attention to Kafka's representation of the telephone.

10. In Walter Benjamin, "Berlin Childhood" (*Gesammelte Schriften*, IV, 284, in "Schranke"), translated as a separate unit in Shierry Webber Nicholson's English version of the Paris edition, "The Stocking": "The first cabinet that opened when I wanted it to was the bureau. I had only to pull on the knob and the door clicked open for me. Among the underclothing stored there was the thing that made the bureau an adventure. I had to make a path to the farthest corner; there I found my stockings piled, rolled up in the old-fashioned way. Each pair looked like a small pouch. Nothing gave me more pleasure than plunging my hand as deep as possible into the inside of that pouch. I did not do so for the sake of the warmth. It was 'The Dowry,' which I held in my hand in the rolled-up interior, that drew me into its depths. When I had got my hand around it and confirmed my possession of the soft woollen mass to the best of my ability, the second part of the game, which brought the revelation, began. For now I began working 'The Dowry' out of its woollen pouch. I drew it closer and closer to me until the amazing event occurred: I had extracted 'The Dowry,' but 'The Pouch' in which it had lain no longer existed. I could not test this process often enough. It taught me that form and content, the veil and what it hides, are one and the same. It led me to extricate the truth from literature as cautiously as the child's hand brought the stocking out of 'The Pouch.'"

11. Lacan uses the term "foreclusion" for the way in which, in psychosis – where language or the Symbolic Order is not available to organize such impulses – the sufferer's thoughts return as it were from the outside, in the form of disembodied voices, for example. See "On a Question Preliminary to Any Treatment of Psychosis," in Jacques Lacan, *Ecrits* (New York: Norton, 1977), pp. 179–225.

12. See my "Third-World Literature in the Age of Multinational Capitalism," *Social Text*, no. 15 (Fall 1986), pp. 65–88.

13. See Jameson, *Postmodernism*, pp. 12ff.

6

THE IDEOLOGY OF INITIATION

THE FILMS OF HOU HSIAO-HSIEN

William Tay

Five films by Hou Hsiao-hsien (Hou Xiaoxian) before his magnum opus *City of Sadness* [*Beiqing chengshi*, 1989] deal with initiation in one way or another. The five are *The Boys from Fengkuei* [*Fenggui lai de ren*, 1983], *A Summer at Grandpa's* [*Dongdong de jiaqi*, 1984], *A Time to Live and a Time to Die* [*Tongnian wangshi*, 1985], *Dust in the Wind* [*Lianlian fengchen*, 1987], and *Daughter of the Nile* [*Niluohe nüer*, 1987]. This short essay examines the various aspects of initiation as represented in these five films.[1]

The term "initiation" was used by U.S. New Critics Cleanth Brooks and Robert Penn Warren in their comments on Ernest Hemingway's "The Killers" and Sherwood Anderson's "I Want to Know Why" in the pioneering textbook *Understanding Fiction*.[2] Brooks and Warren used the term to describe a theme and to classify a type of short story. Other formalist critics adopted this usage from the 1940s through the 1970s.[3] Entire anthologies and portions of anthologies have been organized around the initiation theme for pedagogic purposes.[4]

This formalist discussion and anthologizing over a forty-year period established a fictional genre or subgenre based on the initiation theme. Among the definitions of this theme, perhaps the most encompassing is that given by Isaac Sequeira, who takes into consideration the diverse emphases and the minor variations of the different critics:

Initiation is an existential crisis or a series of encounters in life, almost always painful, with experience during which the adolescent protagonist gains valuable knowledge about himself, the nature of evil, or the world. This knowledge is accompanied by a sense of the loss of innocence and a sense of isolation, and if it is to have any permanent effect at all, must result in a change in character and behavior; for if knowledge does not change an individual's thinking and behavior, no learning – an acquisition of knowledge, per se – has taken place. In almost every case, the change leads toward an adjustable integration into the adult world.[5]

Applying this definition to Hou's films, one can argue easily that *The Boys from Fengkuei, A Summer at Grandpa's,* and *Daughter of the Nile* are cinematic equivalents of verbal initiation texts. At the end of *Boys,* the young protagonist finally gains knowledge about himself, his desires, and the vicissitudes of the world. In *Summer,* the young boy witnesses the oppressive forces of social stratification and the punitive consequences of transgressing social norms. In *Daughter,* which, most unusually, features a young girl as the initiate, the heroine encounters the "evils" of the world, a crucial aspect of the discovery process particularly emphasized by the early scholars of the initiation theme.

The two other films, however, cannot be described as initiation films, because the time frame is much too long. *A Time to Live and a Time to Die* spans almost two decades and covers the growth of its protagonists from childhood to young adulthood. *Dust in the Wind* focuses on a shorter period, but the stretch of time is still longer than that depicted in the usual initiation stories. Both films, however, take their forms and structures from the developing personalities of the protagonists. At least in this respect, both can be seen as cinematic analogues of the *Bildungsroman,* which typically incorporates the initiation theme into its plot as a moment of the maturing process.

By using such terms as *Bildungsroman* and initiation story, one inevitably runs the risk of doing violence to texts from a vastly different cultural tradition. But formalist critics would undoubtedly argue that, since initiation and its concomitants of self-discovery and self-knowledge are "universal" in the human process of growing up, such terminology is not inappropriate.[6] Mythopoeic critics who see initiation as an archetype deriving from ancient rites of passage would certainly argue in the same vein. Indeed, as far as the outcome of initiation is concerned, these critics do not sound much different than the formalists. Leslie Fiedler, for example, gives this archetypal view of initiation: "A fall through knowledge to maturity; behind it there persists the myth of the Garden of Eden, the assumption that to know good and evil is to be done with the joy of innocence and to take on the burdens of work and childbearing and death."[7] This notion of the initiation archetype can also be found in the works of Joseph Campbell, Northrop Frye, and Mircea Eliade.[8] But both critical groups, in stressing common humanity and its innate constants, have erased the sociocultural and historical-specific dimensions of initiation in different times and places. As such, the problem lies not with cultural divergences, but with methodological inadequacy. And if indeed "all third-world texts are necessarily . . . to be read as . . . national allegories,"[9] then the history alluded to in Hou Hsiao-hsien's texts has to be excavated and explicated so that the meanings of initiation in Taiwan society can be more fully comprehended.

The developmental history of Taiwan constitutes a subtext in the films under discussion. In *Summer,* the island economy is still underdeveloped and unindustrialized. The agricultural base of the economy can be seen as a homology of the traditional hierarchy and order in human relationships, thus partially explaining the outcome of the plot. It is in this period of economic underdevelopment that the government begins to lure foreign investments and multinational corporations by organizing special economic zones where import and export taxes are lifted, inexpensive land for construction and basic infrastructure are provided, and the cheap labor force of the agricultural area is enticed to migrate to these zones.

When the boys from Fengkuei (Fenggui) go to Kaohsiung (Gaoxiong), they take part-time menial jobs in an electronic factory. This brief stint for the young protagonist, from the spectator's perspective, is a sobering experience not because of the work, but because his future is hereby portended. The messy love affair that the protagonist observes – a crush on an older woman is a popular motif in initiation stories – features another young worker who is forced to steal from the factory in order to save for his marriage. True to the Chinese tradition, both the factory worker and the young protagonist perceive education to be an important means of upward social mobility. The former goes to night school and the latter tries to study Japanese on his own; however, the former's efforts are finally derailed by the law, and the latter's are mocked by his peers as futile. The film ends with the Fengkuei boys about to be conscripted and shies away from a pessimistic prognosis of their future. Just before this open-ended conclusion, the young protagonist, who has been thrust into maturity during his stay at Kaohsiung, is shown to be swallowed up by the heavy city traffic – a scene in which the camera remains still while the crisscrossing traffic wipes out the solitary image of the protagonist. Besides connoting a strong sense of alienation, this scene poignantly epitomizes the fates of many young rural men and women who desert their villages and opt for life in the cities and factories.

The same kind of migration is portrayed in *Dust,* except that the young hero, like many teenagers who seek a better future, ends up in Taipei with a menial job at slave wages. It is this process of migration from the country to the city that deprives the Taiwan agricultural base of human resources. What is being depicted in an objective way in this film is what all Third World countries have experienced; the results are usually squalid living conditions in the cities and polarization between the urban and the rural. As a chronicle of two youngsters growing up together, the film refrains from making explicit references to unsettling economic issues, with the exception of the miners' strike in which the young man's father participates, but the protagonist's quest is so typical and familiar that the issues stand out almost immediately.

If *Dust* is only a glimpse of the larger changes to come, *Daughter* is a visualization of a quintessential Third World metropolis: myriad forms of North American mass culture proliferate, though indigenous traditional ideologies in their last gasps are not yet entirely ineffectual; the newly discovered consumerism exists coterminously with the more conventional conspicuous display of wealth. It is this schizophrenic moment in Taiwan's economic development that the film uses as a backdrop. Working for a U.S. fast-food chain – a time marker, since U.S. fast-food franchises did not move into Taipei until after McDonald's 1984 gamble, which grossed an unheard-of NT$1.4 million a week – the young heroine in *Daughter* is mainly a peripheral observer as rapidly changing events overwhelm her and her family. Whether she attains any self-knowledge in the process remains ambivalent – formalist critics would have called this "uncompleted initiation,"[10] but she is undoubtedly representative of her generation of young workers who are being absorbed by a service economy and are moving away from the sweat shops. As the plot becomes more entangled, the heroine's sense of alienation becomes more acute, and her inability to comprehend, not to say control, the events around her makes her more vulnerable and helpless. This loss of control not only is symptomatic of the youthful mentality torn between the East and the West, but is also indicative of the disintegration of the traditional social order and system of values.

The young heroine is a member of a minority on the island consisting of second-generation mainlanders whose fathers usually have been in exile from the mainland since 1949 and whose mothers are Taiwanese. For her and others of

25. Hou Hsiao-hsien, *The Boys from Fengkuei* (1983). COURTESY OF CHANG HUA-K'UN

this second generation, Taiwan is home and they are bona fide Taiwanese though their identity cards may tell them otherwise. But to the older generation, despite the long stay on the island, Taiwan is no more than a temporary stopover, and they, mere passers-by or stranded travelers. This absence of a sense of belonging is powerfully articulated by two scenes in *Time.* The first scene uses the bamboo furniture in the house to foreground the father's feeling of transience: this furniture is inexpensive, so that when the mainland is recovered the family will not have to ship it home. The second scene is perhaps the most memorable of the film: the grandmother takes a stroll with her grandson in a Taiwan village as if she were back in her hometown. The mock seriousness imbues the scene with both emotional intensity and dramatic irony.

This film, perhaps the most historical of the five films under discussion, traces the growth of the protagonist in the 1950s and 1960s. Like the other films, this one is seemingly apolitical; but in its quiet manner, it confronts the sensitive issue of provincial identity differences. A historical consequence of the Kuomintang (Guomindang) debacle in 1949, the issue still haunts current electoral politics and threatens the social stability of Taiwan. By delineating this issue without being partisan, this film, like the other films with different subtexts, raises a highly charged question but refrains from answering it. But in this mode of being polemical lies the key to the art of Hou Hsiao-hsien, that is, an art of indirect, suggestive presentation in an episodic structure rather than a straightforward, dramatized statement in a strong, causal plot.[11] This mode of presentation allows Hou's works to be read at different levels because they are more open and indeterminate than other films of the same period.

However, a constant tension between two worlds, or perhaps between two value systems, runs through Hou Hsiao-hsien's vision. In *Summer,* the reminiscent narration romanticizes childhood happiness and conjures up a memorable pastoral moment despite the rude intrusion of a traditional society and its norms into an innocent love affair. Similarly, *Time* is also full of nostalgic fondness in spite of the poverty, sickness, and death.

But besides the usual psychological inclination to romanticize childhood and to embellish the past, Hou Hsiao-hsien's unstained and innocent countryside always remains in idealistic opposition to, if not an alternative to, the city, which is usually portrayed as the embodiment of deception, corruption, and exploitation. This binary opposition is first seen in *Boys* and is repeated in *Dust.* In both films, the journey from the country to the city results in the loss of innocence and a process of disillusionment.

In *Daughter,* however, there is a twist to this theme of initiation and its subsequent disillusionment. For characters who lived through the ingenuous and pastoral days of an agricultural Taiwan, the past was at least a cherished moment to be invoked against the present. But for the young heroine in *Daughter,* who knows no such past but only a present characterized by compulsive materialism, commodity fetishism, and self-alienation, there is no looking back in nostalgia.

26. Hou Hsiao-hsien, *A Summer at Grandpa's*, (1984). COURTESY OF CHANG HUA-K'UN

Her mental haven is the "mythic" and faraway Egyptian world in Japanese-style comic books. For her, retrospection is replaced by introspection.

The young heroine in *Daughter* is exceptional in another way. Nearly every single one of the many Chinese and U.S. initiation stories that I have come across over the years features a young male protagonist as an initiate – the most prominent exception being Carson McCullers's *The Member of the Wedding* (1966). In fact, in some of the "classic" initiation stories, women are often presented as femmes fatales, part of the "evil" to be discovered or to be overcome in the initiation process.[12] But this is certainly not the case in *Daughter*, where the quiet and observant heroine, though unable to alter the course of events, endures a demimonde of violence and death where men are the problem. In this film the sons, traditionally responsible for familial continuity and prosperity, are either abject failures or social outcasts, whereas the daughters are self-supportive and responsible.

While *Daughter* is narrated from the heroine's point of view, the earlier films are from the male initiates'. One characteristic that stands out in these films is the absence of a powerful and dominating patriarchy. In *Summer*, the father makes only two brief and inconsequential appearances. In *Boys*, the father is medically a vegetable who is totally dependent on the family. The mother becomes the head of the household and is in charge of raising the male protagonist. Similarly, the father in *Time* is an invalid who eventually succumbs to tuberculosis. The mother is another resilient character who shoulders the burden of the family. Again, in *Dust*, the father is a miner who has difficulty holding his job, leaving the mother in charge of the household. The fathers in these films are all nominal heads who,

27. Hou Hsiao-hsien, *A Summer at Grandpa's* (1984). COURTESY OF CHANG HUA-K'UN

for one reason or another, have to leave the reins of power in the hands of their wives. These patriarchs clearly contradict their conventional images. One can even argue that the films are rather subversive in their constructions of the patriarchs. They can play ball (*Boys*), give orders to their children (*Time*), and get drunk (*Dust*), but the real work lies mainly with the mothers.

No doubt one can contend – and one Chinese deconstructionist critic has indeed done so[13] – that the quiet demeanor and meek submissiveness of the young man's girlfriend in *Dust* reduce her to an object entirely at his whims. But this reading appears to be a Western critical rewriting of the girl's image along the lines of earlier North American feminist positions where the key issue is gender as universalized sexual difference.[14] Such an interpretation does not take into consideration national and cultural differences among women, nor does it recognize the differences between women and the abstract, universal concept of woman. In this instance, if the girl's image had been fashioned so as to be more in tune with U.S. feminist positions, the film would have rewritten history rather than reconstructed the then-dominant behavioral norms of young girls from rural Taiwan. On the other hand, the girl finally chooses, entirely against the wishes of her family, a postal worker as her husband, demonstrating a rather unorthodox behavior. Though the film remains silent about this change of heart, the decision itself and the will to exercise a choice allow one to propose an interpretation of the girl as an independent person capable of making up her own mind.

It is such attempts to be "evenhanded" in the narration of history in his own way, to be untendentious to the point of being ambivalent at times, that have allowed Hou Hsiao-hsien to produce a corpus of works that are in sharp contradiction with the many films sponsored by the government over the years. Although the initiation theme as explicated in the West is an individual experience, Hou Hsiao-hsien's realization of this theme is subtly contextualized so that the collective memory of growing up in and with Taiwan as it progressed from an agricultural society to a newly industrialized economy is quietly reconstituted. Taken together, these films have accomplished a feat that no other Chinese director in the post-1949 period has done so far: a mediated retrospection of the historical sea changes that one Chinese society has gone through during the past four decades.

NOTES

I thank Professor Teresa de Lauretis and Professor Donald Wesling for their incisive comments on an earlier version of this essay.
1. "Ideology" is used in this essay to suggest "a deformed representation of the object – a 'screen' or 'filter' which we can nonetheless peer behind to obtain a glimpse of the object as it really is." Terry Eagleton, "Ideology, Fiction, Narrative," *Social Text*, 2 (1979), p. 62.
2. Cleanth Brooks and Robert Penn Warren, *Understanding Fiction* (New York: Crofts,

1943). Warren's own "Blackberry Winter" is not actually discussed in this anthology, but the "exercise" questions strongly imply that the story is concerned mainly with initiation.
3. Adrian Jaffe and Virgil Scott, *Studies in the Short Story* (New York: Norton, 1949); Carl Benson, "Conrad's Two Stories of Initiation," *PMLA,* 69 (1954), pp. 46–56. Albert J. Guerard, Introduction to *Heart of Darkness,* by Joseph Conrad (New York: Signet, 1950); James W. Johnson, "The Adolescent Hero: A Trend in Modern Fiction," *Twentieth Century Literature,* 5 (1959), pp. 3–11; Ray B. West, *The Short Story in America, 1900– 1950* (Chicago: Henry Regnery, 1952); Mordecai Marcus, "What Is an Initiation Story?" (1960), revised version in Charles E. May, ed., *Short Story Theories* (Columbus: Ohio University Press, 1976); Gorman Beauchamp, "The Rites of Initiation in Faulkner's *The Bear,*" *Arizona Quarterly,* 28 (1972), pp. 319–25; Isaac Sequeira, *The Theme of Initiation in Modern American Fiction* (Mysore: Geetha, 1975).
4. Robert Gold, ed., *Point of Departure: 19 Stories of Youth and Discovery* (New York: Dell, 1967); Robert Gold, ed., *Stepping Stones: 17 Stories of Growing Up* (New York: Dell, 1981); Arthur and Hilda Waldhorn, eds., *The Rite of Becoming: Stories and Studies of Adolescence* (New York: New American Library, 1969); Oliver Evans and Harry Finestone, eds., *The World of the Short Story* (New York: Knopf, 1971); Thomas West Gregory, ed., *Adolescence in Literature* (New York: Longman, 1980); David Thorburn, ed., *Initiation: Stories and Short Novels on Three Themes* (New York: Harcourt, 1976).
5. Sequeira, *The Theme of Initiation,* pp. 23–4.
6. Ibid., pp. 9–10.
7. Leslie Fiedler, "From Redemption to Initiation" (1958), in his *No! In Thunder* (New York: Stein, 1960), p. 281.
8. Joseph Campbell, *The Hero with a Thousand Faces* (New York: Pantheon, 1949), p. 10; Northrop Frye, *Anatomy of Criticism* (Princeton, N.J.: Princeton University Press, 1957), pp. 192–6; Mircea Eliade, *Rites and Symbols of Initiation,* trans. Williams Trask (New York: Harper, 1958), pp. x–xi.
9. Fredric Jameson, "Third-World Literature in the Era of Multinational Capital," *Social Text,* 15 (1986), pp. 65–88. Here the term "allegory" refers to the decoding and interpreting of the "personal fantasy, collective storytelling, and narrative figurability" of the film texts in order to expose their larger contextual meanings, which are often sociocultural and politicoeconomic. See Jameson, *Signatures of the Visible* (New York: Routledge, 1990), p. 38; cf. idem, *Postmodernism, or the Cultural Logic of Late Capitalism* (Durham, N.C.: Duke University Press, 1990), p. 168.
10. Marcus, "What Is an Initiation Story?"; Sequeira, *The Theme of Initiation.*
11. Cf. *Growing Up* [*Xiao Bi de gushi,* 1983]. Hou Hsiao-hsien took part in the directing, though only Chen Kun-hou (Chen Kunhou) was credited.
12. For a feminist analysis of Sherwood Anderson's stories, see Judith Fetterly, *The Resisting Reader: A Feminist Approach to American Fiction* (Bloomington: Indiana University Press, 1978).
13. Liao Ping-huei [Liao Binghui], "Nüxing yu taifeng" [Women and Typhoons], *Chung-wai wen-hsüeh* [*Zhongwai wenxue*], 17, no. 10 (March 1989), pp. 61–70.
14. Teresa de Lauretis, *Technologies of Gender* (Bloomington: Indiana University Press, 1987), pp. 1–3.

7

THE RETURN OF THE FATHER

HONG KONG NEW WAVE AND ITS CHINESE CONTEXT IN THE 1980S

Li Cheuk-to

A review of Hong Kong cinema in the 1980s must begin with the rise of the Hong Kong "new wave" in 1979. The achievements of this new wave are patently not up to those of the new cinemas of mainland China and Taiwan. It did not produce directors of the caliber of Hou Hsaio-hsien (Hou Xiaoxian), Edward Yang (Yang Dechang), Chen Kaige, or Tian Zhuangzhuang – or works with serious historical resonances such as the masterpieces *City of Sadness* [*Beiqing chengshi*, 1989], *Taipei Story* [*Qingmei zhuma*, 1985], *Yellow Earth* [*Huang tudi*, 1985], and *Horse Thief* [*Daomazei*, 1986]. In the context of Hong Kong cinema, however, the importance and influence of the Hong Kong new wave – whether in terms of the systematic industrialization of the 1980s, modes of creativity, film culture, or its dialectic with tradition – cannot be underestimated.

Even before it became a reality, the Hong Kong new wave – unlike the new cinemas of China and Taiwan – was eagerly awaited and anticipated by critics. This was not only because the new wave directors, including Ann Hui (Xu Anhua), Allen Fong (Fang Yuping), Patrick Tam (Tan Jiaming), Tsui Hark (Xu Ke), Yim Ho (Yan Hao), and Alex Cheung (Zhang Guoming), were recognized as a new generation of filmmakers who had undergone vocational training in film schools in the West, but also because they had the opportunity to display their talent in television before they entered the film industry.

As a result, before their first feature films appeared, the public had clear aspirations for these directors, not the least of which was that they would represent a break with tradition. This was, in effect, what the Fifth Generation directors in mainland China and the new wave directors in Taiwan achieved. In their case, however, no one could confidently predict that they would produce work that broke significantly with the past. The break with the past in Hong Kong cinema had a more complex significance. In the thirty years after World War II, Hong Kong cinema did not develop in uniform fashion. Not only was there the problem of dialects (the Cantonese cinema had a different tradition than Mandarin cinema), there was the question of how Hong Kong as a British colony could develop its own cultural base for cinema while acting as a branch of the larger family of Chinese cinema.

The expectations generated by the rise of the new wave also had to do with the fact that the directors were genuinely local filmmakers who had been born and had grown up in the territory and had received a Hong Kong–style education. The generation of filmmakers who had achieved prominence before the new wave emerged were largely from the mainland, specifically from the industry based in Shanghai, and had come to Hong Kong throughout the 1940s and 1950s. Hence, the new wave embodied a consciousness, experience, and memory that were markedly different from what had come before. In the area of aesthetic preferences, they were more Westernized – or internationalized – in outlook. They tended to view problems or societal questions from the Hong Kong perspective. The territory, not traditional Chinese culture, was their main frame of reference. Hence, the cinematic gap between Hong Kong and China grew wider.

History has shown that the Hong Kong new wave failed to establish a self-sustaining model that did away with tradition. Yet Hong Kong cinema is constantly criticized for being too "Westernized" or for lacking historical perspective and attention to tradition. Such criticism is probably not unreasonable, especially that aimed at the new wave at the point when it surrendered to commercial pressure, but it could not be applied to the total oeuvre. The early work of the new wave is its most representative. The focus is on the abyss between tradition and modernity.

A prime example is Allen Fong's first film, *Father and Son* [*Fuziqinq*, 1981]. Its story is similar to that of a 1954 film of the same name directed by Wu Hui. Both films feature a white-collar office worker whose career prospects are hampered by a poor academic background (e.g., lack of fluency in English) or proper connections with the upper class. He projects all of his ambitions and hopes on his son, ensuring his education and growth. The narrative of Wu Hui's *Father and Son* develops wholly from the father's perspective. The portrayal of a father enduring misery to ensure a good future for his son is drawn with remarkable sensitivity. The father–son relationship is based on the authority of the father – a traditional concept in Chinese society. It does not offer even a hint of the son's feelings or his own hopes.

Allen Fong's film, in contrast, focuses on the son and his memories by means of a flashback in which we see the love–hate relationship between him and his father. Aside from taking a sympathetic attitude to the father's plight in society as a poor working-class male, the film deals with the son's dissatisfaction with the father, who appears to dictate the son's interests and ambitions. (The son's interest in movies leads him to ignore his studies while the father exerts strong discipline over him, forcing him to concentrate on his studies.) It would appear from this film that the new directors have found an avenue for expressing their own voice by reviewing and reminiscing about their pasts.

Unfortunately, although Fong's film expresses the son's mild criticism of the family system in which the patriarch predominates (and oppresses the female members of that family – the daughter/sister gives up her own education to earn money so that the son may advance), in the end the film must be regarded as a highly sentimental work. The son is invariably portrayed as passive, even weak. He yields to his father's authority and generosity and never for a moment questions the one-sided nature of the relationship.

A scene in a restaurant in which the father makes plans for the elder daughter's wedding in a trade-off for his son's education makes evident the son's opposition to his father. It is the climax of the conflict between father and son. In the subsequent scene, however, the son has received a letter notifying him of his successful application for work as an actor at a television station. In torrential rain, he goes out looking for his father. Facing him, he tears the letter to shreds, signifying his obedience to the father. Fong describes the son's inner struggle in a fantasy scene: having joined the ranks of a firing squad made up of Japanese soldiers, he holds up his gun to shoot a common Chinese citizen – his father. The implications are ambiguous, but the son at least recognizes that his father is a victim (both because of his low social status and the sense of defeat he suffers as a result of the son's opposition). From this point on, the son suppresses his urge to rebel against his father's wishes and abandons his own ambitions.

A moment's tolerance does not, of course, compensate for a lifetime of compromise. The problem is that the son, having now become representative of a modern Hong Kong man, is apparently as passive and weak as his father (revealed in the opening scene when the son is reunited with his family to mourn the dead father). The son's education in the West obviously did not make him an independent person. The shadow of his father's patriarchal authority, even in death, weighs heavily on his shoulders.

In point of fact, the ending of the first-edited version of *Father and Son* is different from that of the released version. In the final scene of the first version, the son leads his family to pay their respects at the father's grave. The implication is that the son has now taken over the role of patriarch. The notion of time in the present is not entirely subjugated to reminiscences of the past. In the released version, the whole film is composed of one long flashback. The final frames do not revert back to the present. The film stops in the past with the family seeing the son off at the airport. The frame freezes on a plane as it takes off into a gray, foreboding sky.

When we analyze this narrative structure, the recollection of the past seems only a superficial expression of the son's point of view. It is really concerned

28. The family is devastated by a fire. Allen Fong, *Father and Son* (1981). SIL-METROPOLE ORGANISATION, LTD.

with the father; his death in the opening scene acts as a catalyst for a kind of homage to him. That the narrative remains in the past without ever reverting to the present signifies victory for the father. (When he receives the son's certificate of graduation, his joy leads to a fatal heart attack and he dies with no regrets.) To put it another way, although the film attempts to balance the conflicting emotions – and also to avoid being too melancholic – in its reminiscences of the past, it still cannot detach itself from the shadow of patriarchy. Fong's *Father and Son* acts as a mirror image of the increasing gap between China and Hong Kong in the 1960s and 1970s and the very frustration and anxiety it caused, very much like the son's distress over the loss of his father. Yet the father's influence remains, leaving the son with no recourse for affirming the present and, ultimately, with no hope for the future. In an unconscious way, the film prophesied the tragic destiny of a Hong Kong in the 1980s facing the intractable problem of 1997.

Apart from Allen Fong, only one other first-time new wave director has tackled the problem of tradition and history with brevity. Ann Hui's *The Secret* [*Feng Jie*, 1979] is a crime-of-passion story cloaked in a psychological thriller format. Based on a real incident that occurred in 1970, the film utilizes locations in the Western District with its seedy old-world streets and back alleys to emphasize a mood of darkness and decay. Further, it effectively plays up the traditional rites and ceremonies, the superstitions and long-standing customs of Chinese society as they are practiced in Hong Kong. Hence, every frame of *The Secret* is shrouded in the spirit of Chinese tradition, from the opening ceremony of expiating the sins of the dead, to the moment when the mother of the wrongly accused murder suspect – a lunatic – decapitates a chicken as a ritualistic curse, to the final scene when the same woman cuts open the stomach of the pregnant protagonist with a cleaver.

The tragedy of the crime of passion in *The Secret* is not that Li Wan, the central protagonist, is involved in a triangular relationship, but that she has become pregnant while unmarried. As such, she has violated the traditional code of modesty and chastity of Chinese womanhood. In addition, she is deserted by her lover, who falls for another woman. With no way to turn – and concerned for the future of her unborn baby – she treads the path of tragedy and murder. The pressures of traditional Chinese ethics complicate her emotional odyssey. This is the true tragedy of *The Secret*.

Through narrative structure, Ann Hui contrasts a modern sensibility with the sentiment of nostalgia. Through Li Wan's friend (the role played by Sylvia Chang [Zhang Aijia]), who is compelled to search for the truth (the real murderer), a series of short flashback sequences conveys the feeling of an exciting pursuit thriller. Intermittently, there are flashes of subjective camera shots, as well as transitions between scenes that are deliberately far from clear. These build to a spectacular effect. Such a modern cinematic sensibility serves the narrative and its themes perfectly. Objective and subjective realities are frequently placed in the same cinematic space, making the point that the ghosts of humankind ceaselessly appear to haunt our present.

This theme is further explored in Hui's next film, *The Spooky Bunch* [*Zhuang dao zheng*, 1980]. The story deals with a company of Cantonese opera performers who meet up with mischievous and revengeful ghosts in a theater. These are the ghosts of a whole battalion of soldiers in the Republican era who died accidentally en masse by drinking tainted herbal medicine. They have sworn revenge on the perpetrator and all his descendants, one of whom happens to be involved with the leading lady of the troupe of opera performers. The sins of one's ancestors must be paid for by succeeding generations.

In their first films, both Allen Fong and Ann Hui have taken a look at Hong Kong's past. In their different ways, both have pointed out the oppressiveness of Chinese tradition. *Father and Son,* however, retains a sense of nostalgia and sentimentality. In *The Secret*, the old world is characterized by mystery and madness. Similar films produced by the new directors of Taiwan such as *A Time to Live and a Time to Die* [*Tongnian wangshi*, 1985], *Ah Fei* [*Youma caizi*, 1984], and *Growing Up* [*Xiao Bi de gushi*, 1983] have adopted a more tolerant, even fondly sentimental, attitude toward the past. There are the oppressiveness and bitter memories to be sure, but past and present are not presented in stark contrast with each other. This difference of attitude in the new cinemas of Hong Kong and Taiwan reflects the social and cultural differences between the two societies. It also testifies to the fact that Hong Kong lacks local roots, that, as a British colony, it had cut itself off from the Chinese motherland both culturally and politically in the 1960s and 1970s.

Another important factor is that the postwar generation in Hong Kong had come of age by the 1960s and that leading members of the largely refugee community that made up the previous generation were starting to withdraw or retire from active life. Young adults in the 1960s and 1970s had grown up locally and had been educated in the colonial system, with no natural ties to or memories of the Chinese mainland. Chinese nationalism, which was already peripheral, became irrelevant as Hong Kong began to prosper economically and the city became an international financial center. What in fact grew out of all this was a local Hong Kong consciousness.

The ten-year Cultural Revolution on the mainland widened the gap between Hong Kong and China. The colonial government in Hong Kong experienced the biggest challenge to its rule in 1967 during riots instigated by leftist groups and inspired by the Cultural Revolution. The riots were violent and lasted a period of several months. As the territory recovered from them, the population at large began to develop a lingering fear of instability and the notion of a stable and prosperous society became a sacred catchword.

Regrettably, this important chapter in Hong Kong's history was, until 1988, the forbidden zone of Hong Kong cinema. Tsui Hark's *Dangerous Encounter – First Kind* [*Diyi leixing weixian*, 1980] originally included scenes of three high school students making bombs and, without any motive, setting them off all over Hong Kong (including cinemas). Because these scenes reminded authorities of the 1967 riots, when homemade bombs were exploding everywhere, the film was banned by the censors (Figure 29). It was eventually released with these scenes cut out and new scenes included.

This form of political censorship represents the greatest threat to the creativity of filmmakers. The most sensitive area is the political relationship between China and Hong Kong. As the 1980s rolled by and the issue of Hong Kong's return to mainland China in 1997 became the bugbear in every household, Hong Kong was forced to face the historical reality of a China that had become a stranger over the years. During the negotiations between Britain and China, the latter had frequently taken a nationalist position. However, the performance of Chinese negotiators and leaders during this period reminded Hong Kong people of the long feudal, patriarchal tradition of China and the country's backwardness. If the new wave directors, when they first became active, could not avoid the embrace of tradition, this was because they had the power of foresight, for in the 1980s if one was even slightly sensitive to the realities of the day one could not avoid the shadow of China hanging over one's head.

Such was the background of Ann Hui's controversial *Boat People* [*Touben nuhai*, 1982]. Earlier in her career, Hui had already been concerned with the problem of Vietnamese refugees. She had made *The Boy from Vietnam* [*Laike*, 1978] for the television series *Below Lion Rock*. This and *The Story of Woo Viet* [*Hu Yue de gushi*, 1981], plus *Boat People*, are commonly thought of as Hui's "Vietnamese trilogy." *The Story of Woo Viet* borrows the conventions of a thriller of the underworld-killer mode to tell the story of Woo Viet, an ethnic

Chinese from Vietnam who escapes to Hong Kong as a refugee. He becomes involved with two women: a social worker from Hong Kong and a fellow refugee from Vietnam. This triangular relationship essentially reflects the rootlessness of overseas Chinese communities (naturally including that of Hong Kong). Woo Viet flees to Hong Kong in the hope of going on to the United States but ends up in the Philippines. In the end, he finds himself going out to sea again and the vicious circle is complete. Woo's predicament is similar to that of Hong Kong Chinese, who in anticipation of 1997, are starting to flee the territory as a more orderly parallel of the tide of Vietnamese refugees in the 1980s.

Boat People is even more forthright in dealing with Vietnamese refugees. It is also one of the few films that gives us a picture of postrevolution Vietnam. The importance of the film lies in the remarkable way in which today's Vietnam is used as a metaphor for tomorrow's Hong Kong. In this way, it avoided problems with the territory's censors and won the sympathy of an audience who immediately saw the analogy. (The timing of the film's release was impeccable. It opened on October 1982, after Margaret Thatcher had visited Beijing and differences had begun to emerge between Britain and China over how to resolve the issue of 1997. China had all along remained firm in its resolve to recover Hong Kong in 1997.) The film broke the attendance record for films of its genre (as a "political" melodrama and a non-*gong fu,* comedy film).

29. His friends killed by Hong Kong police and American gunrunners, the sole survivor breaks down completely. Tsui Hark, *Dangerous Encounter – First Kind* (1981). FOTOCINE FILM PRODUCTION, LTD.

Boat People is a political film because, on the one hand, it achieved the attention – the support – of a mass audience through its distribution via the commercial network of cinemas and, on the other, it clearly, although indirectly, touched a collective nerve among Hong Kong people who were by now becoming increasingly worried over their future, indeed over the fact that a capitalist society would be incorporated by an authoritarian political power.

Ironically, the film was shot on location in China's Hainan Island. At that time, Sino-Vietnamese relations were at a low point. Chinese authorities had given their support to the production of the film, no doubt because they had hoped it would be used as anti-Vietnamese propaganda. The roles of the Vietnamese Communist cadres, officials, and soldiers were played by Chinese actors. When the film was released in Hong Kong, the local audience had no trouble in equating the Vietnamese Communist characters with their Chinese counterparts. Postliberation Vietnam was tantamount to post-1997 Hong Kong. When word began to circulate that *Boat People* was really an anti-Communist film, the Chinese authorities who were planning to release the film on the mainland canceled all plans for distribution, effectively banning it. After its initial release in Hong Kong, it is believed that they also exerted pressure on the producers to curtail its further circulation. The film has not been seen again since its release in 1982.

If *The Secret* dealt with the oppressiveness of Chinese tradition, *Boat People* transformed this theme to one of political oppression. It was a work that represented the climax of the new wave movement in Hong Kong, its aesthetics reverting to the melodramatic instincts that color the early realism of Hong Kong cinema in the 1950s and 1960s. In contrast with the modern style of *The Secret*, the style of *Boat People* could very well be considered a reversion to conservatism. Its vision is limited to the liberal humanism of the middle class, showing, as it does, sympathy for the oppressed masses and a mild protest against the totalitarian system. It offers no objective or logical analysis, however, of the great historical tragedy that is Vietnam.

Paradoxically, this weakness is also the film's strength. Precisely because the Vietnam depicted in the film lacks a specific historical dimension, the Hong Kong audience could empathize with the characters. The Vietnamese Communists represented the universal bogeyman. They stood for all Communists in the world.

Through the character of the Japanese journalist (the role played by singer Lam), the film conveyed a strong sense of disillusionment with politics, which was also reflective of the disillusionment with Communist China felt generally by Hong Kong people. The ending of *Boat People* is similar to that of *The Story of Woo Viet:* in both cases, the leading characters are forced to the open seas, to cast their destinies with the unknown. But whereas in Woo Viet a sense of aimless wandering is implied, in *Boat People* there is a sense of hope as signified in the freeze-frame shot of the young girl hugging her brother, both staring into

30. Today's Vietnam as a metaphor for tomorrow's Hong Kong. Ann Hui, *Boat People* (1982). PANASIA FILMS

the distance at dawn (Figure 30). On them lies the hope of all in the audience who feel they may be facing an impasse but who have not lost their will to live and therefore to hope.

From the local history of Hong Kong and Chinese tradition in general, Ann Hui has progressed naturally to the reality of China – the China factor – in Hong Kong's affairs, not least because of the 1997 issue. The metaphorical approach of *Boat People* enabled the film to escape censorship and thereby to speak to the collective anxiety of Hong Kong residents in the early 1980s. Its influence can be seen in the more recent film by Tsui Hark, *A Better Tomorrow, Part III* [*Ying-xiong bense III,* also known as *Love and Death in Saigon,* 1989]. Shot on location in Vietnam, the film is set in Saigon just before it fell to the Communists in 1975. It is a love story in a dangerous setting and an obvious rehash of the themes explored in *Boat People.* However, some of the scenes – such as those of demonstrating students being suppressed by the army, the dead and wounded lying in the hospital – are apparent references to the June 4, 1989, Tiananmen Massacre in Beijing. The success of *Boat People* led to the production of such movies as Tsui Hark's *Shanghai Blues* [*Shanghai zhi ye,* 1984] and *Hong Kong 1941* [*Dengdai liming,* 1984], directed by Leong Po-chih (Liang Puzhi). These utilize the eight-year anti-Japanese war and the fall of Shanghai and Hong Kong to the Japanese as further metaphors for 1997. Ann Hui herself made a contribution to this "fallen-city" genre with the appropriately titled *Love in a Fallen City* [*Qingcheng zhi lian,* 1984]. However, the concept of using the past to reveal the present soon became a chiché: these movies are stiff and lacking in interest. They also lack a mature understanding of politics and at the same time show a knack for self-pity. *Hong Kong 1941,* for example, with its fixation on Communist phobia and the feeling of betrayal by the colonial master Britain was out of line with the muted optimism – the sense of making the best out of a poor thing – felt generally by the population after the signing of the Sino-British Joint Declaration in 1984. (The film was released hot on the heels of this event.) As for *Shanghai Blues* and *Love in a Fallen City,* both films avoided tackling politics realistically, emphasizing instead that sympathy and goodwill would solve the problem. Indeed, both films went so far as to display an optimism arising from deep despair – happiness arising from disaster, bad luck turning to good.

At least two excellent works dealing with the China–Hong Kong relationship came out in 1984. They were *Homecoming* [*Sishui liunian,* 1984], by Yim Ho (Yan Hao), and *Long Arm of the Law* [*Shenggang qibing,* 1984], by Johnny Mak (Mai Dangxiong). *Homecoming* deals with the experiences of a young woman from Hong Kong who visits relatives in her hometown on the mainland. She meets two of her childhood friends, now married to each other, and a triangular relationship develops. In the process, the different values of the two societies – the materialistic ones of Hong Kong, the spiritual ones of the mainland – are examined. The conclusion seems to be that love for one's home village and friendship can overcome all differences. *Long Arm of the Law,* in contrast, deals with the Hong Kong "Big Circle" gangs whose members are refugees or immigrants from China. A spasm of violent crime in Hong Kong awaits a group of such transient visitors in the film. *Homecoming* and *Long Arm of the Law* were released at about the same time and served as the positive and negative poles of people's perceptions of the mainland in Hong Kong. The former was a gentle, romantic melodrama featuring women characters, while the latter was a violent thriller whose leading characters were macho types.

Homecoming was produced by the same company – Bluebird (Qing niao) – that produced Ann Hui's *Boat People.* While Hui's film dealt with the theme of refuge from political oppression, Yim's film – as is obvious from the title – dealt with the theme of homecoming and the affirmation of feelings toward one's native country. This theme was so pronounced that some people suspected it to be "United Front" propaganda once disseminated by the Communist Party and now resurfacing in the countdown to 1997. At the time, it tied in with the general populace's tendency to be more compromising with Communist powers and the film was seen as a subtle attempt to show the superiority of the socialist system over capitalism. Yim Ho himself has explained that the character of Shan Shan (the woman from Hong Kong) is a projection of his own character and personal experiences. He had not intended to show one political system in a more favorable light than the other, but to utilize the two leading female characters to compare the two life-styles: the austere self-reliance of the mainland and the frenetic pace, with its frequent setbacks and advances, of Hong Kong.

Shan Shan's urge to return to her native village on the mainland comes more from her inner self – her need for self-discovery – than from a compulsion to search for a new environment. She is disappointed and stultified by her life in Hong Kong, but her motive for returning to China is only to seek a temporary respite that will afford her time to think. As a Hong Kong citizen – hence, only a marginal Chinese – she finally decides to leave her native village for Hong Kong and to face up to reality. One can accept the film's ending as logical and sensible, unlike the conclusions of most films of the West that deal with similar intellectual characters in search of self and who go "on the road." *Homecoming* also avoids the conventional one-sided affirmation of the country over the city, common in so many films.

However, the problem of the "sojourning" mentality arises. Since Shan Shan is only "passing through" and her only concern is self-discovery, her vision of the backward country life is obscured by romanticism. The presentation of certain aspects of village life comes across as too aestheticized. Yim Ho's own experiences in making the film were precisely those of Shan Shan's. Her journey was the filmmaker's journey.

Yet another problem is that Shan Shan was not really in search of a way out. In the end, she can decide to leave her native village and return to Hong Kong with

31. Sentiments instead of politics or reality. Ann Hui, *Love in a Fallen City* (1984).
SHAW BROTHERS (HK) LTD.

32. Feeling of betrayal by Britain mixed with Communist phobia. Leong Po-chih, *Hong Kong 1941* (1984). D & B FILMS CO., LTD.

a greater sense of fulfillment. One is not sure whether her views on life or her ability to relate to people have changed for the better. In any case, if one were to stick to the motif of the search for the quality of human beings or the common longings of two societies, one could easily fall into the trap of prematurely ascribing blame for each social or environmental grievance on the cry of *c'est la vie*. It would be especially easy to fall into this trap in the context of the countryside and one's home village and to become virtually depoliticized.

It is perhaps understandable why *Homecoming* had such a wide following among the intellectuals of the territory. For one thing, the idealized portrayal of country life evoked a deep nostalgia in Hong Kong's city dwellers. Also, China at the time had reached the apex of its economic reforms and "open-door" policy. Shan Shan's homecoming was a symbolic journey that allowed Hong Kong people – who had by and large accepted the fact that China would be their overlord in 1997 – to equate the concept of home village with that of nation. It reaffirmed the relationship between the two societies and the possibility that the contradictions between the two could be resolved.

On the surface, Johnny Mak's *Long Arm of the Law* is a crime thriller. Seeping through its violent action scenes is a political consciousness that is perhaps unintentional. Its depiction of the "Big Circle" gangsters who come down to Hong Kong from Guangzhou and then return after a series of robberies, loaded with the latest leisure goods, hints at the material gap between China and Hong Kong. Before they leave Guangzhou, the protagonists – who were once members of the Red Guards – engage in a comradely bout of singing. The song is one sung by illegal immigrants who seek to cross the border between China and Hong

Kong, a phrase of its lyrics intoning, "A small river divides two worlds." The gangsters' former status as Red Guards brings up the specter of the Cultural Revolution – a further sign of the huge political gap between the two worlds. The last violent confrontation is set in the Kowloon Walled City, where the robbers are ensconced and from which they must fight their way out with the Royal Hong Kong Police. The Kowloon Walled City is a deeply significant setting. A historical anomaly, it is, in effect, a Chinese island in the heart of British-ruled Hong Kong. This last battle scene, therefore, is associated with the notions of a China–Hong Kong conflict as well as past against present, sovereignty against territory.

This scene has a direct bearing on the collective subconscious of Hong Kong people; indeed, it plays up the collective sense of fear. Their differences create a standoff and a feeling of animosity between the two worlds. Hong Kong people in general have been very vocal in their complaints against the entry not only of Vietnamese refugees but of illegal immigrants from the mainland. There is a strong perception that these unwanted guests will seriously harm the territory's flaunted sense of "stability and prosperity" (Figure 33).

In addition to this strong prejudice against mainlanders – who are dismissed as Big Circle gangsters – the film's narrative gives vent to their social predicament and the no-choice decisions they ultimately make. There is, after all, an affinity here with Hong Kong's own predicament in the face of 1997. A number of examples illustrate this point:

1. The protagonists are given only forty-eight-hour passes into Hong Kong. They use this limited time to indulge in the pleasures that a decadent capitalist society can provide.
2. After the robbery, the protagonists are torn between leaving and staying. The prosperity of Hong Kong has eroded their feelings of home and duty.
3. A series of betrayals ensue. The protagonists are betrayed by local gangs, who are in turn betrayed by the police. (The sense of betrayal by the Sino-British Joint Declaration has become prevalent among Hong Kong people.)

The world the film depicts is one full of deceit, animosity, crisis, and brutality. Any display of humanity by the protagonists is only a moment's brilliance in a dark world. Survival and self-interest are paramount, leading to situations in which one must kill or be killed. No one can be trusted. The three power groups presented in the film (the Big Circle gang, the police, and the local triad society) are superficially different from one another but their ways of life ensure similarity. They all abide by the law of the jungle in their dedication to violence. In the end, all three are entangled in a deadly game of survival where the means justify the ends. The final scenes spell the end of all hope, even though one of the Big Circle members pathetically implores "Could we try to talk peace with them?" Although pathetic, this plea does not lessen the tragedy. The finale of *Long Arm of the Law* is a testament to the fatalism that marks Hong Kong people's feeling of a no-win, no-choice situation.

33. Visitors marking the material and political gap between the People's Republic and Hong Kong. Johnny Mak, *Long Arm of the Law* (1984). GOLDEN HARVEST (HK) LIMITED

Long Arm of the Law also subverts the heroic-mold thriller genre. It harbors no illusions about humankind; it is completely cynical. As such, the film reminds one of Tsui Hark's *Dangerous Encounter – First Kind.*

Tsui Hark's film was, in fact, one of the very first films in the new wave to utilize violence and controversial subject matter. The irrationality, indeed the fanaticism, of its violent scenes are an integral part of the absurd, emotional world it presents. Its pulse beats along with the antiestablishment, rebellious values of youth that are inherent in everyday life. Other films of this genre produced by the new wave, such as Yim Ho's *Happenings* [*Yeche*, 1980] and Patrick Tam's *Nomad* [*Leihuo qingchun*, 1982], lack the extreme edge of Tsui's and Mak's films where the pent-up sensations of frustration, defeat, and insecurity ultimately result in no-holds-barred violence and fatalistic destruction.

This group of "violent" directors, not surprisingly, distance themselves from "tradition." The defeat and frustration they portray may be related to the gap between the values and aesthetics of the middle class and those of the vast majority of Hong Kong people. It is also possible that these directors were deeply sensitive to the daily heartless pressure faced by Hong Kong society and that they foresaw the inherent violence of an oppressed consciousness which results from the return of Hong Kong to mainland control in 1997. Hence, the violent films they produce are expressions of a tragic mentality.

The interrelationships among the characters portrayed in *Dangerous Encounter – First Kind,* the four youths, the police, the Special Branch, the foreign gun runners who symbolize the overbearing influence of foreign powers in Hong

Kong affairs, are a faint shadow of the power relationships that will emerge over the 1997 issue. These interrelationships also hint at the behind-the-scenes deals and political chicanery of Hong Kong officials and the way such deals are swept under the carpet, leaving Hong Kong people with a sense of no control over their own destiny.

Though the film conveys a hatred for the world and its ways in a cynical, satirical fashion, it also expresses dissatisfaction and anger. Four years later, the same dissatisfaction and anger expressed in *Long Arm of the Law* find a clear target – China. Behind the violent excesses of *Long Arm of the Law* is an empty vision harboring no illusions toward anyone or anything.

The two main themes of the Hong Kong new wave culminated in the year 1984 (the year in which the future of Hong Kong was sealed) with Yim Ho's *Homecoming* and Johnny Mak's *Long Arm of the Law*. The former is seen from the perspective of the intellectual middle class, the position of humanism, in its review of tradition and Hong Kong's relationship with China. It affirms the values of goodwill, tolerance, as well as country life and love for one's home village. At the time it was released, who could argue with such sentiments? But with the deterioration of China–Hong Kong relations and the continuing political animosity, the sentiments of *Homecoming* were now in danger of being anachronistic. In any case its limited vision does not reflect the present helplessness felt by Hong Kong people. *Long Arm of the Law* is an extension of the violent thriller genre as typified by Tsui Hark's *Dangerous Encounter – First Kind*. Its subconscious urgings – as expressed through violence – hide a deeper political message. But Johnny Mak's extreme cynicism and overindulgence in violence finally steer the film away from analyzing the problem or finding solutions.

There is, however, no denying the commercial popularity of the genre with its violence and fast action. The blockbuster – *A Better Tomorrow* [*Yingxiong bense*, 1986], directed by John Woo (Wu Yusen) and produced by Tsui Hark, which was a major box office hit at the time – started a fad of romantic hero movies (crime thrillers of *The Godfather* mold). If nothing else, this new fad broke the monopoly of comedy films. Apart from its sensational violence, the success of *A Better Tomorrow* counted on the way in which audiences empathized with the character played by Chow Yun-fat (Zhou Yunfa), an underdog character who can take no more insults and fights back – the underworld romantic hero type (Figure 34). It is no accident that the film satisfies the audience's need to vent its frustration and anger.

The key to the film's popularity may lie in the Daya Bay Incident, which occurred in August 1986. Daya Bay is situated in Guangdong Province, not too far northeast of Hong Kong. It was here that Chinese authorities started to build a nuclear power plant. A pressure group in Hong Kong organized a petition-signing campaign against the construction of the plant, but the wishes of the million people who signed the petition were ignored by China. It was at this juncture that *A Better Tomorrow* was released. What better way for a frustrated

34. Chow Yun-fat as underworld romantic hero in a modern-dress version of the old martial arts movies. John Woo, *A Better Tomorrow* (1986). FILM WORKSHOP CO., LTD.

public to give vent to pent-up feelings? On this level, *A Better Tomorrow,* like *Boat People* before it, was a lucky coincidence, one that touched sensitive nerves but allowed the audience to identify with its romanticization of violence even though all the film offered was a means of letting off steam rather than a sympathetic response to the predicament of Hong Kong people.

The facts, of course, are never simple. The film itself may not have deliberately set out to mirror the social conditions of its day, but the sentiments expressed by the Chow Yun-fat character – we must personally fight to regain what we have lost – have won the audience's acceptance. The concept of heroism that underlines such sentiments confirms the tenet that only the individual can control his or her own destiny. Yet it is a heroism tinged with a pessimistic melancholy – the fear that betrayal will cause everything one has achieved to be lost. Such anxiety – the sense of "here today, gone tomorrow" – no doubt reflects the average Hong Kong person's own anxieties over the future.

Because *A Better Tomorrow* is a romantic gangster thriller, its world is a mirror image of Hong Kong's materialistic riches. The nighttime shots of the waterfront docks are a symbol of Hong Kong's prosperity. Chow Yun-fat's

statement as he looks down at Hong Kong harbor perfectly expresses the sentiments of Hong Kong residents: "I never knew Hong Kong by night could be so
beautiful. To lose such a beautiful thing . . . that's something that breaks the
heart."

It is worth noting here that part of the plot and some of the characters of *A
Better Tomorrow* were borrowed from an earlier film, *The Essence of Heroes*
[*Yingxiong bense*], made in 1967 by director Long Gang (the Chinese title is also
taken from another film). In *A Better Tomorrow* the role of the underworld "big
brother" (played by Di Long) who comes out of jail resolved to turn over a new
leaf, but who eventually acts as the fall guy for his brother and returns to jail, is
borrowed from the old version. The new film introduces a new character, "Brother" Mark, played by Chow Yun-fat, who is allowed to steal the film from the
lead, Di Long. The mutual devotion of these two characters is played out with
relish, and it is a relationship the audience also delights in. The "romantic
drifter" characteristics of Brother Mark remind the audience of previous films
directed by martial arts director Chang Che (Zhang Che) that also star Di Long,
but whose sidekick there was David Chiang (Jiang Dawei). This allusion to
the Chang Che films is understandable when we remember that the director
of *A Better Tomorrow,* John Woo, was once Chang's assistant director. The
romantic-hero ideology of *A Better Tomorrow,* its use of slow motion to accentuate violence, the bloodbaths, and the description of male friendships all have
antecedents in Chang Che's martial arts *gong fu* films. The influence of another
strand of martial arts movies made in the 1970s – the sword-fighting series of
romantic knights-errant directed by Chu Yuan and written by Gu Long – must
also be mentioned. These films attempt to update the settings and the ideology of
the characters, to incorporate the passing of romantic heroes and keep up with
modern notions of bravery and heroism.

Hence, although *A Better Tomorrow* is adapted from a Cantonese production
of twenty years ago, it departs from its mode of social criticism and realist
aesthetics and transforms itself into a modern-dress version of the old martial arts
movies. Its characters use guns instead of swords. The difference is that where
the old version tends to pit one individual hero against the oppressive world, the
new version adopts twin heroes who engage in a life-or-death struggle with their
environment. The significance of this new mold is revealed in the recent remake
of another classic Cantonese film, *The Orphan* [*Renhai guhong,* 1960], directed
by Li Chenfeng.

The Orphan stars a young Bruce Lee (Li Xiaolong) as the orphan of the title.
He is separated from his father during World War II and, while in the charge of a
foster mother, grows up on the wrong side of the tracks. He becomes a pick-
pocket and is one day caught by his father, now in charge of a rehabilitation
center for delinquent youths. Though the two are unaware of each other's identities, a father–son relationship develops. This becomes the basis for the orphan
boy's redemption. The 1989 remake of *The Orphan,* titled *City Kids* [*Renhai*

guhong, 1989], directed by Poon Man-kit (Pan Wenjie), downgrades the father figure to little more than a cameo role. He appears only at the beginning and end of the movie. In his final appearance there is animosity between father and son, perhaps signifying that the son has come of age. The movie eschews the father–son relationship for a buddy–buddy relationship between the orphan and his friend, which forms the crux of the movie.

From the remake of *The Orphan,* we see a transformation in the paradigm of Hong Kong cinema – from father to friend, from family ethics to a code of brotherhood – which reflects the ongoing evolution of that cinema (and its society). Where the model is father and family, its underlying philosophy affirms the continuity and harmony between generations, an affirmation of history. As the postwar generation of Hong Kong youth was growing up in the 1960s, their attachment to tradition became loosened. After the 1967 riots, the gap between Hong Kong and China grew wider, resulting in a "historical black hole" for Hong Kong while also positioning the territory in its awkward, modern state. It passed through a short period of chaos and anxiety that gave rise to a feeling of helplessness, but it is now attempting to establish a new set of values based on a sense of common destiny held by the postwar generation. Its future is uncertain; there seems nothing to look forward to.

Although a modern consciousness took root in the 1970s, there was an attempt at the same time to develop a local culture to fill the vacuum left by the demise of traditional ways. From this perspective, the popularity of the "romantic-hero" genre and the resurfacing of the idea of a new paradigm reflect the crisis of confidence felt by Hong Kong people in the late 1980s, as does the genre's preoccupation with such themes as betrayal of friendship and fatalism.

In 1988, many young directors – mostly graduates of film school – made their debuts: Lawrence Ah Mon (Liu Guochang) with *Gangs* [*Tong dang*], Wong Kar-wai (Wang Jiawei) with *As Tears Go By* [*Wangjiao kamen*], Alex Law (Luo Qirui) with *Painted Faces* [*Qi xiao fu*], Jacob Cheung (Zhang Zhiliang) with *Lai Shi, China's Last Eunuch* [*Zhongguo zuihou yige taijian*], and Clara Law (Luo Zhuoyao) with *The Other Half and the Other Half* [*Wo ai taikongren*]. The last time so many new directors had made such an impact was 1979, the year of the Hong Kong new wave. Though these young directors exhibited a refreshing new touch in the handling of both subject matter and style, their status and achievements could not compare with those of the new wave directors in 1979. However, it is worth mentioning Lawrence Ah Mon's *Gangs,* a film notable for its attitudes toward reality and tradition.

Before his debut film, Ah Mon had worked for Hong Kong's official broadcasting unit, Radio Television Hong Kong, making "socially aware" television dramas. *Gangs* was produced by the same company, Sil-Metropole, that had produced Allen Fong's *Father and Son.* The "leftist" tendencies of the company meant it had a preference for "social realist" subject matter, unlike other production companies operating in the mainstream, which preferred sex and violence.

The realism of *Father and Son* was that of the past. *Gangs,* in contrast, was firmly set in the present and dealt with contemporary problems – youth gangs and the restlessness of neglected "problem" youths marginalized by society in the 1980s (Figure 35).

The youthful protagonists of *Gangs* live in the slumlike housing projects built by the government in the 1960s. There, they are co-opted into illegal activities by triad societies. Utilizing the talents of unknown actors, director Ah Mon recorded all dialogue synchronically while shooting (a practice given up by the industry in the 1960s and rarely used since). This synch-sound recording technique heightened the film's realistic atmosphere and the naturalism of the actors, but it also created a sense of unease: it was "too real." The censors demanded cuts not only of portions of the dialogue but of entire scenes in at least thirty places.

However, although the film's subject matter dealt with the problem of triads and secret societies, unlike most films of the same genre, it avoided depicting its characters in a romantic, heroic way as a device to win the audience's sympathy. The film also refused to acknowledge the notions – indeed the myth – of brotherhood and individual heroism perpetrated by more popular films. Its relationships are based entirely on self-interest and ruthless behavior. Plots, betrayal, and suspicion are routine.

In this cold, unsentimental world, the only hope for redemption lies in blood

35. Unsentimental depiction of marginalized "problem" youths. Lawrence Ah Mon, *Gangs* (1988). SIL-METROPOLE ORGANISATION, LTD.

ties – between father and son, entailing the sacrifice of the father so that the son may be saved. The father–son relationship depicted in *Gangs* reminds one of that in *Father and Son*. Both fathers are dissatisfied with their sons and constantly scold them. This dissatisfaction bespeaks their deep love for their sons and a horror of seeing them retread their own worthless paths. But the sons have different motives for their rebellious opposition. In the 1960s, the conflict in the father–son relationship grew out of the overbearing patriarchal authority that tended to suppress the son's aspirations. In the 1980s, the son's premature independence, with both father and son sticking stubbornly to their own views, led to a communication gap and worsening of the relationship.

The father in *Gangs* does not wish to see his son entangled in a life of crime. He himself was a member of a triad but is now unwilling to let his son "become bad." He does not realize that the son may have been inspired by his own example. In the same vein, the youngest son is inspired by the elder brother, who in turn is inspired by the father. The son loves the father after all and sees in him a role model. He soon comes to realize, however, that this inspiration will most likely lead to tragedy. His estrangement from the family intensifies his involvement in the youth gang of which he is a part and from which he finds it difficult to escape.

Fong's *Father and Son*, in cherishing the memory of the father, exposes the lingering fear of Chinese tradition and hence has a bearing on the present indecisiveness society feels when it is called upon to make a stand. The oppressiveness of the patriarchy in *Gangs* has all but disappeared, but society's ills remain and have worsened. Thus, traditional values are reaffirmed: the ethics of the family are preserved, as is the relationship between boy and girl (which must be wholesome, even chaste – a point made more poignant by the scene in which a gang member forces his girlfriend into prostitution) and the requisite obedience to the father.

Lawrence Ah Mon's coolheaded attitude lapses into sentimentality only in the last moments of his film. The father's final sacrifice is heavily compromised. It seems there was no getting around the mainstream commercial paradigms of Hong Kong cinema after all, as can be seen in the work of other new directors, such as the nostalgic, sentimental *Painted Faces* and the stylistically "packaged" *As Tears Go By*. All these traits reflect the commercial pressure that young new directors face in their careers. At the same time, they are an expression of the new conservatism that has befallen Hong Kong cinema – the tendency to embrace "tradition." It is possible that in the last years of the 1980s, reality was a disappointment to many people. However, Hong Kong cinema has come full circle in its dealings with tradition. From 1981, with Allen Fong's *Father and Son*, to 1988, with Lawrence Ah Mon's *Gangs*, a cycle has been completed.

8

BORDER CROSSING

MAINLAND CHINA'S PRESENCE IN HONG KONG CINEMA

Esther Yau

When they ask me for my nationality or ethnic identity, I can't respond with one word, since my "identity" now possesses multiple repertories. . . . I am a child of crisis and cultural syncretism.

Guillermo Gómez-Peña (1989)[1]

In many respects, Hong Kong appears to be an inappropriate place for post-colonial arguments. Since the early 1900s, residents of mainland China have left their own country for the British colony. Although the natives challenged colonial authority in the early years and are still negotiating with the government for better political representation, since the late 1970s, many of them have also become compliant. One of the most impressive capitalist enclaves in Asia, Hong Kong has an expanding middle class, which, well-educated and articulate, serves the administration effectively. The dominant cultural mode is a syncretic one: Chinese customs and values are being observed, forgotten, revived, passed on from one generation to the next and modified while Western forms of social organization are practiced. The ideology of acquiescence dominates, and in the late 1980s, an extension of British rule was even proposed by local residents. Reluctance to return to the motherland reflects the popular support for colonial capitalism, while the socialist experience next door is not favored. In short, the Hong Kong people seem more or less satisfied with their situation and have few postcolonial interests.

Yet this impression needs to be revised, and film provides a suitable medium for approaching the complexities of Hong Kong's cultural identity. Often trivialized as "cheap violence" by Western critics and local elites, Hong Kong films fit the derogatory label by their relatively low production costs and the frequency of martial art sequences in popular genres. Seen more carefully, however, the films demonstrate a skillful adaptation of the ideological codes and functions of Hollywood to a context in which the public's preoccupations are survival and upward mobility. Many films address and capitalize upon the frustrations and fantasies of the working class; they also rationalize the modes of existence available within the social context as much as express, often in narrative terms, the breakdown and redefinition of these modes. In broad terms, Hong Kong films are actively engaged in producing the meaning of existence for the local population. This essay argues that the Hong Kong films participating in the 1997 discourse construct the complex dynamics and symbolic structures that mark the cultural repositioning of a population whose ambivalence toward the colonial administration is accompanied by nationalistic sentiments toward China.

The 1997 Consciousness

Following British Prime Minister Margaret Thatcher's visit to Beijing in September 1982, formal diplomatic negotiations were undertaken to arrange for Hong Kong's official return to the People's Republic of China in the year 1997.[2] Subsequent Sino-British talks indicated that these two countries would reach a final settlement on Hong Kong on the basis of their mutual political and economic interests. The blunt reminder that Hong Kong has no self-determination contradicted the government's policy and rhetoric of localization since the riots of the late 1960s and tested the residents' tenuous sense of belonging.[3] If the prospering residents have entered a more or less complacent "postexile" phase since the late 1970s, Thatcher's historic visit brought back memories of a refugee past and created collective anxieties regarding Hong Kong's unknown political future. Clearly, the year 1997 has become a horizon beyond which few are able to locate themselves.

In addressing the "1997 consciousness" of its spectators, films participate in public contemplation of Hong Kong's changing "identity."[4] Films like *Burning of the Imperial Palace* [*Huoshao Yuanming Yuan,* 1983] and *Hong Kong 1941* [*Dengdai liming,* 1984], for example, recall well-known incidents of China's losses under imperial forces and recount survival stories from the early colonial period respectively. In retracing and reconstructing the past, these films acknowledge explicitly or implicitly that Hong Kong's historical destiny has always been intertwined with China's. Historical representation thus provides an allegorical space for contemporary sentiments to be conveyed without presenting the 1997 question on a realistic plane. These films provide different positions, which range from patriotic engagement to cynical distance, from which one looks at a revived past. Nevertheless, viewers' responses are far from uniform, and such factors as age, class, and political stance come into play.[5] Viewers' varying emotional responses to the reenacted past testify to Hong Kong's perception of its relationship with China as distinct (i.e., dictated neither by Britain nor by China) and mediated by social and personal factors, including class, expressed as the ability (or lack thereof) to emigrate overseas. Of course, films made in the early 1980s that have 1997 as an implied point of reference were subjected to government censorship that discouraged direct representation of this sensitive subject.[6]

Emotional bonds between Hong Kong and mainland China still exist, of course. Though quite obvious, it needs to be said that the exiles' loyalty toward the motherland is different from allegiance to the regime(s) in power in the past or at present. That is, while not every Chinese feels the same toward the country's political leadership, many agree on nationalist principles of some sort. Benedict Anderson's discussion on the magical power of nationalism in his *Imagined Communities* (1983) is relevant here considering that "China" refers to at least five different Chinese political entities that either existed in the past or still exist: the Middle Kingdom (with multiple identities) under imperial rule before 1911; Republican China led by the Nationalists; socialist China under the Communists after 1949; Taiwan under the Nationalists after 1949; and Hong Kong ruled by the British since 1842. In each case, the emotional association between the people and the rulers has been neither uniform nor unchanged.

Yet in most people's minds, all these "Chinas" signify one and the same nation – Zhongguo (the Middle Kingdom). Zhongguo, symbol of an abstract community, is to most the motherland where Chinese peoples of the past, present, and, conceivably, the future believe that they share a civilization, a written language, a general culture, and a continuous history.[7] As one identifies with this nation (i.e., as one imagines being within it by responding to the interpellating power of Zhongguo), the similarities and differences among the histories and lives of the peoples otherwise distinguished by region, dialect, class, gender, generation, and so on become integral parts of a totality. It is on such a basis of symbolic oneness that the political boundaries separating Chinese peoples appear arbitrary and inconsequential to national identification. On a similar basis, the regimes can rightfully make calls for unification to Chinese subjects who are living in divided political territories.

This essay focuses on the importance of the border and the act of border crossing in considering the character and complexity of Hong Kong's popular perception of its relationship with China as 1997 approaches. The terms "self" and "other" are significant concepts with which to approach the mixed modes of identification, differentiation, and distance in this changing perception. Conceivably, the difficulties for collective maintenance of strict boundaries between Hong Kong as "self" and mainland China under socialism as totally "other" point toward an ambivalence that can be attributed to a nationalistic logic. Stuart Hall has defined cultural identity as "a matter of 'becoming' as well as of 'being.'"[8] Adapting Hall, I suggest that the in-between political positioning put forth by certain Hong Kong films of the 1980s is connected to the collective anxiety over the Colony's imminent return to socialist mainland China. Such a collective anxiety toward an inevitable "becoming" directs filmic exploration of history and change. In this sense, Hong Kong films in the 1980s both expressed and constructed the identity crisis of a society that, during the last years of its colonial experience, seeks to redefine its relation to the still-distanced mother country.

This essay proposes an understanding of the films' complex dynamics and symbolic structures through the Althusserian concepts of "conjuncture" and "mediation."[9] It approaches film as the textual site of contradiction and negotiation informed by the historical conjuncture. Institutional, formal, and textual terms serve as mediating levels between the conjuncture and each individual film. Thus, though one may describe certain correspondences between the constructed "present" of the film texts and the analyzed "present" of history, the correspondences are mediated by narrative and filmic terms including the codes of popular genres. The consideration of history as instantiated in the texts enables one to define and describe more fully the meaning and position(s) produced for the spectator-subject. Such an approach to textual functions justifies the reading of the fictional character as a figure of historical and social agency. I would submit that the symbolic import of popular Hong Kong films of the 1980s that address the 1997 issue lies in their appeal to the spectators' shared understanding of historical references and in their creation of compelling figures of historical and social agency. It is within this framework that the films are considered for their symbolic relevance to the "being" and "becoming" of Hong Kong as well as for their symbolic resolution of contradictions.

Colonial–Chinese Cultural Syncretism

Before the full implications of the border can be comprehended, it is necessary to contextualize Hong Kong's political ambivalence in relation to its cultural syncretism. Metonymic of Britain's imperialist forays in Asia in the nineteenth century, Hong Kong bears witness to the Middle Kingdom's failings in the expansionist era.[10] In the late twentieth century, however, the city has achieved competitiveness, prosperity, and attractiveness to investors in ways that go beyond Britain's and the People's Republic of China's own appeal. While late Qing and Republican intellectuals, as well as economists, wanted China to build wealth and strength, it is the colonized territory that has efficiently and steadily produced them.

The economic environment of Hong Kong is the result of international collaboration. British laissez-faire policies gave incentives to local and overseas investors, while daily imports from mainland China supplied the city with subsistence goods. For four decades, as a thriving entrepôt trade brought income to both Britain and the People's Republic, neither nation wanted to jeopardize its interests by making either capitalist democracy or socialist revolution a serious issue in this extraterritorial site. The political identity of Hong Kong is thus the product of a pragmatic kind of complicity conducive to ideological ambivalence or dubiety. The residents' political indifference, often associated with an inherently Chinese attitude, is, in fact, an expression of this pragmatic complicity.

Nevertheless, explicit challenges to the colonial government have been raised from time to time. In 1951, 1956, and 1967 respectively, local demonstrations and confrontations with the Royal Hong Kong Police brought to the surface class and other political tensions in the territory. The vigor of these and other labor and student movements in the early 1970s can be attributed to those who believed, for one reason or another, in the inevitability of an increasingly prominent Chinese presence in world politics (which coincided with Western attention to the Cultural Revolution.) Demands that the Chinese language be given the same official status as the English language, however, were made by university students and white-collar workers who shared nationalistic sentiments and marked an important step in the "decolonizing" direction. An eclectic politics, inspired by both local interests and Communist China's example, informed protests that demanded localization and equal rights between expatriates and indigenous residents. Members of the indigenous, Westernized middle class, who became important political players in the late 1980s, emerged out of this period, an important moment of political and social change alluded to in *Starry Is the Night* [*Jinye xingguang canlan,* 1988], directed by Ann Hui [Xu Anhua].

Cultural syncretism in Hong Kong is possible not only because of colonial policies (e.g., regarding school curriculum) but also because the colonial presence has become less direct and not visibly oppressive during the past decade. Even if there are areas with little freedom of choice (such as qualification for certain positions), mixed linguistic and cultural codes are used on an everyday basis. Interpretation aside, the coexistence of mixed codes in the same social space mandates adaptative work within their parameters. In the semiautobiographical *Father and Son* [*Fuziqing,* 1981] of Allen Fong [Fang Yuping], relationships in the workplace and at home are structured respectively according to Westernized and traditional standards. Apparently, the father is subordinate in the former context and dominant in the latter; but in fact his authority at home is threatened by colonial standards and his struggles exemplify the complex dynamics involved. Denied promotion in the 1960s because he lacked English language skills, the father supervised his son's English homework in an authoritarian manner and later sacrificed his daughter's marital freedom so that his son could receive a university education overseas – a gesture that pushes the son to succeed in a Western system on behalf of the family. The son, however, rebels against both formal colonial education and traditional paternal desires; attracted by visual images instead, he adapts Chinese pulp fiction to amateur film projects and later pursues a degree in filmmaking at the University of Southern California in the United States. In other words, if the older generation has succumbed to colonial standards for economic reasons, the inscription is perceived as cultural for the younger generation. Interestingly, U.S. popular culture in Fong's films provides an imaginary alternative to the constricting conditions, and in *Father and Son* film education becomes a self-actualizing alternative to both traditional patriarchy and colonial authority. Though it is beyond the scope of this essay, the Americanization of Hong Kong as a notable aspect of colonial–Chinese cultural syncretism is worth exploring.

The Vanishing Border

The Hong Kong–China border, closed on June 16, 1951, to prohibit undocumented travel, became a more fragile divider of Chinese people living on both sides by 1978. Continued southern migration of mainlanders promoted Hong Kong's diversity in dialects and habits. The reverse northern movement of capital and businesses into the mainland's special economic zone, Shenzhen, accelerated southern China's modernization and enhanced its capitalistic outlook. By the late 1980s, as many as 11,000 trucks and cars traveled daily across the border, and as many as 27 million people did the same annually.[11]

In the climate of increasing exchange between Hong Kong and China's southern provinces, mutual awareness of each other's proximity and difference was enhanced by media on both sides of the border. Hong Kong cinema and television, through co-production projects and other ventures, took advantage of mainland scenery. This touristic gaze is implicitly complemented by a narcissistic look at the successful self that supports a condescending attitude toward new mainland immigrants.[12] In a comparable spirit, mainland studios chose commercial districts in Shenzhen for location filming to display China's modernization and Westernization. The gaze of fantasy in this case was often complemented by a warning of the criminal nature of materialistic Hong Kong. In Hong Kong television's *The Good, the Bad and the Ugly* [*Wangzhongren*, 1979], Pearl River Studio's *Sunshine and Showers* [*Taiyang yu*, 1986], and *Escape to Hong Kong* [*Taogangzhe*, 1988], media imaging of each other mirrors the defensive ways in which each acknowledges the increasing presence of the other in its own territory.

Ambivalence and Border-Crossing Figures: Invaders or Tourists?

In a state of mind where one loves and hates China, one also loves and hates Hong Kong. Hong Kong is a haven where one takes refuge from oppression but it is also a desert, both a paradise and a forever insecure place.

Ng Ho[13]

Two Hong Kong films, *Long Arm of the Law* [*Shenggang qibing*] and *Homecoming* [*Sishui liunian*], both made in 1984, place border crossing and its consequences at the center of the narrative. Though censorship makes it impossible to portray what it will be like when Hong Kong is returned to the PRC, the films that feature border crossing so as to place Hong Kong and mainland residents within the same imaginary space, in fact, amount to efforts to do so. By representing two activities that characterize the period of the vanishing border, the films provide grounds for popular assessment of values and social behavior that are products of economic and political realities. Explicit as well as subtle tensions are brought to light, while the films express different notions about the mainlanders and the state of Hong Kong's being.

The directors of both films began their media career in television. Johnny Mak (Mai Dangxiong), director of *Long Arm of the Law,* produced and directed very macho, Peckinpah-type television drama series in the 1970s that gave sensational treatment to police investigation, criminal violence, and prostitution. Yim Ho (Yan Hao), the director of *Homecoming,* completed a number of government-funded projects in the 1970s on student movements, teenage delinquents, and corruption. The differences in the backgrounds of Mak and Yim are apparent in these two films as well. *Long Arm of the Law* is a local, purely commercial production that derives its material from news stories of Hong Kong's recent robberies carried out by armed *daquanzai* gangsters ("Big Circle" guys) from the mainland. *Homecoming,* in contrast, involves mainland and Hong Kong personnel in both screenwriting and acting and expresses a nostalgic view of the mainland, the basis of which is autobiographical and poetic.

Disturbed Condescension in *Long Arm of the Law*

In *Long Arm of the Law,* mainland border crossers enter the territory as armed robbers. *Qibing* (bannermen) in the film's Chinese title alludes to the Red Guards of the Cultural Revolution. *Qi* in *qibing* can also refer to the Manchus (as in *Qiren*). In either case, Hong Kong is represented as vulnerable to a military entity coming from the north; that is, it is being transgressed by a physically threatening "other" (Figure 36). *Shenggang,* a shorthand combining *Guangdong sheng* (province) and *Xianggang* (Hong Kong) can be taken to mean the visitation or inspection of Hong Kong (in which case the same characters should be pronounced *xinggang* instead). The film makes it clear that it is the glittering gold of the capitalist city that captures the greed of the Big Circle gangs in Guangdong, who want to "cross the river that divides the two worlds" for money. It attributes the mainlanders' readiness to use armed violence to their Red Guard experience in the Cultural Revolution. In this way, the disparity between the mainland people's lack of material comforts under a socialist system and the Hong Kong people's enjoyment of it under a different system is clearly laid out. This becomes the basis for dramatic conflicts culminating in armed confrontation. The conventions of the crime/gangster film are thus invoked to differentiate between those who have settled down in Hong Kong and the newcomers from the mainland.

In a mildly revisionist manner, *Long Arm of the Law* undermines its scheme of clear contrasts between Hong Kong residents and mainland intruders. By making

36. Mainland gangsters were former Red Guards. Johnny Mak, *Long Arm of the Law* (1984). GOLDEN HARVEST (HK) LIMITED.

the local gangsters a double of the Big Circle who are in some ways inferior to the latter, the film acknowledges comparable elements of illegality and violence between these two groups. Colonial law, figured in the Royal Hong Kong Police, is implicated in this comparison and shown to be as violent as the other parties. Hence, the narration does not operate on a simplistic logic of complacency and superiority that distinguishes the self and the other; instead, it operates on the logic of transgression and cynicism.

Consistent with undermining the law as theme, the film's narration moves back and forth between the position of the law and that of the criminal. It is through the Big Circle members' eyes that one sees and experiences life in Hong Kong. The mainland's gaze – that of the have-nots – on Hong Kong's plenitude is full of envy and the desire to possess. The criminal perspective common to films of the gangster genre has, in *Long Arm of the Law,* an additional dimension of "cultural difference," represented by the mainlanders' lack of urban sophistication and an unruly appetite for vulgar sensual pleasures. This characterization makes the Big Circle members objects of the condescending voyeurism of the Hong Kong spectator already situated within the discourse of plenitude. As shifts in perspectives continue to take place in the film, the "raping" of Hong Kong is seen from both the rapist's and the rape victim's experience, a double perspective duplicated in a scene where a mainland gangster points his gun at a snobbish prostitute.

Consistent with the playful attitude toward generic conventions in popular films of the 1980s, criminal interest in Hong Kong's wealth is given a subtly humorous treatment in *Long Arm of the Law.* When the mainland gangsters attempt their first armed robbery of a jewelry shop in Tsimshatsui, the plan is thwarted because another criminal is already robbing the place. This unexpected circumstance draws attention to the temptations that show windows have for mainland and local outlaws alike. As the gangsters run away, the viewer stays with them, sharing their disappointment, confusion, desperation, and loyalty to one another. This strategy of narration, common to the gangster genre, partly humanizes the mainlanders and reduces their "alien" character to some extent. Yet as the film attributes crime to greed and focuses on criminal fraternity, it displaces any possibility of analyzing deprivation and political difference and simply sensationalizes the superficial action effects.[14]

By romanticizing the mainland criminal fraternity, *Long Arm of the Law* actually mobilizes a kind of "developed sector" sentiment concerning an "underdeveloped sector." In the film, the Big Circle members are loyal to one another while Hong Kong gangsters are selfish. In addition, relationships between the latter and local police are characterized by mutual exploitation and treacherous betrayal. The film makes such a "self-indictment" possible by showing the superior aspects of the (otherwise inferior) outsiders. This treatment echoes the "First World's" idealization of the "Third World" as a closely knit community whose members have shared needs and feelings. Thus, loyalty and community are values necessary for survival under economically deprived conditions, while (First World) economic progress mandates individualism and manipulation con-

37. A Hong Kong prostitute, condescending yet vulnerable. Johnny Mak, *Long Arm of the Law* (1984). GOLDEN HARVEST (HK) LIMITED.

ducive to internal destruction. The film reveals a self-perception of industrialized Hong Kong as having lost the previous values still held by members of preindustrialized China. Though self-critical, the implications of the difference are not explored by the film beyond this schematic contrast.

The local gangster informant, Ah Tai (A Tai), plays the role of both manipulator and victim of the breakdown of trust in a society that is ruthlessly pragmatic. As an unsympathetic figure of the local underworld, Ah Tai makes it difficult for the spectator to identify with either the "outsiders" or the "insiders." The following scenes are most relevant. As the gang members refuse to help, Ah Tai goes through the humiliating process of seeking police help and offers himself as bait so that the Big Circle members can be arrested. Shortly after, Ah Tai, who has played double entendre with the Big Circle members, is discovered and, as the escaping gangsters use him as a human shield, he is gunned down mercilessly by police officers. The death of Ah Tai dramatizes the readiness of the police to abandon an "associate." The pact of complicity that quickly disintegrates under trial is driven by self-interest and treachery. Ah Tai's mobility between criminals and the law, between Hong Kong and mainland, is more than a simple generic feature. Rather, the in-between position set up by his trajectory in the narrative inspires an analogy that points to a pessimistic vision of the 1997 future. Ah Tai is the narrative agent that refers to a Hong Kong caught between merciless British and mainland forces (Figure 38).

The deliberate implication of politically sensitive matters in *Long Arm of the Law* is evident in the choice of the Kowloon Walled City for the film's climactic final scenes. For decades before its strategic demolition and transformation into a public park in 1992, the Kowloon Walled City had been an "illegitimate" territory of Hong Kong. Since the area had not been included in any of the Sino-British treaties signed in the nineteenth century, it was isolated from the rule of the Qing court and later from that of the Republican and the People's Republic governments, and was likewise left alone by the colonial administration.[15] As a domain immune to the jurisdiction of the police, it was nicknamed a *san buguan,* or "three no-control" district, and was not officially serviced with water or power. The Kowloon Walled City, an anomalous urban ghetto where unlicensed doctors and dentists operated and where drug and other illegal operations flourished, was a temporary shelter for struggling new immigrants. The film fully exploits its narrow and tortuous alleys leading to abrupt dead ends in chase sequences between the police and gangsters; the Walled City thereby becomes a metaphor for repressed political disorder – it disrupts colonial authority and unravels Hong Kong's myth of affluence by revealing the marginalized and underdeveloped sector within this materialistic paradise.

Li Cheuk-to, a notable local film critic, once suggested that Hong Kong films in the 1970s were more cynical than films of other decades.[16] To a large extent, such cynicism reflects the films' inscription of working-class ambivalence toward the status quo. The prominent mode of that inscription is demonstrated in

38. Ah Tai as manipulator/victim caught between mainland gangsters and British law. Johnny Mak, *Long Arm of the Law* (1984). GOLDEN HARVEST (HK) LIMITED.

Long Arm of the Law in the disavowal of any illusions of Hong Kong's political autonomy and respectability. Arguably, generic coding of the film depoliticizes, relatively speaking, the disavowal as it constantly displaces the potential force of the political critique into a mode of narrative action. Still, the process is not a simple one, and the concluding scenes in *Long Arm of the Law* function to reinstate law and order to the territory while representing the process as a murderous and traumatic one.

In the ending scenes, the entry of the police squad into the Walled City is obviously a transgression. Strictly speaking, the squad has crossed over into "noncolonial" territory – the realm of potential political disorder. The death of innocent people during the ambush further underlines the "illegitimate" nature of the police's armed presence. Still, the mainland gangsters' readiness to use excessive force calls for rightful intervention of the law. Before the gang is exterminated, however, the film introduces an immigrant couple whose role as helper/betrayer/victim is a variant of that of Ah Tai. The gangsters seek medical help and shelter in the home of an unlicensed doctor from mainland China who is studying for his qualifying examination. The doctor has agreed to help, but his wife, who feels no responsibility for the mainlanders, leads them to an attic and locks them in. This incident dramatizes the dilemma of struggling immigrants who try hard to become legitimate insiders. Like Ah Tai, as the reluctant couple get in the way of a confrontation between the Hong Kong police and the mainland gangsters, they are shot to death, the husband by the police, the wife by the gangsters.

In the ending sequence, the police firing squad shoots continuously at the ceiling until they can hear no more movement from the attic. This merciless display of deadly force is the culminating moment of the action film's trajectory toward magnified violence. Again, not only do the shifts in camera position throughout the sequence offer privileged views of the attic above, they also ensure an experience so violent and traumatic that it is hard to welcome the reestablishment of law and order. Spatially speaking, the sequence is extremely claustrophobic and the attic is literally a death trap. The gunshots fired by the squad are depicted, by special effects, as coming through the floor. More significantly, the view of dying criminals reeling in pain and falling through space in slow motion onto a floor littered with bleeding rats is denied to the firing squad. The officers, satisfied with proof of death by blood dripping from the ceiling above, simply leave. The camera and the spectator, however, stay with the scene of muted death inside the attic as sunlight shines through a tiny window. The shot, echoing the strange serenity of violent death conjured by the ending shot of *Sophie's Choice* (1982), epitomizes the film's ambivalence toward the self and the other.

The Mythic Nation in *Homecoming*

The release of *Homecoming* in 1984 brought a delightful surprise to both filmmakers and critics in Hong Kong and mainland China. Reviews of the film that appeared in major newspapers and film magazines in both regions were unanimously positive, a phenomenon quite unusual for Hong Kong films. In October 1986, China Film Press in Beijing published the film's screenplay together with a selection of reviews and interviews written by both mainland and Hong Kong critics in an anthology titled *"Sishui liunian": cong juben dao yingpian* [*Homecoming:* From Screenplay to Film].[17]

Such critical attention, reserved in China for its own notable status productions that meet the criteria of artistic quality and political interest,[18] was unprecedented for a (co-produced) Hong Kong film. Undoubtedly, *Homecoming* was and continues to be one of the rare art films made within the commercial constraints of Hong Kong cinema. This widely acknowledged achievement, which, moreover, was based on the film's poetic engagement with rural life on the mainland, appeared uniquely comforting at a time when other productions such as *Long Arm of the Law* were busily capitalizing on hostility toward the People Republic's claims of sovereignty. China's official film institutions' appreciation of *Homecoming* thus reflected their members' recognition of the film's unusual capacity to accommodate mainland China's reunification goals in artistic and human terms – a recognition that partly accounts for the content of some of the essays only and does not explain director Yim Ho's original creative motives.

Noticeably, many essays in the anthology attempt to recapture the poetic mode of *Homecoming* by choosing a vocabulary usually reserved for the discussion of Chinese poetry and painting. Words such as *yijing* (mood and sense emerging from presented images), *yunwei* (subtle meaning and sense), and *qing* (human feeling or emotional content) that are specific to traditional aesthetic and poetic discourse recur throughout. Some essays make an additional effort to correlate the film's aesthetic attributes, characterized as conducive to understanding subtle intent and underlying meaning, with a *Zhongguo hua* (sinified) or *minzu hua* (national-cultural) character. In addition to form, these critics share an appreciation of the film's depiction of interpersonal exchanges to convey the cultural characteristic of subtle expressiveness (*hanxu*).[19] As the critics respond to the film's sensitive, complex, yet stylistically low-key rendering of differences between the Hong Kong visitor and her mainland hosts, they respond to the film's approach to life on a human and existential level rather than on a political one. The critical discourse on *Homecoming* re-created the dialogic space in the film's "cross-cultural" venture.

History in *Homecoming* is couched mainly in terms of personal experience rather than political incidents. In the film, two childhood friends, Coral (Shan Shan) and Pearl (A Zhen), who have been separated from each other for twenty years since Coral moved to Hong Kong in the 1960s, meet again in the 1980s when Coral travels back to visit Zhuangyuan village. In the interim years, as the two women put it in plain terms, one has moved from farming in the New Territories to managing a publishing business in Kowloon, while the other has continued teaching at the same rural school and become headmistress. The striking political contexts in which their different lives have unfolded, including such events as the student movements in Hong Kong and the Cultural Revolution in China, are virtually absent from the diegesis. The political events, if they did in fact have an impact on many Chinese in real life, are of no thematic significance in the film, as they are eclipsed by Coral's stories of survival as a new immigrant in Hong Kong and by Pearl's daily routine in the countryside (Figure 39).

As the film's narrative point of view in the present is carried by Coral, who is in the process of retracing her childhood and reexperiencing her ancestors' village, the historical sense is conveyed through objects and situations that revive the faded yet nostalgic memories of a woman-child. Through her memory, the views of the countryside that characterized the 1980s and the 1960s are merged. Thus, narration in the film shows Chinese history as personal, existential, emotional, and to some extent timeless – an ideological context that makes it possible for mainland China to be called "home." However, though the film's ideological context seems susceptible to the charge of political calculation on the part of its mainland sponsors, who would like Hong Kong viewers to become more comfortable about rejoining the People's Republic, its "imperceptible politics" should not be reduced to such calculation.

39. Pearl and Coral, intimate yet uncomfortable. Yim Ho, *Homecoming* (1984). EDKO
FILMS LTD.

I would suggest that *Homecoming* constructs China as a timeless cultural
(read: anthropological) entity that transcends political and social distance and
unifies differences. Visualized through a poetic rendering of the spring landscapes of the southern Chinese countryside, a mythic nation is constructed and
imaged through an ethnographic sensitivity that gives presence to the details of
everyday living and to emblematic features and objects. Individual moments,
features, and objects are woven into the rural fabric, which resonates with
symbolic significance – critics who connect the film's poetic discourse with
traditional painting codes immediately allude to a (transcendental) Chinese sensibility. There are numerous such memorable details, including housewives rub-
bing clothes on washboards together in public; a woman standing up from her
sewing to let someone walk past in a narrow alley; Pearl, the headmistress,
seating her family on a school bench to have their picture taken by Coral with her
Polaroid camera (Figure 40); the attempt to measure a huge ancient tree by both
Coral and the twin great-grandfathers (with the symbolic names Han and Tang),
who wrap their arms and bodies around it; sails that flow gracefully along the
edge of the paddy fields while children are flying kites; a pool of rainwater lying

in the middle of a dirt road around which Coral and Pearl's husband Tsong (Xiao Cong) walk on either side; and an old village house with a pigsty in the open courtyard where one rests after a day's work. From time to time, sounds of nature such as the splattering rain or croaking frogs add to the ambience, while a child's rhyme sung in *chaozhou* dialect gives musical expression to the self-contained rural order of things.[20] Some of the images may be described, in Roland Barthes's terms, as containing an "obtuse meaning" (one that arises from the author's "manner of reading 'life' and so 'reality' itself").[21] In director Yim Ho's words, the details become a symphony of life.[22] Hence, their "third meaning" contributes to the mythic quality of China's countryside; in addition, their emotional and poetic qualities exceed their signifying role and ideological function and cannot be simply reduced to an analytical language alone.

Insofar as *Homecoming* tapped an "exotic" countryside for its healing power, the film shared similar interests with mainland films of the same period that were engaged in cultural introspection. Whereas mainland Chinese films sought the magical power of minority cultures in the process of recovering from the trauma of the Cultural Revolution, *Homecoming* found its formal and existential inspiration in the long-abandoned home village. In particular, I am reminded of Zhang Nuanxin's *Sacrificed Youth* [*Qingchun ji*], made two years later, in 1986, in which the female protagonist Li Chun reexamines her rigid Han upbringing and adopts spontaneous Dai ways of living while working among minority peasants in Yunnan Province. Li Chun's entrance into the realm of the "minority other" makes possible an internal renewal and gives her the most memorable days of her life.[23] In *Homecoming*, Coral is a disheartened professional with a failing business, a disintegrating family, and broken relationships, who takes a vacation away from Hong Kong to pay tribute to her grandmother's grave. Her temporary immersion in a preindustrial setting enables her to come to terms with the disappointments of a materially oriented society and to savor the paradoxical complexities of life. In both films, a crisis of self-definition (both partly based on the authors' past)[24] precedes a nourishing "cross-cultural" encounter which is, strictly speaking, an internal experience found inside a mythic "China" that encompasses racial and political differences and transcends arbitrary boundaries. It is a natural China from which both films draw inspiration for their visual design. The protagonists' sojourns into the natural, "otherly" realm are temporary in both films: in the end, they depart, only partly recuperated, expecting to go on to an economically more advanced, socially more complex, and emotionally less gratifying Chinese world. "Like water the years flow by," the literal translation of *Homecoming*'s Chinese title *Sishui liunian*, lyrically condenses a pervasive sense of loss shared by *Sacrificed Youth*.[25]

Integral to the "cross-cultural" venture in *Homecoming* is the representation of "difference," whose textual significance is as important as its intended reception. Given that the film was co-produced by Hong Kong and mainland Chinese personnel, its inscription of difference that emphasizes existential and ahistorical

40. The rural family posing for Coral's Polaroid. Yim Ho, *Homecoming* (1984).
EDKO FILMS LTD.

aspects is not without social relevance. Hence, fictional characters, though not rigidly typified, are distinguished by a set of social and familial references meant to reflect certain basic differences between capitalist urban Hong Kong and socialist rural China. Coral and Pearl, who are both economically independent professional women in their respective societies, for example, are still differentiated in the following ways: unmarried–married; childless–with child; greater ability–lesser ability to consume, and bold–conservative. These differences inform some of the subtle and not so subtle conflicts and tensions in scenes in which the women attempt to relate to and help each other while making each other uncomfortable at the same time. A similar set of differences underscores the urban versus rural dichotomy that overlaps a capitalist versus socialist form of economy and life-style.

In spite of such a dichotomy, the film also incorporates other axes of difference to show that the countryside is not monolithic and that changes are already taking place in the villages as well. As a rural couple, Pearl and Tsong do not hold the same views on changes. Distinguished by their statuses as headmistress versus peasant and their temperaments as dominating versus acquiescing, their responses to Coral are also different. The better-educated wife expresses her reservations about Coral quite openly, while the inarticulate husband is quietly supportive. Pearl's defensiveness is exploited by the film, which, in a melodramatic vein, links it with her jealousy of Coral's friendship with her husband. Negotiation between tradition and change within the village is given substance in the father–son conflicts between the village elder Uncle Zhong and little Qiang. In the film, Uncle Zhong's traditional wisdom, adherence to farming, and conservative outlook are challenged by little Qiang's eagerness for modern knowledge, his aspiration to be educated in the city, and his desire for new experiences. The modernizing tendencies in the rural imagination have produced Miss Wang and little Qiang, who are intermediaries between the conservative but wise village elder and the urbane yet disillusioned Coral. The nation's intention to modernize informs the breakdown in the urban–rural dichotomy and, by implication, the differences between an industrial Hong Kong and a preindustrial Chinese village. With the obvious and subtle changes taking place in the 1980s, Coral's ways are no longer "otherly," nor is China a stagnant nation dissociated from the demands of the modern world. The scene that depicts little Qiang's bold and rebellious behavior during the schoolchildren's visit to Guangzhou reinforces what has been hinted at: though not without frustrations, China is taking slow but sure steps toward a modernizing phase.

The tension between Coral and Pearl is in counterpoint to the estrangement

41. Tsong follows Coral uneasily as she takes him to a shop for rainboots. Yim Ho, *Homecoming* (1984). EDKO FILMS LTD.

between Coral and her sister. Ironically, the sister, who is not separated from Coral by familial, social, or political boundaries, is in fact emotionally and spiritually distanced, and a source of deep frustration. In the film, sisterly communication is brief and indirect – by telephone, letter, and a legal suit. The estrangement, moreover, is consistent with other alienating relationships in Hong Kong that Coral alludes to, including loveless sexual relationships that end in abortions and manipulative social exchanges conducted on the basis of mutual use. Outright hostility between Coral and her sister defines life in Hong Kong as an experience of alienation. The colonial experience is presented as clashing with the national sensibility, and the visual contrast between a cluttered urban apartment and the open countryside supports this comparison.

The colonial experience as alienation supports the border-crossing visit as homecoming that is, in reality, home visiting. Coral, the border-crossing figure, becomes situated between her "doubles," a rural "Chinese" version rooted in a culturally rich community, and an urban, Hong Kong (read: Westernized) version grounded in cultural poverty. For a person whose origins are in the countryside, the urban version becomes a distortion of an early, healthy experience. Thus, even though there are conflicts in the rural–rural or rural–urban contacts, in the film they are somehow self-revolving, while such is not the case with conflicts among the urban residents. Within this system of cultural difference, Uncle Zhong's traditional wisdom and the twin great-grandfathers' charismatic optimism are, within the film text, an integral part of the mythic nation and thus superior to the legal institution in the colony. Given both the characterization of Coral's sister as foreign-educated and the representation of Hong Kong by a noisy, urban apartment room, the film evidently idealizes rural relationships. Interestingly, the film does not find a permanent resolution in China's countryside either, and Coral's inability to identify fully with either side significantly underlines her in-between position. That is, from Coral's point of view, she is beyond the point of return. This decision, at work from the very beginning (i.e., Coral is simply having a vacation) means that alienation, no matter how painful it is, has been accepted as an everyday reality. This implicit acceptance accounts for a touristic and idealistic approach to Chinese social reality. Traditional stereotypes furnished by the socialist realism of the People's Republic in the 1950s had depicted Hong Kong people as spies, degenerate businessmen, and prostitutes. *Homecoming*, though it does not follow any simplistic political or moralizing logic, nonetheless envisions Hong Kong as lifeless and empty.[26] This time, however, Hong Kong residents are self-critical, and they consciously seek recovery and inspiration from cultural life in the mainland.

Concluding Remarks

In different ways, Hong Kong films have expressed ambivalence toward the city's postcolonial future. The China to which Hong Kong will be returning in the year 1997 is visualized along three related registers – formal, generic, and in terms of social reception. Through images and icons of violence derived from the gangster/action film, *Long Arm of the Law* creates criminal types out of country hicks. Through images integral to the poetic/painterly tradition, *Homecoming* portrays a pastoral beauty. In other words, guns and gore in the first film reinforce Hong Kong viewers' fear of and repulsion toward greedy and uncouth mainland intruders, while paper butterflies and rice paddies invoke the residents' nostalgia for the mainland's unperturbed preindustrial tranquility. Not coincidentally, the narrative point of view in these two films is differentiated by a masculine (and, indeed, chauvinistic) versus a feminine (or, rather, "feminized") perspective. Yet while an "ethnocentric" outlook dominates the first film and a cultural understanding is pervasive in the second, the sensibility in each film is not monolithic; mixed feelings of empathy and distance are articulated in both films as well. Thus, internal to each film and common to them, the encounter with mainland China (or its metonymic figures) is presented as both appalling and rejuvenating. In this way, these two films of the mid-1980s mark the range of local sensibilities regarding Hong Kong's return to China.

The complexity of the return derives from the simple self–other opposition that undergoes dissolution in these films. That is, the Hong Kong as "self" and mainland China as "other" are not sustained by the film texts as absolute antinomies. This internal textual deconstruction of the pair comes from the shared racial and national heritage between the people in Hong Kong and those on the mainland. Therefore, even though colonial-capitalist Hong Kong may view socialist China as the "other," on the basis of a shared Chinese heritage with the mainlanders, the colonial component in Hong Kong can also be seen viewed as an imposed, "otherly" element. The composite identity of the Hong Kong "self" becomes more evident when, as a result of 1982, contemporary China is incorporated into the configuration. The composite identity includes a colonial-capitalist/Westernized component, which serves as the basis by which Hong Kong can view mainland China as the "other" (and for mainland China to see Hong Kong as the "other"), and a national/racial component, which allows the Hong Kong and mainland Chinese to have a shared opposition to the colonizers. Hong Kong films' ambivalence toward its postcolonial future can thus be ascribed to the composite nature of Hong Kong's cultural identity. Therefore, it is not inconceivable that, in a film as hostile toward the mainlanders as *Long Arm of the Law* is, one finds instances that undermine the colonial police's authority; while in a film as nostalgic toward the mainland countryside as *Homecoming* is, one identifies an urban superiority and a lack of interest in long-term relocation. In other words, as the films connote an anxiety about postcolonial transformation and express discontent with the current state of things, they also reproduce the composite identity's paradoxical inclinations and cannot be simply reduced to either "anti-Communist" or "pro-Communist" labels.

Evidently, the 1980s, conceived as a historical conjuncture in this essay, cannot be reduced to any single cultural problematic. Still, the public's sense of betrayal by Britain and of Hong Kong's helplessness after Margaret Thatcher's visit to China in 1982 constitutes a notable collective interpretation of the significant political events unfolding during the decade. Popular films' construction of disadvantaged and weary in-between characters is a trope of this collective interpretation and, as such, constitutes a narrative/filmic response to the historical conjuncture. Seen this way, the cynicism in *Long Arm of the Law* has a popular as well as political basis outside cinema – in the distrust of and disenchantment with the nature and development of the Sino-British talks – while the sentimentality in *Homecoming* appeals to a nationalistic type of thinking that is being appropriated by the discourse of the People's Republic on reunification. Once again, the coexistence of cynicism and sentimentality testifies to the ambivalence and syncretism of Hong Kong cinema of the 1980s.

By supporting the demonstrations in Beijing's Tiananmen Square in 1989, Hong Kong residents have introduced changes in the situation. Having identified with the protesters on the mainland, the residents have begun to empower themselves by participating in altering, however slightly, the terms by which they will be ruled at present and after 1997. The 1989 experience and the changes thereafter have brought about a much more intense political experience, which has implications for Hong Kong cinema and which remain to be explored.

NOTES

1. Guillermo Gomez-Peña, "Documented/Undocumented," *L.A. Weekly* (Summer 1989), pp. 23, 26, 29. See also idem, "A Binational Performance Pilgrimage," *Drama Review*, 35, no. 3 (Fall 1991), pp. 22–45.
2. A very informative collection of papers documenting the negotiation process in the 1980s is Joseph Y. S. Cheng, *Hong Kong: In Search of a Future* (Oxford: Oxford University Press, 1984). See also Joseph Man Chan and Chin-chuan Lee, *Mass Media and Political Transition: The Hong Kong Press in China's Orbit* (New York: Guilford Press, 1991).
3. A less interesting but still useful reference on the political attitude of Hong Kong residents before the 1980s is Lau Siu Kai, *Society and Politics in Hong Kong* (Hong Kong: Chinese University Press; New York: St. Martin's Press, 1983).
4. Special studies on Hong Kong cinema published in association with the annual Hong Kong International Film Festival are essential to any serious study of Hong Kong cinema. They represent consistent and systematic efforts on the part of local curators, critics, and scholars.
5. This statement is based on the author's personal observations rather than any formal audience studies.
6. The thorny issue of Hong Kong film censorship was openly discussed in the Hong Kong periodical *Dianying Shuang zhou kan* (Film Biweekly) in the late 1980s.
7. See Benedict Anderson, *Imagined Communities: Reflections on the Origin and Spread of Nationalism* (New York: Verso, 1983); Thomas Elsaesser, *New German Cinema: A*

History (New Brunswick, N.J.: Rutgers University Press, 1989); and *New Formations*, special issue on nation, migration, and history, no. 12 (Winter 1990).

8. "Far from being eternally fixed in some essentialized past, [cultural identities] are subject to the continuous 'play' of history, culture and power . . . identities are the names we give to the different ways we are positioned by, and position ourselves within, the narratives of the past." Stuart Hall, "Cultural Identity and Cinematic Representation," *Framework*, no. 26 (1989), p. 70.

9. Louis Althusser and Etienne Balibar, *Reading Capital*, 2nd ed. (Surrey: New Left Books, 1977).

10. Immanuel C. Y. Hsu, *The Rise of Modern China* (New York: Oxford University Press, 1970).

11. Daniela Deans, "The Vanishing Border: As 1997 Approaches, Is China Taking over HK? Or Vice Versa?" *L.A. Times Magazine*, August 4, 1991.

12. Cheng Yu, "Uninvited Guests," in *The China Factor in Hong Kong Cinema*, the 14th Hong Kong International Film Festival special study (Hong Kong Urban Council, 1990), pp. 98–101.

13. Ng Ho, "Exile: A Story of Love and Hate," in *The China Factor in Hong Kong Cinema*, pp. 31–41.

14. See Thomas Elsaesser's argument in "Social Mobility and the Fantastic: German Silent Cinema," in James Donald, ed., *Fantasy and the Cinema* (London: British Film Institute, 1989), p. 29.

15. China's claims on Hong Kong since 1949 are discussed in Lin Tong's "Neiqing guijue de Zhonggang guanxi" [The Enigmatic Inside Story of the China–Hong Kong Relationship], *Ming bao yuekan* [Ming Bao Monthly (Hong Kong)], 24, no. 12 (December 1989), pp. 12–22.

16. Li Cheuk-to, "Postscript," in Li Cheuk-to, ed., *A Study of Hong Kong Cinema in the Seventies*, the 8th Hong Kong International Film Festival (Hong Kong Urban Council, 1984), pp. 127–31.

17. Critics' responses discussed here were taken from various essays in the anthology *"Sishui liunian": Cong juben dao yingpian* [*Homecoming: From Screenplay to Film*] (Beijing: Zhongguo dianying chuban she, 1986).

18. Examples are Xie Jin's *Red Detachment of Women* [*Hongse niangzi jun*, 1961] in the pre–Cultural Revolution era and Huang Jianxin's *The Black Cannon Incident* [*Heipao shijian*, 1986] in the "new period."

19. Examples include essays by Zhou Chengren (pp. 160–7), Yu Mowan (pp. 240–9), and Ni Zhen (pp. 333–41), in *"Sishui liunian": Cong juben dao yingpian*.

20. I have not considered the musical dimension of the film. Kitaro's music appears to me to have made the images more "sexy" for modern taste, whereas Anita Mui's theme song expresses a weary acquiescence. The use of both, arguably, also demonstrates the modern Hong Kong art film's distrust of the strength of the Chinese rural discourse on its own.

21. Roland Barthes, "The Third Meaning: Research Notes on Some Eisenstein Stills," in *Image, Music, Text* (New York: Hill & Wang, 1977), pp. 52–68.

22. Yim Ho (Yan Hao), "Shengming de zugu" [The Symphony of Life], in *Sishui liunian: Cong juben dao yingpian*, p. 169.

23. Esther Yau, "Is China the End of Hermeneutics? Or, Political and Cultural Usage of Non-Han Women in Mainland Chinese Films," in Diane Carson, Linda Dittma, and

Janice Welsch, eds., *Multiple Voices in Feminist Film Criticism* (University of Minnesota Press, 1994).

24. Yim Ho says in "Shengming de zugu," "Other than that I am not a woman, and have not had any abortions, I admit the emotional crisis and state of mind that the woman protagonist Coral went through is to a large extent my own." *"Sishui liunian": Cong juben dao yingpian,* p. 169. *Homecoming*'s other screenwriter, Kong Liang, was dispatched to work in the countryside, as Zhang Manling, *Sacrificed Youth*'s author, was during the Cultural Revolution.

25. The original titles of both *Homecoming* and *Sacrificed Youth* are explicitly nostalgic. One is *Paper Butterfly* [*Zhi hudie*] and invokes memories of the paper kites one used to fly as a child; the other is *There Is a Beautiful Place* [*You yige meilide difang*] and invokes the lush Dai village in one's memories where grass is always green and streams keep flowing.

26. Leung Noong-kong, "The Long Goodbye to the China Factor," in *The China Factor in Hong Kong Cinema*, pp. 66–70.

9

TWO FILMS FROM HONG KONG

PARODY AND ALLEGORY

Leo Ou-fan Lee

"Films from Hong Kong" – the phrase establishes an almost immediate association with mass entertainment. For years the Hong Kong film industry was dominated by two tycoons: Run Run Shaw (Shao Yifu) and Raymond Chow (Zhou Wenhuai), whose moneymaking "factory productions" have become trademarks for what may be called typical Hong Kong movies. Roughly, I would divide them into two basic subgenres – the "hardcore" *gong fu,* or martial arts, movie in a pseudohistorical setting or its contemporary counterpart, the gangster film whose obvious mass appeal is violence, and the "softcore" sexual or romantic comedy featuring a beautiful actress/songstress singing the obligatory number of songs. In the United States, the two types of film often form a double-feature presentation at the local Chinese cinema on a Saturday night. (It was in fact on such a typical evening in San Francisco's Chinatown that I discovered *Rouge* [*Yanzhi kou,* 1987], one of the surprises of artistic filmmaking disguised as a "softcore" comedy, a film I will discuss in this essay.)

It is not my intention here to give a conventional sociological analysis of these two subgenres as typical products of Hong Kong's urban popular culture. In recent years, the Hong Kong film has undergone some drastic transformations, and no simple catchall phrase like "popular entertainment" or the usual division between the "low-brow" commercial movie and the "high-brow" art film is likely to do justice to its complexities of form and content. On the production side, I attribute the transformations to the emergence of new talent: first, a new type of male actor epitomized by Jackie Chan (Cheng Long) and Chow Yun-fat (Zhou Yunfa), whose acting style combines a healthy physical prowess with a cunning sense of self-parody (contrasting sharply with the sickly, vengeful seriousness of, say, Run Run Shaw's "one-armed swordsman"); second, and even more important, a younger generation of producer-directors who have attended film schools abroad or had considerable experience in television, or both. Their most successful representative is certainly Tsui Hark (Xu Ke), whose recent film, *Peking Opera Blues* [*Daoma dan*, 1986], may be considered his hallmark. To put it simplistically, I think the style of the younger directors like Tsui Hark also exhibits a high degree of self-parody in the sense that their films often consciously borrow elements from earlier films and mock their generic conventions, so that what we see is a kind of filmmaking that does not seem to take itself seriously but nevertheless manages to appeal to both popular audiences and film buffs schooled in the histories and styles of Chinese and world cinema.

How do we explain this new phenomenon? Before I invoke any theoretical paradigms of "postmodern" culture, I would like to give some analysis of two of my favorite films of this new, mixed genre: *Rouge* and *Peking Opera Blues*. And before I delve into their individual styles I wish to make some "commonsensical" remarks about Jackie Chan, whose acting popularized the style of self-parody in Hong Kong filmmaking.

Clearly, the success of Jackie Chan owes a great deal to Bruce Lee (Li Xiaolong): it was Lee's enormous popularity as a media idol that paved the way for Chan. Beyond this obvious genealogy of *gong fu* expertise, the similarity ends. For all his genuine martial arts skills, Lee is not a good actor: in most of his films he is much too serious and his style of acting is easily traceable to the "one-armed swordsman" movies. At his best, *The Chinese Connection* [*Jing wu men*, 1973] and *Enter the Dragon* [*Meng long guo jiang*, 1973], Lee is capable of nurturing a simmering wrath that explodes at the final climactic moment. The process leading to that final outburst is often painful to watch in terms of both the excessive violence contained therein and the formulaic story, in which the hero is invariably a masochist who suffers violent beatings by the "bad guys." Jackie Chan's films, in contrast, are potentially more enjoyable for the viewer because he clearly (on the film's surface, that is) enjoys his roles, making all kinds of narrow escapes throughout the film. Even when he is severely treated or badly tricked, his body nevertheless maintains the quirky rhythm of comedy as his face turns anxious and anxiety-ridden. Sometimes the opposite happens: the acrobatic scenes are deadly serious because they require enormous concentration of the body, but Chan's facial expression retains a comic nonchalance. (It is known that Chan was injured many times doing these scenes, and the outtakes appear at the end of his films during the final credits.) I am suggesting, in other words, that in all his roles Jackie Chan constantly maintains two levels of acting – he is both serious and comic, often at the same time, and his double-layered acting matches perfectly the content of the story (Figure 42).

Aside from his acting, much of Jackie Chan's parody – since he is also the director – consists of his imitation of Hollywood action movies, especially the swashbuckling kind. The plot device of piracy on the high seas reminds us of *The Crimson Pirate* (1952), in which Burt Lancaster's acrobatic feats also figure

42. Jackie Chan, serious and comic at the same time. Jackie Chan, *Project A, Part II* (1987). GOLDEN HARVEST (HK) LIMITED.

prominently. But the action in Jackie Chan's films moves even faster. The tavern brawl scene in *Project A* [*A jihua*, 1983] is, of course, derived from countless army/navy soldier films from Hollywood in the 1940s and 1950s, yet it looks more exciting because of the careful choreography of movements inspired by both Chinese and Western traditions. Thus, the typical, chaotic energy of the Hollywood prototype is combined with a wonderful use of the indoor space characteristic of the best films by another veteran director, King Hu (Hu Jin-quan). In fact, Jackie Chan is so assured of his skills of acrobatic mise-en-scène that the last twenty minutes of *Project A: Part II* [*A jihua xuji*, 1987] become a nonstop rollercoaster ride of action-packed sequences (Figure 43). The plot is almost irrelevant at this point of self-indulgence – as if he wanted to show that he could do better than all previous action sequences "formalistically," thus defying all conventions.

Still, it cannot be said that Jackie Chan's films are all flashy form, lacking in serious content. Again we can take his most popular works, *Project A* and its sequel, as examples. The story of both films is, on the surface, funny, silly, and entertaining, but upon closer examination, we soon realize that it constructs a historical legend about colonial Hong Kong (with the sequel containing refer-ences to the Republican Revolution in 1911) – at a time when the Chinese takeover in 1997 is imminent. Thus, in both films contemporary messages are

43. An acrobatic scene requiring an enormous concentration of the body. Jackie Chan, *Project A, Part II* (1987). GOLDEN HARVEST (HK) LIMITED.

intentionally intercut into the plot, giving the local audience a sense of immediacy and shock of recognition that is normally out of place in a popular genre film of historical fantasy. Here, in some very brief moments, we find the hero arguing with his friends or opponents about the meaning of colonialism and the fate of its colonized servants – the Hong Kong police force. Here, too, we find that Jackie Chan does, indeed, insert his own point of view, very seriously defending the status of Hong Kong as one of its responsible citizens and guardians (in his film guise as a policeman). (Since I do not believe it has anything to do with the plot, I would not be surprised if the hero, at such inserted moments, in fact speaks for a sizable segment of Hong Kong's contemporary population.) As we shall see, in *Peking Opera Blues* this consciousness of the contemporary debacle becomes the central metaphor that is woven into the film's story and style.

In Hong Kong, *Peking Opera Blues* and *Rouge* were both box office hits in 1987. They also proved popular in Chinese communities abroad, though they were never released in the commercial film circuits in the United States. It is not hard to see that for the Chinese audience the films' box office success has something to do with the drawing power of their female stars: *Rouge* features a famous Cantonese opera singer, Mei Yanfen; *Peking Opera Blues* features among its three female leads two of the most popular stars, Lin Qingxia from Taiwan and Zhong Chuhong from Hong Kong. For film scholars and film buffs, however, the appeal lies elsewhere. *Peking Opera Blues,* together with films by Jackie Chan and others, were shown in the Hong Kong film festivals at the Film Center of the Art Institute in Chicago in 1988 and 1989, chiefly through the efforts of Barbara Scharres, the Center's director, who professed that she is a great fan of Hong Kong films because, like the Hollywood films of the 1950s, they manifest such obvious relish and sophisticated skill in filmmaking itself. [1]

If I may venture a preliminary "reading" of the two films, I would like to begin by arguing that my sense of "pleasure of the text" is derived from two kinds of familiar responses, which in turn come from my recognition of largely generic conventions. *Rouge* contains the familiar frame of the ghost story and the literary-scholar-meets-courtesan (*caizi jiaren*) formula in its characterization. Both conventions are traceable to traditional Chinese fiction. (The film is based on a novel of the same name by Li Bihua, a Hong Kong writer originally from China who has authored a dozen other semipopular novels based on Chinese historical and literary sources.) This traditional frame is contained in the film as a series of flashbacks that recount the familiar story of a pair of doomed lovers – he a rich dandy and she a romantic courtesan – who cannot marry each other because of his family's objections. They decide to commit suicide by swallowing opium. He, however, survives the suicide attempt, whereas she dies. The early parts of the film give an extremely opulent presentation of the decadent world of old Hong Kong, a most fitting milieu for the lovers' ritual enactment of courtship and suicide. The "real" story, however, begins in present-day Hong Kong, where the forlorn and frustrated ghost-beauty comes back from the "netherworld" to find her lover. Her sudden appearance in a newspaper office trying to place a personal notice introduces the subplot of a separate, modern pair of lovers whose lives become intertwined with her romantic search.

To some extent, the story of the young lovers presents an even more familiar picture, that of the typical middle-class existence of young urban professionals. A jarring and somewhat unfamiliar effect is created, however, by this intrusion of a figure from a past world – and seemingly from another film, for the flash-back sequences are done with a totally different cinematic style, a "narrative diagesis" [2] fraught with colorful and lavish symbols and markers, signifying an imaginary world far removed from the quotidian reality of the present. It is

44. A pair of doomed lovers. Stanley Kwan, *Rouge* (1987). GOLDEN HARVEST (HK) LIMITED

45. Ghostly beauty visits plain urban professional: a unique juxtaposition of fantasy and realism. Stanley Kwan, *Rouge* (1987). GOLDEN HARVEST (HK) LIMITED

definitely a cinematic tour de force for the film's director, Stanley Kwan (Guan Jinpeng), and its cameraman. In contrast, the life of the two young lovers in present-day Hong Kong is depicted in a prosaic and utterly unflashy realism. This juxtaposition of realism and fantasy achieved through a mixture of two generic styles is, in my view, what makes the film so unique and interesting.

Whatever intentions may have guided the director's design, this two-films-in-one device has created the (almost intentional) effect of incoherence by splitting the narrative form of the film. In fact, the ghostly woman with her gaudy costume is portrayed as noticeably uncomfortable in the "real world," the realistic narrative seeming to imprison the flame of her passion as well as the stylistic flare of the flashback sequence. Yet it is precisely her ghostly presence that serves as a reminder of another world – and another film style. Near the end of the film the two incongruent elements are reunited when the female ghost finally finds her old lover, who turns out to be a decrepit old man working in a modern film studio. As we watch the scene of another film being made in the studio (another film-within-a-film), with costumed figures flying up and down from the props, we are brought back once again to the fantasy world as represented by the flashback sequences and to an awareness of the function of filmmaking itself— to create make-believe fantasies. Thus, by juxtaposing and interweaving two familiar but different worlds – one derived from past convention, the other reflecting "real life" – the film succeeds in both entertaining and challenging its viewers.

In what ways does it challenge our expectations as viewers? For one thing, it hard to categorize the film generically, as it draws upon and mixes two traditions: ghostly/fantastic and mimetic/realistic. High-brow film critics might like the fantasy sequences and dismiss the realistic part of the film as uninteresting, perhaps because the evocations of decadence convey a more "literary" flavor reminiscent of the fiction of Eileen Chang (Zhang Ailing) and Pai Hsien-yung (Bai Xianyong).[3] Yet the realistic segment can inspire a popular imagination as it harks back to the precedents of other popular films: there are many Hollywood and Chinese movies in which a ghost who looks like a typical human being intermingles with other human characters in a realistic setting. Without a frame of reality, the comic and ironic effects would be lost: the romantic quest leads to a rather unromantic ending as the female ghost becomes totally disillusioned with the sight of her old lover. And the scenes in the movie set also become a parody of the flashback sequences: romantic passion is but the product of fabrication, of self-induced fantasy and self-referential filmmaking.

Peking Opera Blues represents a different world, that of the warlords in Beijing, but creates a similar cinematic effect. Although its story clearly refers to the warlord era of the 1910s and 1920s, a period familiar to most Chinese audiences from their history books or memory, the film does not give us any specific time markers, nor do the sets or decor convey the realistic feel of old Beijing (as, for instance, is the case of films based on Lao She's novels, *Rick-*

shaw and *Teahouse,* produced in the People's Republic). One could easily consider it a world of commercial escapism and dismiss its lack of historical authenticity as sloppiness. In my view, however, this omission of a "realistic" historical frame serves a more pointed purpose: it does not refer so much to any historical "facts" as to another popular subgenre – the warlord–courtesan films popularized by director Li Hanxiang, which in turn hark back to an older tradition of urban popular fiction and drama in the 1930s and 1940s (e.g., *Xiao Fengxian* and *Qiu Haitang*).[4] Thus, again, in generic terms the element of parody is also present in Tsui Hark's film as it seeks to add a more contemporary edge to the old formula of "softcore" sexual escapism.

In a way, the imagined milieu of *Peking Opera Blues* seems to have more in common with the glamorized old Hong Kong in Jackie Chan's *Project A;* there is a romantic gloss in its representation of another world. As in Chan's films, the plot moves, somewhat confusingly, at a fast pace. Scenes of action and escape abound. The ploy of mistaken identities, especially between the warlord's concubine and the opera company manager's daughter, only adds to the general confusion. But the unique features of the film are that, true to the implication of its title, everything is extremely stylized and artificial – plot, acting, decor, camera setup, movement, and mise-en-scène. Whereas several important twists of plot take place on and off stage, one has the overall impression that the entire film is set on an artificial stage – or a movie lot. Every time I watch the film, I am struck by the up-front angle of the camera placement: most shots seem to be either close-ups or medium shots. Background setting is often left out or blurred. This is definitely contrary to the celebrated "sequence shot with deep-focus, long take" that, according to André Bazin, draws out the essential realism of cinema.[5] Nor does the style approach the intensity of a Bergman film, which likewise favors the close-up angle. Rather, the film's composition and camera angle tend to accentuate its surface glitter, its pervasive artifice.

I am not sure this is a Tsui Hark trademark, since I have seen very few of his works. In this particular film, however, the artificial style makes perfect sense, for it fittingly evokes the make-believe world of the Beijing opera, a popular art form that is characteristically highly stylized. The Beijing opera stage is never "deep," and there is no need, so to speak, to lay out a realistic background. But I think there is another implication. The plots of traditional Chinese operas, including the Beijing opera, frequently draw on historical subjects and events. But history undergoes a noticeable "spatial" change on the Beijing opera stage: the sequence of "real" time is all but "synchronized" in space into connected acts and scenes; the passage of years is obliterated, and the past is brought "up front" to the present, to the duration of the performance itself. In short, the Beijing opera is as atemporal as it is unrealistic. This is not necessarily the case with the subgenre of the historical film, however, since there are many ways to create the illusion of passing time on the screen (long fade-outs, superimposed lines like "three years later," etc.). Tsui Hark does not seem to follow this long-established convention except at the very end of the film. Rather, *Peking Opera Blues* does indeed imitate the atemporal stylization of Beijing opera by giving us an artificial sense of the present – by the frequent and adroit use of close-up and medium shots that not only destroy the mimetic depth of the background but also collapse both past and present onto the same contemporary plane.

Does this serve any purpose? Does form imply a new message beyond the film's surface content? Before I attempt to answer this question, I shall refer to a few other relevant details in order to point out the film's contemporary relevance. First, the central female figure (played by the famous actress Lin Qingxia), the daughter of the warlord and also an underground revolutionary, dresses like a man and has short hair. She does not conceal her female identity (as did the historical "Woman Warrior" Hua Mulan, for instance), but gives a barely plausible excuse that dressing like a man makes it easier to do things. This does not seem to make any sense, if we do not seek out the role's references. In Beijing opera, of course, the established convention is to have men play all parts. (The legendary Mei Lanfang has immortalized the female role.) In the film, this convention is parodied by a conscious role reversal: instead of a man playing a female role, a woman wants to play a man. (On the other hand, when the male actor playing female operatic roles is approached by a thug on behalf of his boss for his/her sexual favors, he plays it straight and becomes scared, contrary to the conventional formula in popular Chinese novels in which such homosexual episodes are commonly accepted.)

The sexual confusion assumes a contemporary relevance because the female revolutionary apparently exhibits no romantic interest in her male revolutionary comrade, but rather prefers to form warm friendships with the other two women. There are at least two scenes of "unusual" interest: one involving the three women relaxing and playing in nightgowns in her bedroom, the other showing, partly in slow motion, how she is tortured in prison. The former may or may not imply a lesbian intent, but the sexual sadism of the latter is conspicuous. (The torture chamber scene is immediately followed by a seduction scene.)

We may charge the director with catering to prurient interests, but another explanation may be that he plays with the comic potential of sexual role reversals and, like Blake Edwards in *Victor/Victoria* (1982), cynically mocks the contemporary problem of sexual identities. More significantly, I think, lurking behind this play of sexual identity is a more serious reference to history: the model for Lin Qingxia's role may have been derived from Qiu Jin, the renowned female revolutionary of the late Qing era who, as legend has it, likewise wished to dress as a man. If indeed the role is a takeoff on Qiu Jin, then it again becomes a parody of the real historical figure. Lin Qingxia plays the role straight, without much comic flair, thus intentionally or unintentionally becoming a foil – a "straight man" – for the comic acts of the two female characters. One wonders if this is due to a certain residual reverence for a revolutionary legend. But placed within the film's make-believe milieu, the "real" historical reference becomes short-changed: can we take her seriously as a revolutionary leader, or is she merely playacting, like the rest of the characters? Her manly short hair becomes an operatic mask. Her two sides – as a revolutionary and a warlord's daughter – are clearly in conflict, since the unfinished task of the Nationalist revolution at the time was to get rid of the warlords. What, then, are we to make of this enigmatic role of an aristocratic-looking male/female revolutionary? What is implied here about the meaning of the revolution?

At the very beginning of the film, before the credits appear, a figure of the Beijing opera with a heavily painted face emits several roars of laughter directly at the audience. It reminds me, curiously, of Leoncavallo's *verismo* opera, *Pagliacci*, in which the baritone in a clown's costume sings an aria of sustained pathos about his life as an actor. In *Peking Opera Blues*, there is hardly any pathos (or "blues" – hence, the translated title is a misnomer). Indeed, the laughter sounds like a sneer: behind the masked face we detect the gesture and attitude of a seasoned cynic who wants to laugh at all the follies of the world. This dramatic posture is not so unique unless we place its "identity" realistically in a Hong Kong context. It may not be total coincidence that the film was made in 1987, ten years before the final takeover of the colony by China. I think its historical references also conceal an utterly cynical outlook on modern Chinese history. The film's story about "revolutionary" activities reminds me of the words of Lu Xun in 1927, a time of great uncertainty and confusion:

Revolution, counter-revolution, anti-revolution. Revolutionaries are killed by counter-revolutionaries, counter-revolutionaries are killed by revolutionaries. Anti-revolutionaries are taken to be revolutionaries and killed by counter-revolutionaries, or taken to be counter-revolutionaries and killed by revolutionaries, or not taken to be anything and still killed by revolutionaries or counter-revolutionaries.[6]

The film presents a merry-go-round of "revolutionary" activity that hardly signifies anything: two major warlords (surnamed Cao and Duan in reference to the historical Cao Kun and Duan Qirui) are both killed while fighting each other. Although the "revolutionaries" and some members of the opera troupe make a narrow escape from the stage, their eventual fate remains uncertain at the film's end. As the protagonists go their separate ways, a few lines on the screen, paraphrasing history, inform us that the revolutionary effort failed and Yuan Shikai won; then Yuan died and the "democratic revolution began all over again." There seems to be no bright future in store – and no happy ending. This is, in my view, definitely a contemporary and cynical reading of history from Hong Kong's present vantage. Neither Communist nor Nationalist, the majority of Hong Kong residents may well see history, especially when "repeated" on the screen, as meaningless farce. It is indeed an unexpected message brought about by the film's artificial and parodistic style.

What can one say in general terms about the current Hong Kong cinema on the basis of two films? If I have argued that *Rouge* and *Peking Opera Blues* are in some ways distinctive in style, I have in mind an implicit comparison with the films I have seen from mainland China and Taiwan. This much may be stated on the gut level: had the two films been made in Taiwan, they would have tended to be more vulgar and commercial, without the energy of high camp; and had they been made on the mainland, they would have been too serious in outlook and slow in rhythm (like *The Black Cannon Incident* [*Heipao shijian*, 1986]), without the cynicism and the exaggerated form of parody.

I have used the word "parody" several times to refer to a kind of generic derivativeness and imitation combined with a conscious mocking of earlier precedents largely in matters of style and form. I have also argued, especially with regard to *Rouge,* that parody may also contain a mixture of film genres. Following Fredric Jameson, I could also call this mixed style "pastiche."[7] Is there a difference between parody and pastiche and, for that matter, between high camp and pop or kitsch? These terms are obviously drawn from the current theoretical discourses on postmodernism, and these questions lead me to the inevitable theoretical query: can we regard Hong Kong films as in some way products of a Chinese postmodern culture? To answer it affirmatively would necessitate a full-fledged discourse on the nature of Hong Kong culture itself and the role of the film artist in it – a daunting task indeed.

Although I am not prepared to engage in such a cultural analysis in this essay, I am nevertheless convinced that the styles of the two films I have discussed here do have something to do with the infrastructure of Hong Kong's urban culture. Any casual visitor to this British colony can see that it is a contemporary culture of multiple styles, combining both "high" and "low," East and West. This "erasure of the historical boundaries between high and low culture," according to Steven Connor, is one of the symptoms of the postmodern in film.[8] Another interesting phenomenon of Hong Kong filmmaking is that, as the success of Tsui Hark (who is often both director and producer of his films) has shown, the notion of a cinematic auteur no longer applies; Tsui Hark is not Truffaut or Godard, nor is he much interested in evolving a new art form. His major concern, obviously, is money and like some, if not all, commercial artists he hopes to make money by giving the consumer an appealing product. Does this form of filmmaking confirm Benjamin's worry about the loss of the "aura" of art in an age of mass production or subvert the modernist position of the independent artist as originator? I am not sure, but I can say that in Hong Kong there does not seem to be a tradition of modernism to begin with, nor are Hong Kong filmmakers concerned about originality in the sense of forging a unique, unmistakable style as a statement of their individual artistic stance, as the so-called Fifth Generation directors from China are inclined to do.

The simple reason is that, unlike China, Hong Kong does not have a history of Party control over art and literature. Insofar as we can speak of a prevailing "official ideology," it is obviously constituted by the forces of money and market. To be sure, films in Hong Kong are a commodity, but it does not mean that the parameters of commercial transaction leave no room for the production of individual styles and visions. If the art of high modernism is predicated on the conception of a "unique self and private identity,"[9] the talent of Hong Kong's "postmodern" filmmakers lies perhaps in their seemingly effortless probing and public representation (in the form of a commercial product) of the collective "political unconscious" of the average Hong Kong resident and filmgoer.

To give a preliminary view of the contours of this particular mentality, let me quote a relevant commentary on Western contemporary culture:

As in other areas of contemporary culture, the collapse of the modernist ideology of style, therefore, brings with it a culture of multiple styles, which are combined, set against each other, rotated and regenerated in a furious polyphony of decontextualized voices. This brings about a flattening of the sense of historical origins, so that what are circulated in this art of pastiche are not only stylistic individualities, but also dislocated histories.[10]

According to Connor, whose commentary is in turn based on the theory of Jameson, the result of this act of decontextualization and flattening of history is the nostalgia or "retro" film (like *American Graffiti* [1973], *Star Wars* [1977], *Chinatown* [1974], and *Body Heat* [1981]), which sets out "to recreate not a particular historical setting but the cultural experience of a particular period."[11] In the case of the Hong Kong films, however, this seeming "retro" mode contains within its "dislocated histories" something more than merely another extension of the postmodern West. If what is being evolved in *American Graffiti* seems to typify the cultural experience of the United States in the 1950s, the three Hong Kong films – *Project A, Peking Opera Blues,* and *Rouge* – combine to evoke a "narrative experience" marked by three historic moments: late-nineteenth-century colonial Hong Kong, early-twentieth-century China during the warlord period, and contemporary Hong Kong (with flashback to the 1920s). It seems that they offer a peculiar allegory about the dislocated history of Hong Kong under the shadows of Western and Chinese colonialisms. The "flattening" of all three moments in the formal confines of the cinema brings out a contemporary sense of anguish and anxiety that goes beyond the simple nostalgia of a "retro" mode. In fact, given their parodistic bent, there is very little nostalgia; even in a film like *Rouge,* the ending serves to sever the present from a (re-created) romantic past as the disillusioned woman ghost leaves her decrepit lover forever. Rather, the cultural experience of contemporary Hong Kong does not particularly relish its colonial past, which seems to situate Hong Kong as a ground of struggle among various forces of chaos and war. With the flattening of the past into the present, the parodistic form of the films also becomes a form of cultural critique – that is, it turns these historic moments into ironic parables of Hong Kong's uncertain future. As discussed earlier, this future message is especially pronounced in *Peking Opera Blues.* If one may still discern any sense of nostalgia, it is directed at the present from a future perspective. In one of the recent popular

46. The disillusioned woman ghost looking for her lover of the past life. Stanley Kwan, *Rouge* (1987). GOLDEN HARVEST (HK) LIMITED

cop-and-gangster films (*A Better Tomorrow* [*Yingxiong bense*, 1986]), two brothers stand on the Hong Kong harbor facing the glittering nighttime skyline and are suddenly seized with nostalgia: after 1997, will they ever be able to witness a scene of such beauty and splendor? The scene captures vividly Hong Kong's fin-de-siècle mood – a mood punctuated by the realization that the "postmodern" present can itself become a dislocated "history" by marking the end of an era. In another recent film by Tsui Hark, *Love and Death in Saigon* [*Yingxiong bense, III*, 1989] (which is intended as a "pre-sequel" to the gangster film just mentioned), this obsession is carried forth in a magnificent re-creation of the last moment of the withdrawal of the United States from Saigon, down to the last detail. Thus, the film's plot becomes an imaginary prefiguration by telling within it a separate allegorical story about the fate of Hong Kong.

Whether or not there is any validity to my reading, I can certainly claim that as both an academic and a film buff I have derived great pleasure from watching these contemporary films from Hong Kong.

NOTES

1. From the publicity brochure prepared by Barbara Scharres for the Hong Kong film festival at the Art Institute of Chicago (January–February 1988).

2. Bill Nicholas, *Ideology and the Image* (Bloomington: Indiana University Press, 1981), pp. 82–5. "Somewhat impressionistically, the diegesis can be defined as all that contributes to the look and feel of the imaginary world of the narrative" (p. 84).

3. Both novelists also set their stories of passion and decadence against a background of the past re-created through the narrative. The heroine as passionate courtesan is a recurring trope in the fiction of Pai Hsien-yung. The works of these two writers are especially popular in Taiwan and Hong Kong, but not in the People's Republic.

4. The legend of the romance between the courtesan Xiao Fengxian and the warlord Cai E was itself made into a film in the 1950s, starring Li Lihua and Yan Jun. The play, *Autumn Quince* [*Qiu Haitang*], based on the story by a butterfly school writer, was a box office hit and the most popular work in Japanese-occupied Shanghai in the early 1940s. For a discussion, see Edward Gunn, Jr., *Unwelcome Muse: Chinese Literature in Peking and Shanghai, 1937–45* (New York: Columbia University Press, 1980), pp. 141–5.

5. Stephen Heath, *Questions of Cinema* (Bloomington: Indiana University Press, 1981), pp. 42–3.

6. Lu Xun, "Xiao zagan" [Mini-thoughts], quoted in Leo Ou-fan Lee, *Voices from the Iron House: A Study of Lu Xun* (Bloomington: Indiana University Press, 1987), p. 139.

7. See Fredric Jameson, "Postmodernism and Consumer Society," in Hal Foster, ed., *The Anti-Aesthetic: Essays on Postmodern Culture* (Port Townsend, Wash.: Bay Press, 1984), p. 114.

8. Steven Connor, *Postmodernist Culture: An Introduction to Theories of the Contemporary* (Oxford: Basil Blackwell, 1989), p. 178.

9. Quoted in ibid., p. 176.

10. Ibid., p. 176.

11. Ibid., pp. 176–7.

CHRONOLOGIES

PEOPLE'S REPUBLIC OF CHINA, BY PAUL G. PICKOWICZ

1978

In December the Third Plenum of the Eleventh Communist Party Central Committee, dominated by supporters of Deng Xiaoping, launches the Four Modernizations program. Massive reforms begin to take place throughout Chinese society. Higher education is restructured to emphasize intellectual "expertise" rather than political "redness." A large number of students are sent abroad for advanced study. Policies that will lead to the decollectivization of agriculture are initiated.

Following more than ten years of Cultural Revolution–era inactivity, the Beijing Film Institute reopens by admitting approximately 150 students in the fields of art, cinematography, direction, sound, and acting. The new students include Zhang Yimou, Chen Kaige, Tian Zhuangzhuang, and Wu Ziniu.

Forty-five feature films are produced by veteran directors, the largest number since 1960. Post-Mao relaxation permits films that criticize the Cultural Revolution.

1979

On January 1, the United States and the People's Republic formally establish diplomatic relations.

In February, Chinese troops stage a brief invasion of Vietnam, "to teach a lesson" to the Soviet-leaning Vietnamese.

Throughout the year, dissidents put up wall posters calling for a "fifth modernization," democracy. This Democracy Wall period also marks a flowering of the arts. Filmmakers experiment with new techniques and equipment. The number of films produced climbs to sixty-two. A few films, such as *Troubled Laughter* [*Kunaoren de xiao*] by Yang Yanjin and Deng Yimin, point to injustices that plague post–Cultural Revolution society.

In the fall, the Democracy Wall movement is crushed by Deng Xiaoping. Wei Jingsheng, a leader of the movement, is arrested and sentenced to a long prison term.

The audience for the revitalized film industry reaches 29 billion.

1980

Opinion polls, a new feature of Chinese life, report widespread dissatisfaction with wages, housing, leader privileges, dullness of life, factionalism, and education.

In September, Premier Hua Guofeng is replaced by Zhao Ziyang. Deng Xiaoping retains behind-the-scenes power.

In November, the Gang of Four is put on trial. Jiang Qing (Mao's widow) and Zhang Chunqiao receive suspended death sentences, which are later commuted to life in prison.

Xie Jin's *The Legend of Tianyun Mountain* [*Tianyunshan chuanqi*] is one of the first films to criticize the Anti-Rightist Campaign (1957) and the Great Leap Forward (1958). Eighty-three features are produced.

1981

The Communist Party issues an official reevaluation of Mao's place in Chinese history, criticizing his role in the Cultural Revolution.

Hu Yaobang formally replaces Hua Guofeng as head of the Communist Party.

In the spring, Peng Ning's *Bitter Love* [*Kulian*] is banned and attacked in the first of several post–Cultural Revolution campaigns against "bourgeois liberalization."

In December, Hu Yaobang addresses 250 film workers, warning them not to attribute "errors in Party work" to the nature of the socialist system itself. Film production soars to 105 features, the most in the history of mainland cinema.

1982

In the fall, the first post–Cultural Revolution class of the Beijing Film Institute completes its B.A. work, and graduates are assigned to work in various state-run film enterprises. Due to an overpopulation of veteran directors at the major studios, promising new directors are often assigned to smaller studios in the provinces, such as the Xian and Guangxi studios.

Film production sets a new record of 114 features. Owing to a surge in television sales, the film audience declines to 10 billion.

1983

Wu Tianming takes over as head of the Xian Film Studio. Wu becomes a major patron of the young directors who soon become known as the "Fifth Generation." Wu devises the strategy of funding their experimental art films with profits made from popular commercial works.

In the fall, a political campaign against "spiritual pollution," a code word for Western cultural influence, is launched and then fizzles.

1984

Economic reform moves ahead; the foreign trade structure is decentralized and enterprises are given more autonomy.

The first Fifth Generation film, Zhang Junzhao's *One and Eight* [*Yige he bage*], is produced at the Guangxi Studio. A record 143 features are turned out nationwide.

1985

Queen Elizabeth II signs an agreement ending the term of British rule over Hong Kong on July 1, 1997.

A new educational reform policy stresses more autonomy for colleges.

Rural people's communes are abolished and replaced by small towns and township governments.

Chen Kaige's *Yellow Earth* [*Huang tudi*], produced at the Guangxi Studio, gets little attention in China but makes a significant impact at international film festivals.

1986

Huang Jianxin's *The Black Cannon Incident* [*Heipao shijian*], made in Xian under Wu Tianming's patronage, is the first Fifth Generation film to win broad popular acclaim.

In December, student demonstrations begin in Hefei and Wuhan and quickly spread to other cities.

1987

In January, student demonstrations continue to grow. The party responds with yet another campaign against "bourgeois liberalization." Leading intellectuals, including Liu Binyan, Fang Lizhi, and Wang Ruowang, are dismissed from the Party. Hu Yaobang is forced to resign his post as Party general secretary. He is replaced by Zhao Ziyang. Li Peng becomes premier. Protests in Tibet turn violent. Up to ten policemen and at least nine demonstrators are killed. At least sixty demonstrators are arrested.

Shi Fangyu, head of the Film Bureau, resists pressure from Party ideologists to resign. The Film Bureau is moved out of the Ministry of Culture and into the new Ministry of Radio, Film, and Television to reduce growing antagonisms between the film and television worlds.

The Xian Studio completes four major films: *Old Well* [*Lao jing*], *King of the Children* [*Haizi wang*], *The Last Frenzy* [*Zuihou de fengkuang*], and *Red Sorghum* [*Hong gaoliang*].

1988

Double-digit inflation caused by the economic reforms creates urban unrest. Attempts are made to reimpose political control over the economy.

The television series *River Elegy* [*He shang*] severely criticizes China's "feudal" political culture.

Zhang Yimou's *Red Sorghum* wins the Golden Bear at the Berlin Festival.

Economic reforms in the film industry encourage studios to make a large number of lightweight, entertaining, and profit-making movies. Subsidies for art films become increasingly scarce. Some commercial films, such as Tian Zhuang-zhuang's *Rock 'n' Roll Youth* [*Yaogun qingnian*], are made by Fifth Generation directors.

The film audience increases to 18 billion.

1989

In April, Hu Yaobang dies. Thousands of students turn out at Tiananmen Square to mourn him and to protest the policies that led to his dismissal. The student movement rapidly spreads to Shanghai and other cities.

In May, Mikhail Gorbachev arrives in China to normalize Sino-Soviet relations. Some students begin a hunger strike. One million demonstrators, now including workers as well as students, fill Tiananmen Square, calling for freedom and democracy, an end to government corruption, and the removal of Li Peng from office.

The government declares martial law. Zhao Ziyang is removed from office. Demonstrators erect a statue of the Goddess of Democracy in Tiananmen Square.

On June 4, on orders from Deng Xiaoping, the army crushes the demonstrators, killing hundreds, possibly thousands, in Beijing. Similar violence by the army against demonstrators occurs in a number of cities throughout China. Widespread arrests and executions take place. Jiang Zemin is appointed new Party general secretary.

Four students from the Beijing Film Institute are arrested. Wu Tianming, head of the Xian Studio, is out of the country but publicly condemns the government. Wu begins a period of exile in the United States.

1990

Teng Jinxian, head of the Film Bureau, charges that filmmakers are guilty of "national nihilism" and "blindly worship Western film theory and artistic genres."

Zhang Yimou makes *Judou* with Japanese funding. *Judou* is banned in China, but in the United States gets nominated for an Oscar for Best Foreign Film. The Chinese government protests the nomination and Zhang is not allowed to attend the award ceremony.

1991

Zhang Yimou makes *Raise the Red Lantern* [*Dahong denglong gaogao gua*] with Taiwan funding. The film is banned in China, but gets nominated (as a Hong Kong entry) for an Oscar for Best Foreign Film.

TAIWAN, BY WILLIAM TAY

1945

Having been ceded to Japan in 1895, Taiwan reverts to Chinese control after World War II.

1947

The Nationalist (Guomindang) government militarily suppresses a popular uprising that started on February 28.

1949

Defeated by the Chinese Communists, Chiang Kai-shek (Jiang Jieshi, 1887– 1975) and the Nationalists move from the mainland to Taiwan. Chiang's son, Chiang Ching-kuo (Jiang Jingguo), takes over the presidency in 1978.

1980

Leading members of the opposition are sentenced to lengthy jail terms for "incitement and treason."

1981

The remaining members of the opposition win approximately 30 percent of the vote of local elections, which results in 20 percent of the seats.

1982

Central Motion Picture Company, financially owned by the Nationalist Party, backs four young, unknown directors – Edward Yang (Yang Dechang), Chang

Yi (Zhang Yi), Tao Te-ch'en (Tao Dechen), and Ko Yi-cheng (Ke Yizheng) –
and produces the film *In Our Time* [*Guangyin de gushi*], which consists of one
episode by each. This film is generally regarded as the beginning of Taiwan "new
cinema."

1983

Growing Up [*Xiao Bi de gushi*], produced by Hou Hsiao-hsien (Hou Xiaoxian)
and directed by Chen Kun-hou, wins the Golden Horse Best Film Award, marking the "official" recognition of the "new cinema." Other major features of this
year: *That Day, on the Beach* [*Haitan de yitian*], directed by Edward Yang; *A
Flower in the Rainy Night* [*Yang chun laoba*], directed by Wang Tung (Wang
Tong); *The Boys from Fengkuei* [*Fenggui lai de ren*], directed by Hou Hsiao-
hsien; *Ah Fei* [*Youma caizi*], directed by Wan Jen (Wan Ren); and *Sandwich
Man* [*Erzi de dawanou*], directed by Hou Hsiao-hsien, Tseng Chuang-hsiang
(Zeng Zhuangxiang), and Wan Jen. Yang's film later wins a Gold Medal at the
Houston Film Festival.

1984

For his second term, Chiang Ching-kuo picks Lee Teng-hui (Li Denghui), a
Taiwanese agricultural economist, as his vice-president.

James C. Soong (Song Chuyu), director of the Government Information Office,
and Ming Chi, general manager of Central Motion Picture Company, leave their
posts and go on to other assignments. Both are supporters of the "new cinema";
their successors are far less enthusiastic.

The initial success of the "new cinema" sparks a trend in adapting established
literary works. Among the critically acclaimed are Chang Yi's *Jade Love* [*Yu-
qing Sao*] (original story by Pai Hsien-yung [Bai Xianyong]) and Tseng Chuang-
hsiang's *Butcher's Wife* [*Shafu*] (original novella by Li Ang). Hou Hsiao-hsien's
A Summer at Grandpa's [*Dongdong de jiaqi*] (story by Chu Tien-wen [Zhu
Tianwen]) is a domestic flop, but his *The Boys from Fengkuei* wins the Best
Picture of the Nantes Film Festival. Li Yu-ning's *Second Spring of Lao Mo* [*Lao
Mo de dierge chuntian*], which touches on the politically sensitive issues of
provincial identity differences and nostalgia for the mainland, wins the Golden
Horse Best Film Award.

1985

On December 1 the Government Information Office formally adopts the new
motion picture rating system: "general admission" and "adults only" (at least
eighteen years of age).

Hou Hsiao-hsien finishes his highly autobiographical *A Time to Live and a Time
to Die* [*Tongnian wangshi*]; and Edward Yang finds private backing for his

Taipei Story [*Qingmei zhuma*], in which Hou plays the male lead. Chang Yi's *Kuei Mei, the Story of a Woman* [*Wo zheiyang guo le yisheng*], however, is almost canceled by Central Motion Picture in the midst of production for being "over budget."

1986

In September the Democratic Progressive Party is formed and becomes the first genuine opposition party.

Hou's *A Time to Live and a Time to Die* wins the International Critics Award at the Berlin Film Festival as well as a Special Jury Prize at the Hawaii International Film Festival. Edward Yang's *Taipei Story* wins the International Critics Award at the Locarno Film Festival.

1987

On July 15 martial law is officially lifted. In November, residents of Taiwan are permitted to go back to the mainland to visit their relatives – this policy marks the beginning of all kinds of contacts and "cooperation" with mainland China. On December 1 all restrictions on newspapers are removed.

A public statement signed by fifty-three well-known intellectuals and film workers urges the government to actively promote film culture and to provide incentives for the film industry. This proclamation is later perceived as the de facto code of the "new cinema" movement.

Wang Tung's *Strawman* [*Daocao ren*, 1987] wins the Golden Horse Best Film Award. Hou Hsiao-hsien's *Dust in the Wind* [*Lianlian fengchen*, 1986] wins awards for best cinematography and best music at the Nantes Film Festival. Edward Yang's *Terrorizer* [*Kongbu fenzi*, 1986] wins second prize at the Locarno Film Festival as well as the British Film Institute special award for the "most original film of the year" at the London Film Festival. This film also gets Yang Best Director Award at the Pesaro Film Festival.

1988

Chiang Ching-kuo dies on January 13; Lee Teng-hui takes over as chairman of the Party as well as president of the Republic.

On January 1 "parental guidance" (twelve years and under) is added to the rating system.

In July the first sex-education film produced locally begins to air on television.

The *China Times Express*, a new evening newspaper, starts its own annual film award as an alternative to the Golden Horse Film Festival, which has become increasingly commercialized. This new award has special categories for independent and noncommercial productions.

1989

The first democratic election after the lifting of the martial law is held in December. The Nationalists win most seats with approximately 60 percent of the popular vote, the lowest in decades.

Hou Hsiao-hsien's *A City of Sadness* [*Beiqing chengshi*, 1989] wins the Golden Lion at the Venice Film Festival, becoming the first Chinese film to capture this major international award. Exploring for the first time the politically explosive February 28 incident of 1947, the film attracts huge audiences throughout the island and is heatedly discussed.

HONG KONG, BY ESTHER YAU AND LI CHEUK-TO

1980

July 30: The British government releases a white paper on the proposed British nationality bill, which redesignates Hong Kong's 2.6 million Chinese who were registered as British subjects as "citizens of the British dependent territory of Hong Kong." The latter will be denied the right of abode in the United Kingdom when Hong Kong ceases to become a British dependent territory.

The Hong Kong International Film Festival Office publishes its third monograph study of Hong Kong cinema. From 1978 onward, a Hong Kong cinema retrospective is presented annually during the International Film Festival.

Several new wave films are criticized for their indulgence in violence and gore, including *Dangerous Encounter – First Kind* [*Diyi leixing weixian*], directed by Tsui Hark (Xu Ke), *The Beast* [*Shan gou*], directed by Dennis Yu (Yu Yunkang), and *Happenings* [*Yeche*], directed by Yim Ho (Yan Hao). An intense public debate on film violence takes place in November after the release of *The Beast* and Mou Dunfei's exploitative *Lost Souls* [*Da she*]. (Mou is not a new wave director.)

Tsui Hark's *Dangerous Encounter – First Kind* is politically censored and released in December only after reshooting and reediting.

1981

Dianying shuang zhou kam [Film Biweekly] and Radio Television Hong Kong co-sponsor the first Hong Kong Film Awards to take place annually. *Father and Son* [*Fuziqing*], directed by Allen Fong (Fang Yuping), wins the Best Film Award.

With the box office gross of *All the Wrong Clues for the Right Solution* [*Guima zhiduoxing*], Cinema City, Inc. challenges Shaw Brothers and Golden Harvest as the third major studio. More new wave directors leave independent production after Tsui Hark joins Cinema City.

1982

September 22: British Prime Minister Margaret Thatcher arrives in Beijing for negotiations on Hong Kong's future. (Between September 1982 and June 1983, Britain hopes that it will be able to continue administering Hong Kong after 1997.) Thatcher stays in Hong Kong from September 26 to 30 and meets with the Council members and local representatives.

Cinema City's *Aces Go Places* [*Zuijia paidang*] grosses HK $26 million, which exceeds the box office record by more than $10 million.

"Problem youth" films such as *Lonely Fifteen* [*Liang meizai*], *Teenage Dreamers* [*Ningmeng kele*], and *Nomad* [*Leihuo qingchun*] are publicly criticized for their negative influence on adolescents. A serious flaw in the Film Censorship Regulations is exposed when the exhibition of *Nomad* is suspended while the "Board of Review" (formed by government censors and other officials together with selected members of the public) considers a petition from a group of teachers. The film industry forms a committee and fights successfully for an amendment of the regulations that allows a film to continue its run during the review period and to be suspended only when the Board of Review reaches a different verdict.

Shaolin Temple [*Shaolin si*], produced by Zhongyuan Company and shot on location in mainland China, brings fame to mainland *gong fu* actor Li Lianjie. For the first time in many years, a film by a Hong Kong left-wing studio becomes commercially successful.

1983 .

April 5: About 140 Hong Kong and Macau residents are appointed to sit on the national or provincial People's Congresses and the Chinese People's Political Consultative Conference.

May 12: Liao Chengzhi states that China will not accept Hong Kong as an independent party in Sino-British negotiations. Instead, members from Hong Kong will be treated as part of the British delegation.

July 30: Xu Jiatun, a member of the Chinese Communist Party's Central Committee, becomes the highest-ranking official to head the Xinhua News Agency (Xinhua she) in Hong Kong, which functions as consulate/embassy for the People's Republic in the Colony.

July 12–13: The beginning of twenty-two rounds of Sino-British negotiations, which will end on September 1984.

September 20: Deng Xiaoping reaffirms China's position that it will recover the sovereignty of Hong Kong upon the expiration of the New Territories lease in 1997, and the future of Hong Kong will be settled to the satisfaction of both Britain and China.

October 15: Hong Kong's financial secretary, Sir John Bremridge, announces that the Hong Kong dollar will be pegged at HK $7.8 to U.S. $1, effective from October 17. On September 24, the Hong Kong dollar falls to a record low of HK $9.55 against the U.S. dollar following the understanding that Hong Kong will definitely be returned to China in 1997.

Director Li Hanxiang completes *Burning of the Imperial Palace [Huoshao Yuanmingyuan]* and *Reign Behind the Curtain [Chuilian tingzheng]*. Location filming in mainland China becomes more viable.

The large-scale use of special effects in Tsui Hark's *Zu: Warriors from the Magic Mountain [Xin Shushan jianxia]* brings Hollywood technology to swordplay and *fantastique* genres.

1984

January 13: Thousands of rioters rampage through Kowloon in the evening, taking advantage of a dispute between taxi drivers and the Hong Kong government.

July 18: The governor of Hong Kong announces a green paper on the development of representative government, which proposes to gradually increase unofficial and elective members of the Executive and Legislative Councils. China reacts negatively.

December 20: Zhao Ziyang and Margaret Thatcher sign the Sino-British Joint Declaration in Beijing. Earlier on, the declaration was endorsed by the Standing Committee of the Chinese National People's Congress and passed by the British House of Commons.

D & B Company becomes the fourth major studio. Financing of less formulaic films such as *Hong Kong 1941 [Dengdai liming]*, directed by Leong Po-chih (Liang Puzhi), becomes possible.

Studios' manipulation of box office receipts to enhance rental value overseas is publicly disclosed.

1985

July 1: The Joint Declaration takes effect. The Basic Law Drafting Committee holds its first meeting in Beijing.

October 17: The British government publishes a white paper on the nationality bill, which denies British subjects registered in Hong Kong the right of abode in England.

D & B rents Shaw Brothers' theater chain in November. Mona Fong of Shaw Brothers announces the studio's plan to produce six to eight films in 1986, about one-fifth of its current output. By October, only 300 employees remain, down from 1,500 in the peak years.

The ghost story genre begun by *The Spooky Bunch* [*Zhuang dao zheng*], directed by Ann Hui (Xu Anhua) (1980), peaks this year as *Mr. Vampire* [*Jiangshi xiansheng*] gains popularity locally (grossing more than HK $20 million) and overseas (including Japan).

With the success of *Winners and Sinners* [*Qimou miaoji wu fuxing*, 1983], *Project A* [*A jihua*, 1983], and *Police Story* [*Jingcha gushi*, 1985], Jackie Chan (Cheng Long) becomes a more popular comedy/martial arts hero than Bruce Lee (Li Xiaolong). The career of actor/director/producer Sammo Hung (Hong Jinbao) also peaks this year.

1986

July to September: Hong Kong Nuclear Investment Company and Guangdong Nuclear Power Joint Venture inform the Legislative and Executive Councils of Hong Kong of plans to build the Daya Bay Nuclear Power Plant. Antinuclear groups gather more than a million signatures for a petition to stop or relocate the Daya Bay Plant. Nevertheless, a contract is signed in Beijing to build the nuclear plant.

From 1982 to 1986, the number of cinemas rises from 89 to 115, and that of minitheaters from 11 to 35. The demand for films increases.

The success of *A Better Tomorrow* [*Yingxiong bense*], directed by John Woo (Wu Yusen), prompts a surge of "hero" movies with male-bonding themes and stylized violence. Actor Chow Yun-fat (Zhou Yunfa) becomes a superstar.

1987

January 14: Plans to demolish Kowloon Walled City (a Chinese territory) are announced.

March 31: In spite of overwhelming opposition from the media and the public, the Legislative Council passes the 1986 security ordinance, which subjects anyone who gives false information that may induce public panic or disturb public security to a maximum sentence of two years in prison and a penalty of HK $100,000. However, before the end of the year, the government cancels the ordinance.

March 17: Confidential government documents are exposed by the *Asian Wall Street Journal* indicating that the legal authority of government film censorship of the past thirty-four years is in doubt. The government releases a new film censorship bill and consults public opinion. The newly formed Motion Picture Industry Association leads the industry in protesting the bill's impractical aspects and political censorship clauses and successfully persuades the government to prolong the consultation period to three months.

Special effects and mixed generic elements are widely adopted in the ghost story genre after the success of *A Chinese Ghost Story* [*Qiannü youhun*], directed by Ching Siu-tung (Cheng Xiaodong).

1988

February 10: The government releases a white paper on the Development of Representative Government, which rules out direct elections in 1988.

June 16: The government implements a screening policy to distinguish "economic refugees" and "political refugees" among the Vietnamese boat people. Economic refugees are to be repatriated to Vietnam.

December 3: The Basic Law Drafting Committee's political system subcommittee approves the "mainstream resolution" in Guangzhou. The resolution, drafted by Louis Cha (Cha Liangyong, publisher of *Ming bao*), calls for postponement of direct elections of executive officials until 2012, or fifteen years after China's takeover of Hong Kong. Pro-democracy groups in Hong Kong hold a month-long hunger strike protesting the passage of that resolution.

The government passes a revised film censorship bill. A three-category system is established to classify film as "universal," "parental guidance," or "restricted" before exhibition.

The Motion Pictures Industry Association and Hong Kong Directors' Guild co-sponsor the Hong Kong Film Awards. The critics-oriented award becomes an industry-oriented one.

Newport Distribution becomes the fourth distribution outlet after Golden Harvest, D & B Company, and Golden Princess. Many independent producers release their previously undistributed films under Newport.

1989

May 21: One million people march in Hong Kong to support students in Tiananmen Square and to protest the imposition of martial law in Beijing. About 40,000 people march the day before despite a typhoon. More than a million U.S. dollars are raised by various Hong Kong groups to support the movement in Beijing.

May 27: Popular singers, television and movie stars help stage a popular concert, which raises U.S. $1 million to support students in Beijing.

October 5: To punish Hong Kong for its role in supporting the Chinese students, China ceases to accept illegal mainland immigrants sent back by the Hong Kong police and resumes acceptance on October 24.

December 20: Britain announces plans to grant the right of abode in the United Kingdom to about 50,000 Hong Kong families.

December 25: Producer/actor John Sham (Cen Jianxun), a leader of the Hong Kong Alliance in Support of the Patriotic Democratic Movement in China, is accused by Xinhua News Agency of helping movement leaders flee from mainland China.

There is a surge of gambling films to emulate the success of *God of Gamblers* [*Du shen*], directed by Wong Jing (Wang Jing).

Annual box office receipts fall more than 12 percent compared with 1988.

GLOSSARY

A jihua A 計劃
A jihua xuji A 計劃續集
A Zhen 阿珍

Bai Xianyong (Pai 白先勇
Hsien-yung)
Bai Xianyong 白先勇本家
benjia
Baimao nü 白毛女
Bashi niandai 八十年代香港電影
Xianggang 筆記
dianying biji
Bei Dao 北島
Beiqing chengshi 悲情城市

caizi jiaren 才子佳人
Cao Kun 曹錕
Cen Jianxun 岑建勳
chaowending 超穩定結構
jiegou
Chao xianshi 超現實
Chen Kaige 陳凱歌
Chen Ruoxi 陳若曦
Cheng Long 成龍
(Jackie Chan)
Cheng Xiaodong 程小東
(Ching
Siu-tung)

Chuilian 垂簾聽政
tingzheng
Cuowei 錯位
Curen shen si de 促人深思的黑炮
Heipao 事件
shijian

Da hong 大紅燈籠高高掛
denglong
gaogao gua
Da she 打蛇
Dangdai dianying 當代電影
Daocao ren 稻草人
Daoma dan 刀馬旦
Daomazei 盜馬賊
Dengdai liming 等待黎明
Deng Xiaoping 鄧小平
Di Long 狄龍
Dianying shijie 電影世界
Dianying shuang 電影雙週刊
zhou kan
Dianying yishu 電影藝術
Diyi leixing 第一類型危險
weixian
Dongdong de 冬冬的假期
jiaqi
Du shen 賭神
Duan Qirui 段祺瑞

Er yi ji	而已集
Erzi de da wanou	兒子的大玩偶
Fang Lizhi	方勵之
Fang Yuping (Allen Fong)	方育平
Feng Jicai	馮驥才
Feng Jie	瘋劫
Fenggui lai de ren	風櫃來的人
Fengkuang de daijia	瘋狂的代價
Furongzhen	芙蓉鎮
Fuziqing	父子情
gaige pianzi	改革片子
gaogan zidi	高幹子弟
Gaoshanxia de huahuan	高山下的花環
gong fu	功夫
gongtong lixiang	共同理想
Guan Jinpeng (Stanley Kwan)	關錦鵬
Guan ni ji (Xianggang dianying pian) (Zhongwai dianying pian)	觀逆集 香港電影篇 中外電影篇
Guangdong sheng	廣東省
Guangming ribao	光明日報
Guangyin de gushi	光陰的故事
guannian de xiandaihua	觀念的現代化
Gulingjie shaonian sharen shijian	牯嶺街少年殺人事件
Guomindang	國民黨
Haizi wang	孩子王
hanxu	含蓄
Heipao shijian	黑炮事件
Heipao shijian zhongheng tan	黑炮事件縱橫談
heise youmo	黑色幽默
heli	合理
Heshang	河殤

Hong gaoliang	紅高粱
Hong Jinbao (Sammo Hung)	洪金寶
Hongse niangzi jun	紅色娘子軍
hongse youmo	紅色幽默
hou gongye	後工業
hou xiandai	後現代
Hou Xiaoxian (Hou Hsiao-hsien)	侯孝賢
Hu Yaobang	胡耀邦
Hu Yue de gushi	胡越的故事
Hua Guofeng	華國鋒
Hua Mulan	花木蘭
Huang Jianxin	黃建新
Huang tudi	黃土地
huangdan	荒誕
Huoshao yuanmingyuan	火燒圓明園
Jiang Jieshi (Chiang Kai-shek)	蔣介石
Jiang Jingguo (Chiang Ching-kuo)	蔣經國
Jiangshi xiansheng	僵屍先生
Jingcha gushi	警察故事
Jing wu men	精武門
Jinye xingguang canlan	今夜星光燦爛
Judou	菊豆
juewang xinqing	絕望心情
Ke Yizheng	柯一正
Kong Du	孔都
Kongbu fenzi	恐怖分子
Kulian	苦戀
Kunao ren de xiao	苦惱人的笑
kunhuo	困惑
Laike	來客
Lao Jing	老井
Lao Mo de dierge chuntian	老莫的第二個春天

Li Chenfeng 李晨風
Li Hanxiang 李翰祥
Li Lianjie 李連杰
Li Lichen 李立晨
  (Li Li-chung)
Li Shuangshuang 李雙雙
Li Tuo 李陀
Li Xiaolong 李小龍
  (Bruce Lee)
Li Yizhe 李一哲
Li Zhuotao 李焯桃
  (Li Cheuk-to)
Liang Puzhi 梁普智
  (Leong Po-chih)
Liangjia funü 良家婦女
Liangmeizai 靚妹仔
Lianlian fengchen 戀戀風塵
Liao Chengzhi 廖承志
Liehchang zhasa 獵場扎撤
Liehuo qingchun 烈火青春
Lin Qingxia 林青霞
Liu Binyan 劉賓雁
Liu Guochang 劉國昌
  (Lawrence
  Ah Mon)
Lunhui 輪回
Luo Qirui 羅啟瑞
  (Alex Law)
Luo Weiming 羅維明
  (Law Wei-ming)
Luo Yijun 羅藝軍
Luo Zhuoyao 羅卓瑤
  (Clara Law)

Mai Dangxiong 麥當雄
  (Johnny Mak)
Maliezhuyi de 馬列主義的電筒光
  diantong 照別人不照自己
  guangzhao
  bieren bu zhao
  ziji
meiyou yongqi 沒有勇氣正視實
  zhengshi xianshi 問題
  wenti
Menglong 猛龍過江
  guojiang

Mingbao wanbao 明報晚報
Mingbao zhoukan 明報週刊
minzuhua 民族化
Mumaren 牧馬人

neiren 內人
Niluohe nüer 尼羅河女兒
Ningmeng kele 檸檬可樂
Nüer lou 女兒樓
Nüren de gushi 女人的故事

Pan Wenjie 潘文傑
  (Poon Man-kit)
Peng Xiaolian 彭小蓮
pizi wenhua 痞子文化

Qi mou miao ji 奇謀妙計五福星
  wufuxing
Qian nü youhun 倩女幽魂
qing 情
Qingcheng zhi lian 傾城之戀
Qingchun ji 青春祭
Qingmei zhuma 青梅竹馬
Qingniao 青鳥
Qiu haitang 秋海棠
Qiu Jin 秋瑾
Qi xiao fu 七小福
qiren 旗人

ren 仁
ren de jiazhi 人的價值
ren de zunyan 人的尊嚴
Renhai guhong 人海孤鴻

san bu guan 三不管
Sha fu 殺夫
Shan gou 山狗
Shanghai wenxue 上海文學
Shanghai zhiye 上海之夜
Shao Mujun 邵牧君
Shao Yifu (Run 邵逸夫
  Run Shaw)
Shaolin si 少林寺
Shenggang qibing 省港旗兵
Shengming de 生命的組曲
  zuqu

Shi Ba	石岜	Wu Hui	吳回
Shi Qi (Sek Kei)	石琪	wu lun	五倫
Shi Xiaoba	石小岜	Wu Tianming	吳天明
Shi Zhecun	施哲存	Wu Yusen	吳宇森
shijie yiyi	世界意義	(John Woo)	
shiwang huixin	失望灰心	Wu Ziniu	吳子牛
Sishui liunian	似水流年	Wutai jiemei	舞台姐妹
Sishui liunian: cong juben dao yingpian	似水流年：從劇本到影片	Xianggang (Hong Kong)	香港
Song Chuyu (James C. Soong)	宋楚瑜	Xianglin Sao	祥林嫂
		Xiangnü Xiaoxiao	湘女瀟瀟
Sun Longji	孫隆基	Xiao Bi de gushi	小畢的故事
		Xiao Fengxian	小鳳仙
Taiyang yu	太陽雨	Xiao jie	小街
Tan Jiaming (Patrick Tam)	譚家明	Xiao zagan	小雜感
		xiao zhong jian da	小中見大
Tao Dechen	陶德辰	Xie Fei	謝飛
Tao gang zhe	逃港者	Xie Jin	謝晉
Tian Zhuangzhuang	田壯壯	Xin Shushan jianxia	新蜀山劍俠
Tianyunshan chuanqi	天雲山傳奇	Xinhuashe	新華社
		Xiyingmen	喜盈門
Tongdang	童黨	Xu Anhua	許鞍華
Tongnian wangshi	童年往事	(Ann Hui)	
Tou e yuan	竇娥冤	Xu Jiatun	計家屯
Touben nuhai	投奔怒海	Xu Ke (Tsui Hark)	徐克
waigong	外公		
waihang lingdao neihang	外行領導內行	Yan Hao (Yim Ho)	嚴浩
waijia	外家	Yang Dechang (Edward Yang)	楊德昌
waipo	外婆		
waisun	外孫	Yang Yanjin	楊延晉
Wan Ren (Wan Jen)	萬仁	yangban	樣板
		Yangchun laoba	陽春老爸
Wang Jiawei (Wong Karwei)	王家衛	yangdaren	洋大人
		yangguizi	洋鬼子
Wang Jing	王晶	Yanzhi kou	胭脂扣
Wang Tong	王童	Yaogun qingnian	搖滾青年
Wang zhong ren	網中人	Yeche	夜車
Wangjiao kamen	旺角卡門	Yeshan	野山
Wenyi bao	文藝報	Yige he bage	一個和八個
Wo ai taikongren	我愛太空人	yijing	意境
Wo zheiyang guo le yisheng	我這樣過了一生	yinyang	陰陽
		Yingxiong bense	英雄本色

yongdongji	永動機	Zhi hudie	紙蝴蝶
You yige meili de difang	有一個美麗的地方	Zhong Chengxiang	仲呈祥
Youma caizi	油麻菜籽	Zhongguo dianying chuban she	中國電影出版社
Yu Yunkang (Dennis Yu)	余允抗		
yuanli xianshi	遠離現實	Zhongguo wenhua de shenceng jiegou	中國文化的深層結構
Yunwei	韻味		
Yuqing Sao	玉卿嫂		
		Zhongguo zuihou yige taijian	中國最後一個太監
Zeng Zhuangxiang	曾壯祥		
Zhang Aijia (Sylvia Chang)	張艾嘉	Zhongguohua	中國化
		Zhongwai wenxue	中外文學
Zhang Ailing (Eileen Chang)	張愛玲	zhongyang wenjian	中央文件
Zhang Che (Chang Che)	張徹	Zhou Xiaowen	周曉文
		Zhou Yunfa (Chow Yun-fat)	周潤發
Zhang Guoming (Alex Cheung)	韋國明		
		Zhu Tianwen (Chu Tien-wen)	朱天文
Zhang Junzhao	張軍釗		
Zhang Nuanxin	張暖昕	Zhuang dao zheng	撞到正
Zhang Yi	張毅	zishen de xiandaihua	自身的現代化
Zhang Yimou	張藝謀		
Zhang Zhiliang (Jacob Cheung)	張之亮	ziwo yasuo	自我壓縮
		Zou Wenhuai (Raymond Chow)	鄒文懷
Zhao Shuxin	趙書信		
Zhao Ziyang	趙紫陽		
Zheng Dongtian	鄭洞天	Zuihou de fengkuang	最後的瘋狂
zhengju	正劇	Zuijia paidang	最佳拍檔

SCHOLARLY WORKS ON CHINESE FILMMAKING IN THE 1980S

Compiled by Li Huai and Paul G. Pickowicz

PERIODICALS

Book-length studies of Chinese cinema appear from time to time, but most new research on contemporary filmmaking is published in periodicals. What follows is a preliminary effort to identify scholarly, quasi-scholarly, and popular journals that devote space to Chinese cinema.

Asian Cinema. Launched in 1985 under the title *Asian Cinema Studies Society Newsletter,* this remarkably useful semiannual is published by the Asian Cinema Studies Society based in Hamden, Connecticut. In addition to listing new publications on Asian cinema, this periodical contains letters to the editor, book and film reviews, interviews, news of scholarly meetings and film festivals, and personal information about scholars who are active in the field. Address: Quinnipiac College, Box 91, Hamden, CT 06518-0569.

Beijing Dianying Xueyuan xuebao [Journal of the Beijing Film Institute]. Launched in 1979, this monthly is the premier publication of the prestigious Beijing Film Institute and often carries the scholarly, theoretical, and critical writings of such faculty members as Dai Jinhua, Ni Zhen, and Zhong Dafeng. It is one of the top two film journals in the People's Republic of China.

The China Quarterly. This scholarly journal, published in London since the 1950s, focuses on contemporary Chinese politics and society, but occasionally carries articles and reviews on Chinese culture, including Chinese cinema.

China Screen. A glossy quarterly published in English (and in Chinese under the title *Zhongguo yinmu*) by the commercially minded China Film Export and Import Corporation (Zhongguo dianying shuchu shuru gongsi). It features brief introductions of new releases.

Dazhong dianying [Popular Cinema]. A nonscholarly popular film monthly that focuses primarily on the lives and careers of actresses and actors, this magazine has a vast readership in China and thus is an important source on the tastes of the film audience. Its publication dates are 1951–66 and 1979–present.

Dangdai dianying [Contemporary Cinema]. This monthly appeared in 1984 and is published by the China Film Art Research Center (Zhongguo dianying yishu yanjiu zhongxin), which is located on the grounds of the Film Archive of China (Zhongguo dianying ziliaoguan) in Beijing. It is one of the two most important scholarly film publications in China and features the research of such resident scholars as Hu Ke, Zhang Wei, Li Xun, and Yao Xiaomeng.

Dianying chuangzuo [Film Creations]. A publication of the Beijing Film Studio, this monthly features the full texts of new screenplays. Most of the screenplays will never be made into movies. In China the "screenplay" (*dianying juben*) is considered to be an independent literary genre. Many texts receive critical acclaim and are widely read, even though they were never intended or considered for actual motion picture production.

Dianying shuang zhou kan [Film Biweekly]. This is a popular film magazine published in Hong Kong. In addition to carrying reviews and production announcements, it contains light features and gossip about Hong Kong film personalities.

Dianying yishu [Film Art]. This is a quasi-scholarly monthly published in Beijing by the state-run Chinese Filmmaker's Association (Zhongguo dianyingjia xiehui). It resumed publishing shortly after the Cultural Revolution ended and carries short articles by critics and filmmakers alike. Its publication dates are 1959–66 and 1979–present.

Dianying yishu cankao ziliao [Film Art Reference Materials]. This is a classified publication of the Chinese Filmworker's Association intended for "internal" (*neibu*) circulation among film professionals. Among other things, it reports on conferences that take up controversial subjects. In July 1980, for example, it reprinted the comments of five speakers who addressed the topic of "human sexuality" at a meeting sponsored by the Association.

East–West Film Journal. A publication of the East–West Center in Honolulu, this biannual scholarly periodical is the most important English-language journal devoted primarily to Asian cinema. Virtually every issue has at least one article on Chinese cinema by such leading scholars as Chris Berry, Paul Clark, Ma Ning, and Tony Rayns.

Modern China. This is the most important scholarly journal in the United States devoted to modern Chinese politics, economy, society, and culture. Published at the University of California, Los Angeles, since 1975, this quarterly occasionally publishes articles on Chinese film and literature.

Modern Chinese Literature. Currently published by the Department of Oriental Languages and Literatures at the University of Colorado at Boulder, this biannual journal was initiated in 1984. The emphasis is on literature, but occasionally an article or even a special issue (see vol. 1, no. 2, Spring 1985) on Chinese cinema appears.

Ying shi wenhua [Film and Television Culture]. This new journal began publishing in Beijing in 1988. It is a publication of the Film and Television Research Section of the Chinese Arts Research Institute.

Zhongguo dianying bao [Chinese Film News]. This news daily, published in Beijing since 1985, is devoted to cinema. Unlike other film publications in the People's Republic of China, this one identifies and discusses controversies as they are breaking. See, for example, the June 18, 1988, issue, which contains heated exchanges regarding *Red Sorghum* [*Hong gaoliang, 1987*].

Zhongguo dianying nianjian [China Film Yearbook]. This important annual volume is published each year in Beijing by the Chinese Cinema Publishing House (Zhongguo dianying chuban she). The first volume in the series covers 1981. In addition to cinema from the People's Republic of China, it reviews the film worlds of Taiwan and Hong Kong.

BOOKS AND ARTICLES

In the early 1980s there was not much writing in English on Chinese cinema. By the mid-1980s a number of important article-length writings began to appear, and by 1986–7 there was a virtual explosion of new work, most of which examined the new wave developments of the 1980s in Hong Kong, Taiwan, and the People's Republic. It is important to note that during the 1980s some scholars were also writing on the longer tradition of Chinese filmmaking, which extends back to the 1920s. But since this volume focuses primarily on the startling developments of the 1980s, no effort has been made to list works that treat Chinese filmmaking before 1979. What follows is a basic list of writings on the 1980s. Needless to say, the list is not complete. With some important exceptions, mention is made of longer scholarly works rather than short reviews, announcements, or popular commentaries.

An effort has been made to survey the voluminous Chinese-language literature. The list of Chinese titles is woefully incomplete, but the editors of this volume believe that it is important for Western scholars to be aware of the ways in which Chinese scholars approach Chinese cinema. Few will be surprised to learn that Chinese approaches are often informed by intellectual agendas that differ markedly from those that preoccupy Western scholars.

Finally, readers will notice that the bibliography mentions works on Chinese cinema written by scholars in various disciplines. Scholars with rich backgrounds in Western film studies and theory often use paradigms that have been used to analyze European and U.S. cinema. Researchers trained in Chinese studies often seek to locate their work on Chinese cinema in the context of current debates on Chinese history, literature, and politics. Others try to combine film studies and Chinese studies approaches. Some scholars write primarily for the film studies audience; others write primarily for the Chinese studies audience. All are making a contribution.

A Cheng. "Xie Jin *Furongzhen* yu ruxue dianying" [Confucian Cinema and Xie Jin's *Hibiscus Town*]. *Jiushi niandai* (May 1987), pp. 10–11.

Anonymous. *"Hong gaoliang* shi chouhua Zhongguo renmin de yingpian" [*Red Sorghum* Defames the Chinese People]. *Zhongguo dianying bao,* June 15, 1988.

Bai Jieming. "You fan zi dao *Haizi wang*" [From Antibourgeois Liberalization to *King of the Children*]. *Jiushi niandai* (January 1988), pp. 94–5.

Bergeron, Regis. *Le Cinéma chinois, 1949–1983.* Paris: Harmattan, 1984.

Berry, Chris. "Chinese Urban Cinema: Hyper-realism versus Absurdism." *East–West Film Journal,* 3, no. 1 (December 1988), pp. 76–87.

"Chinese 'Women's Cinema.'" *Camera Obscura,* 18 (September 1988), pp. 8–41.

"Market Forces: China's 'Fifth Generation' Faces the Bottom Line." In Chris Berry, ed., *Perspectives on Chinese Cinema.* London: British Film Institute, 1991, pp. 114–25.

"Now You See It, Now You Don't: The Arbitrary History and Unstable Future of Censorship in the People's Republic of China." *Cinemaya,* 4 (Summer 1989), pp. 46–55.

"Race: Chinese Film and the Politics of Nationalism." *Cinema Journal,* 31, no. 2 (Winter 1992), pp. 45–58.

"Sexual Difference and the Viewing Subject in *Li Shuangshuang* and *The In-Laws.*" In Chris Berry, ed., *Perspectives on Chinese Cinema.* London: British Film Institute, 1991, pp. 30–9.

Berry, Chris, ed. *Perspectives on Chinese Cinema.* Ithaca, N.Y.: Cornell University East Asia Papers, no. 39, 1985.

Perspectives on Chinese Cinema. London: British Film Institute, 1992.

Cai Hongsheng. "Cheng Long: Xianggang yingtan de baima wangzi" [Jackie Chan: Prince of the Hong Kong Film World]. *Dangdai dianying,* no. 4 (April 1989), pp. 112–18.

Chai Xiaofeng. "Huashuo *Fengkuang de daijia:* Yu Zhou Xiaowen duihua lu" [On *Obsession:* A Discussion with Zhou Xiaowen]. *Dangdai dianying,* no. 2 (February 1989), pp. 75–84.

Chan, Joseph Man, and Chin-Chuan Lee. *Mass Media and Political Transition: The Hong Kong Press in China's Orbit* (New York: Guilford Press, 1991).

Chang Xiangru. "Movies in the Middle Nation: Attitudes of Chinese Audiences." *Independent,* 9, no. 9 (November 1986), pp. 14–19.

Chen Feibao. "Chutan haixia liang an dianying wenhua jiaoliao he yingxiang" [The Initial Interaction of Film Culture Across the Taiwan Straits]. *Dangdai dianying,* no. 1 (January 1990), pp. 96–102.

Chen Feibao, ed. *Taiwan dianying shi hua* [A History of Taiwan Cinema]. Beijing: Zhongguo dianying chuban she, 1988.

Chen Huiyang. *Meng ying ji: Zhongguo dinying yinxiang* [Dream Shadows: Impressions of the Chinese Cinema]. Taibei: Yun chen wenhua, 1990.

Chen Kaige. "Breaking the Circle: The Cinema and Cultural Change in China." *Cineaste,* 17, no. 3 (February 1990), pp. 28–31.

Chen Kaige, Wan Zhi, and Tony Rayns. *"King of the Children" and the New Chinese Cinema.* London: Faber & Faber, 1989.

Chen Ken. "Diwu dai: Chuantou Zhongguo yinmu de youling" [The Fifth Generation:

The Spirit Permeating Chinese Cinema]. *Dianying yishu*, no. 3 (March 1988), pp. 17–23.

Chen Xiaoxin. "Lun *Hong gaoliang* de wenhua jiazhi" [On *Red Sorghum's* Cultural Values]. *Dianying yishu*, no. 2 (February 1989), pp. 29–35.

Cheng, Joseph Y. S., ed., *Hong Kong in Search of a Future* (Oxford: Oxford University Press, 1984).

Chiao Hsiung Ping. "*A City of Sadness:* Interview with Hou Xiaoxian." *Cinemaya*, no. 3 (Spring 1989), pp. 40–2.

"Contrasting Images: Taiwan and Hong Kong Films." *Free China Review* (February 1988), pp. 12–19.

"The Distinct Taiwanese and Hong Kong Cinemas." In Chris Berry, ed., *Perspectives on Chinese Cinema* (London: British Film Institute, 1991), pp. 155–65.

Chiao Hsiung Ping, ed. *Taiwan xin dianying* [Taiwan's New Cinema]. Taibei: Shi bao, 1988.

Xianggang dianying fengmao [The Hong Kong Film Scene]. Taibei: Shi bao, 1987.

Chow Rey. "Male Narcissism and National Culture: Subjectivity in Chen Kaige's 'King of the Children.'" In Ellen Widmer and David Der-wei Wang, eds., *From May Fourth to June Fourth: Fiction and Film in Twentieth-Century China*. Cambridge, Mass.: Harvard University Press, 1993, pp. 327–59.

"Silent Is the Ancient Plain: Music, Filmmaking, and the Conception of Reform in China's New Cinema." *Discourse*, 12, no. 2 (1990), pp. 82–109.

Chua, Lawrence. "*CineVue* Interviews Taiwanese Director Hou Hsiao-Hsien." *CineVue*, 4, no. 3 (September 1989).

Chute, David, ed. "Made in Hong Kong." *Film Comment*, 24, no. 3 (June 1988), pp. 33–56.

Clark, Paul. *Chinese Cinema: Culture and Politics Since 1949*. New York: Cambridge University Press, 1987.

"Ethnic Minorities in Chinese Films: Cinema and the Exotic." *East–West Film Journal*, 1, no. 2 (June 1987), pp. 15–31.

"The Film Industry in the 1970s." In Bonnie S. McDougall, ed., *Popular Literature and the Performing Arts in the People's Republic of China*. Berkeley and Los Angeles: University of California Press, 1984, pp. 177–96.

"Film-making in China: From the Cultural Revolution to 1981," *China Quarterly*, no. 94 (June 1983), pp. 304–22.

"Reinventing China: The Fifth Generation Filmmakers." *Modern Chinese Literature*, 5, no. 1 (Spring 1989), pp. 121–36.

"Cu ren shen si de *Heipao shijian*" [*The Black Cannon Incident* Forces You to Think Hard]. *Dianying yishi*, no. 4 (April 1986), pp. 9–18.

"*Cuowei* cuowei?" [Is *Dislocation* Dislocated?]. *Dianying yishu*, no. 6 (June 1987), pp. 38–46.

Dai, Jinhua. "Xie ta: Zhongdu disi dai" [A Leaning Tower: Stressing the Fourth Generation]. *Dianying yishu*, no. 4 (April 1988), pp. 7–9.

Dianying yishu cidian [Dictionary of Film Art]. Beijing: Zhongguo dianying chuban she, 1986.

Disan ge shiqi de Zhongguo dianying [Chinese Cinema in Its Third Period]. Xianggang [Hong Kong]: Jinhui xueyuan [Baptist College], 1988.

Dissanayake, Wimal, ed. *Cinema and Cultural Identity: Reflections on Films from Japan, India, and China.* Lanham, Md.: University Press of America, 1988.

Du Yuan. "Dui *Hong gaoliang* huo jiang de kunhuo" [Bewilderment Regarding an Award for *Red Sorghum*]. *Dazhong dianying,* no. 6 (June 1988), pp. 2–3.

Eberhard, Wolfram. *The Chinese Silver Screen: Hong Kong and Taiwanese Motion Pictures in the 1960's.* Taipei: Oriental Culture Service, Asian Folklore and Social Life Monographs, 1972.

Farquhar, Mary Ann. "The 'Hidden' Gender in *Yellow Earth. Screen,* 33, no. 2 (Summer 1992), pp. 154–64.

Faubel, Jeffrey. "Cultural Introspection in Chinese Cinema: The Fifth Generation of Chinese Filmmakers," M.A. thesis, Indiana University, 1990.

"*Fengkuang de daijia* bitan" [Criticism of *Obsession*]. *Dangdai dianying,* no. 2 (February 1989), pp. 85–94.

Gao Jun. "A Changed Director: Transcription of a Dialogue with Zhang Junzhao." In Chris Berry, ed., *Perspectives on Chinese Cinema,* London: British Film Institute, 1991, pp. 130–3.

Guo Qing. "Jinnian lai guanyu dianying minzuhua de tantao yu zhenglun" [Debates and Controversies in Recent Years on the Sinification of Cinema]. *Dianying yishu,* no. 11 (November 1985), pp. 33–41.

Hao Dazheng. "Lishi de shi yu chao: *Haitan* guangan" [The Time and Tide of History: Impressions of *The Beach*]. *Dangdai dianyi,* no. 2 (February 1985), pp. 66–71.

"*Heipao shijian*": *Cong xiaoshuo dao dianying* [*The Black Cannon Incident:* From Novel to Film]. Beijing: Zhongguo dianying chuban she, 1988.

"*Heipao shijian* zong heng tan" [Perspectives on *The Black Cannon Incident*]. *Dangdai dianying,* no. 3 (March 1986), pp. 47–66.

Hitchcock, Peter. "The Aesthetics of Alienation, or China's 'Fifth Generation.'" *Cultural Studies,* 6, no. 1 (January 1992), pp. 116–41.

Hoare, Stephanie Alison. "Melodrama and Innovation: Literary Adaptation in Contemporary Chinese Film," Ph.D. dissertation, Cornell University, 1989.

Hollander, Jane. "Jackie Chan: Risking Life for American Approval." *Inside Kung-Fu,* 14, no. 2 (February 1987), pp. 36–41.

Hong Shi. "Guanyu disi, diwu dai dianying daoyan de duan xiang" [Some Distinctions Regarding the Fourth and Fifth Generations of Film Directors]. *Yishu guangjiao* (January 1989), pp. 93–6.

Hsieh Hui-chuan. "Articles for the Censor." *Cinemaya,* no. 4 (Summer 1989).

Huang Ren. "Taiwan shehui de bianqian yu zhipian shiye de fazhan" [The Transformation of Taiwan Society and the Transformation of Its Film Industry]. *Dangdai dianying,* no. 1 (January 1990), pp. 82–91.

Huang, Vivian. "Taiwan's Social Realism: New Cinema Weathers Commercial Pressures and Fickle Audiences." *Independent,* 13, no. 1 (January–February 1990), pp. 24–7.

Jaehne, Karen. "Boat People: An Interview With Ann Hui." *Cineaste,* 13, no. 2 (1984), pp. 16–19.

Jarvie, Ian C. *Window on Hong Kong: A Sociological Survey of the Hong Kong Film Industry and Its Audience.* Hong Kong: Centre of Asian Studies, University of Hong Kong, 1977.

Jiang Hao. *Panni tiancai: Dalu yingtan de liupi hei ma* [Rebel Genius: Six Black Horses of the Chinese Film World]. 2 vols. Xianggang: Guangyaxuan chuban she, 1991.

Jump Cut, no. 31 (March 1986); special issue on Chinese cinema.

Jump Cut, no. 34 (March 1989); special issue on Chinese cinema.

Kaplan, E. Ann. "Melodrama/Subjectivity/Ideology: The Relevance of Western Melodrama Theories to Recent Chinese Cinema." *East–West Film Journal*, 5, no. 1 (January 1991), pp. 6–27.

"Problematizing Cross-Cultural Analysis: The Case of Women in the Recent Chinese Cinema," *Wide Angle*, 11, no. 2 (1989), pp. 40–50.

Lau, Jenny Kwok Wah. "A Cultural Interpretation of the Contemporary Cinema of China and Hong Kong, 1981–1985," Ph.D. dissertation, Northwestern University, 1989.

"Towards a Cultural Understanding of Cinema: A Comparison of Contemporary Films from the People's Republic of China and Hong Kong." *Wide Angle*, 11, no. 3 (July 1989), pp. 42–9.

Lent, John A. *The Asian Film Industry*. Austin: University of Texas Press, 1990.

Leong Mo-ling, ed. *Hong Kong Cinema '84* (9th Hong Kong International Film Festival). Hong Kong: The Urban Council, 1985.

New Hong Kong Films '86/'87 (11th Hong Kong International Film Festival). Hong Kong: The Urban Council, 1987.

New Hong Kong Films '87/'88 (12th Hong Kong International Film Festival). Hong Kong: The Urban Council, 1988.

New Hong Kong Films '89/'90 (14th Hong Kong International Film Festival). Hong Kong: The Urban Council, 1990.

Li Cheuk-to. *Bashi niandai Xianggang dianying biji* [Notes on Hong Kong Cinema of the 1980s], 2 vols. Xianggang: Chuangjian chuban gongsi, 1990.

"Fatal Blow," *Cinemaya*, no. 4 (Summer 1989), pp. 42–5.

"Cinema in Hong Kong: Contemporary Currents." *Cinemaya*, no. 1 (Autumn 1988), pp. 4–9.

"A Review of Hong Kong Cinema, 1988–1989." In *The Ninth Hawaii International Film Festival Viewers Guide*. Honolulu: East–West Center, 1989, pp. 36–9.

Li Cheuk-to, ed. *Cantonese Melodrama (1950–1969)* (10th Hong Kong International Film Festival). Hong Kong: The Urban Council, 1986.

Cantonese Opera Film Retrospective (11th Hong Kong International Film Festival). Hong Kong: The Urban Council, 1987.

Changes in Hong Kong Society Through Cinema (12th Hong Kong International Film Festival). Hong Kong: The Urban Council, 1988.

The China Factor in Hong Kong Cinema (14th Hong Kong International Film Festival). Hong Kong: The Urban Council, 1990.

Li, H. C. "Color, Character, and Culture: On *Yellow Earth, The Black Cannon Incident,* and *Red Sorghum." Modern Chinese Literature*, 5, no. 1 (Spring 1989), pp. 91–119.

Li He, ed. "Chen Kaige yu Nagisa Oshima duihua" [A Conversation between Chen Kaige and Nagisa Oshima]. *Dangdai dianying*, no. 6 (June 1987), pp. 109–16.

Phantoms of the Hong Kong Cinema (13th Hong Kong International Film Festival). Hong Kong: The Urban Council, 1989.

Li Wenbing. "Weile Zhongguo diangying de tongfei" [On the Take-off of Chinese Cinema]. *Dangdai dianying*, no. 4 (April 1987), pp. 6–14.

Li Xun. "Dianying yanjiu de guannian" [Conceptual Approaches to Film Research]. *Dianying yishu*, no. 1 (January 1988), pp. 8–10.

Lie Fu. *Zhidian shi nian: 79–89 dalu dianying zongping* [A Few Pointers on the Last

Decade: A Critical Overview of Mainland Cinema in 1979–1989]. Xianggang: Guangyaxuan chuban she, 1991.

Lin Niantong. *Jingyou* [Wandering Lens]. Xianggang: Suye chuban she, 1985.

"A Study of the Theories of Chinese Cinema in Their Relationship to Classical Aesthetics." *Modern Chinese Literature*, 1, no. 2 (Spring 1985), pp. 185–200.

"Zhongguo dianying de kongjian yishu" [Spatial Form and Spatial Consciousness in Chinese Film]. *Zhongguo dianying yanjiu*, no. 1 (1983), pp. 58–85.

Zhongguo dianying meixue [Chinese Film Aesthetics]. Taibei: Yun chen wenhua, 1991.

Liu Binyan. "Dianying yulexing san ti" [Three Questions on the Entertainment Quality of Film]. *Dazhong dianying* (January 1986).

Liu Gongcheng. *"Haizi wang* bing fei ouxiang" [*King of the Children* Is Really Not Idolatry]. *Zhongguo dianying bao*, December 5, 1987.

Liu, Jerry, ed. *The Hong Kong Contemporary Cinema* (6th Hong Kong International Film Festival). Hong Kong: The Urban Council, 1982.

Hong Kong Cinema '82 (7th Hong Kong International Film Festival). Hong Kong: The Urban Council, 1983.

Hong Kong Cinema '83 (8th Hong Kong International Film Festival). Hong Kong: The Urban Council, 1984.

Liu Wenfeng. "Bashi niandai Taiwan xin dianying yipie" [A Glimpse of Taiwan New Cinema of the 1980s]. *Dangdai dianying*, no. 5 (May 1988), pp. 97–103.

Lu Wei. "Shuoshuo Zhou Xiaowen" [On Zhou Xiaowen]. *Dangdai dianying*, no. 2 (1989), pp. 68–74.

Ma Junrang. "Cong *Hong gaoliang* dao *Judou*" [From *Red Sorghum* to *Judou*]. *Ershiyi shiju*, no. 7 (October 1991), pp. 123–32.

Ma Ning. "Culture and Politics in Chinese Film Melodrama: Traditional Sacred, Moral Economy and the Xie Jin Mode," Ph.D. dissertation, Monash University, 1992.

"New Chinese Cinema: A Critical Account of the Fifth Generation." *Cinemaya*, no. 2 (Winter 1988–9).

"Symbolic Representation and Symbolic Violence: Chinese Family Melodrama of the Early 1980s," *East–West Film Journal*, 4, no. 1 (December 1989), pp. 79–109.

Ma Ning and Linda Ehrlich. "College Course File: East Asian Cinema." *Journal of Film and Video*, 42, no. 2 (Summer 1990), pp. 79–112.

Marchetti, Gina. "Hong Kong Independent Filmmaking: An Interview with Roger Garcia." *Afterimage*, 14, no. 10 (May 1987), pp. 16–17.

"Two from China's Fifth Generation." *Continuum*, 2, no. 1 (1988–9).

Mo Zhong. "A Reader's Letter That Will Make People Think." In Chris Berry, ed., *Perspectives on Chinese Cinema*. London: British Film Institute, 1991, pp. 125–6.

Ni Zhen. "Qitiao de gaodu" [The Height of the Jump]. *Beijing Dianying Xueyuan xuebao*, no. 1 (1985), pp. 88–109.

"Ningyuan zai tansuozhong shibai, buyuan zai baoshouzhong gouan: *Cuowei* chuangzuo gouxiang" [It Is Better to Fail in the Process of Experimentation Than to Play It Safe by Taking No Risks: The Creative Structure of *Dislocation*]. *Dangdai dianying*, no. 3 (March 1987), pp. 111–23.

Nornes, Markus. "The Terrorizer." *Film Quarterly*, 42, no. 3 (Spring 1989), pp. 43–7.

O'Brien, Geoffrey. "Blazing Passion." *New York Review of Books*, 39, no. 15 (1992), pp. 38–43.

Passek, Jean-Loup, and Marie-Claire Quiquemelle, eds. *Le cinéma chinois*. Paris: Centre Georges Pompidou, 1985.

Peng Xinger. "Shei neng lengyan kan shijie? Yong zhiqing yishi xingtai dujie Chen Kaige de yingpian *Haizi wang*" [Who Can View the World with a Cool Eye? Using the Ideology of Young Intellectuals to Explain Chen Kaige's *King of the Children*]. *Dangdai dianying*, no. 2 (February 1989), pp. 103–15.

Pickowicz, Paul G. "Melodramatic Representation and the 'May Fourth' Tradition of Chinese Cinema." In Ellen Widmer and David Der-wei Wang, eds., *From May Fourth to June Fourth: Fiction and Film in Twentieth-Century China*. Cambridge, Mass.: Harvard University Press, 1993, pp. 295–326, 425–8.

"Popular Cinema and Political Thought in Post-Mao China: Reflections on Official Pronouncements, Film, and the Film Audience." In Perry Link, Richard Madsen, and Paul G. Pickowicz, eds., *Unofficial China: Popular Culture and Thought in the People's Republic*. Boulder, Colo.: Westview Press, 1989, pp. 37–53.

"Urban Identities and the Political Economy of Chinese Filmmaking." In Deborah Davis, Richard Kraus, Barry Naughton, and Elizabeth Perry, eds., *Urban Spaces: Autonomy and Community in Contemporary China*. Washington, D.C.: Johns Hopkins University Press, forthcoming.

Rayns, Tony. "Breakthroughs and Setbacks: The Origins of the New Chinese Cinema." In Chris Berry, ed., *Perspectives on Chinese Cinema*. London: British Film Institute, 1991, pp. 104–13.

"The Fifth Generation." *Monthly Film Bulletin* (October 1986), pp. 296–8.

"The Position of Women in New Chinese Cinema." *East–West Film Journal*, 1, no. 2 (June 1987), pp. 32–44.

Semsel, George S., ed. *Chinese Film: The State of the Art in the People's Republic*. New York: Praeger, 1987.

Semsel, George S., Hou Jianping, and Xia Hong, eds. *Chinese Film Theory: A Guide to the New Era*. New York: Praeger, 1990.

Semsel, George S., Chen Xihe, and Xia Hong, eds. *Film in Contemporary China: Critical Debates, 1979–1989*. New York: Praeger, 1993.

Shanghai dianyingjia xiehui, ed. *Shanghai dianying sishi nian* [Forty Years of Filmmaking in Shanghai]. Shanghai: Xuelin chuban she, 1991.

Shao Dan. "Shi kexue fansi ma?" [Is This Scientific Reflection?]. *Dianying yishu*, no. 6 (June 1987), pp. 31–7.

Shao Mujun. "Chinese Film Amidst the Tide of Reform." *East–West Film Journal*, 1, no. 1 (December 1986), pp. 59–68.

"Chun yu feichun: Dangdai dianying lilun zouxiang bianxi" [Pure and Impure: The Trend Toward Analytics in Contemporary Film Theory]. *Dangdai dianying*, no. 3 (1988), pp. 7–16.

"Notes on *Red Sorghum*." *Chinese Literature*, no. 1 (January 1989), pp. 172–80.

Yin hai you [Roaming about the Silver Seas]. Beijing: Zhongguo dianying chuban she, 1989.

"Zhongguo dangdai yule pian wenti poyi" [The Debate on Contemporary Entertainment Films in China]. *Dangdai dianying*, no. 2 (1989), pp. 11–21.

"Zhongguo dianying chuangxin zhi lu" [The Road to Innovation in Chinese Cinema]. *Dianying yishu*, no. 9 (September 1986).

"Sishui liunian": Cong juben dao yingpian [Homecoming: From Screenplay to Film]. Beijing: Zhongguo dianying chuban she, 1986.

Su Bing. "Zisha milian de goucheng: Jiantan *Zuihou de guizu* he *Lunhui"* [Obsession with Suicide: Comments on *The Last Aristocrats* and *Transmigration*]. *Dangdai dianying*, no. 2 (February 1990), pp. 95–9.

Tang Jingguang. "Ruma he konghe jue bushi piping" [Insults and Threats Cannot be Considered Film Criticism]. *Zhongguo dianying bao*, June 15, 1988.

Tian Zhuangzhuang. "Reflections." *Cinemaya*, no. 5 (Autumn 1989).

Wang Dehou. "Dianying de shengji yu weiji" [Vitality and Crisis in Film]. *Wenyi bao*, October 22, 1988.

"Dianying wenhua wenti sui gan lu" [Observations on Questions Regarding Film Culture]. *Dianying yishu*, no. 3 (March 1988), pp. 29–31.

Wang Yichuan. "Mangrang shicuo zhong de shengcun jingzheng: *Hong gaoliang* yu Zhongguo yishi xingtai fenwei" [The Struggle to Survive in a Time of Disorientation: *Red Sorghum* and the Present Ideological Climate in China]. *Dangdai dianying*, no. 1 (January 1990), pp. 41–9.

Wang Yuejin. "The Cinematic Other and the Cultural Self? Decentering the Cultural Identity of Cinema." *Wide Angle* 11, no. 2 (1989), pp. 32–39.

"Mixing Memory and Desire: *Red Sorghum:* A Chinese Version of Masculinity and Femininity." *Public Culture*, 2, no. 1 (Fall 1989), pp. 31–53.

"The Old Well: A Womb or a Tomb?" *Framework*, no. 35 (1988), pp. 73–82.

"The Rhetoric of Mirror, Shadow, and Moon: *Samsara* and the Problem of Representation of Self in China." *East–West Film Journal*, 5, no. 2 (July 1991), pp. 69–92.

Wang Yunman. "Yule pian de zhuti chuangzao he jieshou xinli" [The Creative Essence and Reception Psychology of Entertainment Films]. *Dangdai dianying*, no. 5 (May 1989), pp. 40–6.

Wang Zhongming. *Dachao chudong: Lun Zhongguo dianying yu shehui* [A Great Tide Begins to Swell: Cinema and Society in China]. Beijing: Zhongguo dianying chuban she, 1990.

Wong Kin-yip. "From Page to Screen." *Free China Review* (February 1992), pp. 57–63.

Wu Fang. "*Cuowei* de yiyi" [The Significance of *Dislocation*]. *Dangdai dianying*, no. 3 (1987), pp. 124 8.

Wu Yigong. "We Must Become Film Artists Who Deeply Love the People." In Chris Berry, ed., *Perspectives on Chinese Cinema.* London: British Film Institute, 1991, pp. 133–9.

Xu, Harry Haixin. "Ideological Politics in the Art of China's Film Adaptations." Ph.D. dissertation, Cornell University, 1992.

Yang Jianming. "Lun dianying de shangpin xing" [On Film as a Commodity]. *Dangdai dianying*, no. 5 (May 1989), pp. 47–53.

Yang Ping. "A Director Who Is Trying to Change the Audience: A Chat with Young Director Tian Zhuangzhuang." In Chris Berry, ed., *Perspectives on Chinese Cinema.* London: British Film Institute, 1991, pp. 127–30.

"*Hong gaoliang* meile zhi hou" [After *Red Sorghum* Is Gone]. *Dazhong dianying*, no. 7 (July 1988), pp. 3–4.

Yao Xiaomeng. "Dui yi zhong xin de dianying xingtai de sikao: Shilun dianying yixiang meixue" [Reflections on the New State of Cinema: Exploring the Concept of "Yi-xiang"]. *Dangdai dianying,* no. 6 (June 1986), pp. 42–9.

Yau, Esther C. M. "Cultural and Economic Dislocations: Filmic Phantasies of Chinese Women in the 1980s." *Wide Angle,* 11, no. 2 (Spring 1989), pp. 6–21.

"Filmic Discourse on Women in Chinese Cinema: Art, Ideology and Social Relations (1949–1965)." Ph.D. dissertation, University of California, Los Angeles, 1990.

"International Fantasy and the 'New Chinese Cinema.'" *Quarterly Review of Film and Video,* 14, no. 3 (1993), pp. 95–107.

"Is China the End of Hermeneutics? Or, Political and Cultural Usage of Non-Han Women in Mainland Chinese Films." *Discourse,* 11, no. 2 (Spring–Summer 1989), pp. 115–36.

"*Yellow Earth:* Western Analysis and a Non-Western Text." *Film Quarterly,* 41, no. 2 (1987–8), pp. 22–33.

Yin Hong. "Chong du *Furongzhen*" [Rereading *Hibiscus Town*]. *Dangdai dianying,* no. 2 (February 1990), pp. 33–9.

Yuan Wenzhu. "Dianying de chuantong yu chuangxin" [Tradition and Innovation in Film]. *Dianying yishu,* no. 6 (June 1987), pp. 22–30.

Zhang Chengshan. "Lun Xie Jin de chuangzuo fengge" [On Xie Jin's Creative Style]. *Dangdai dianying,* no. 4 (April 1989), pp. 55–68.

Zhang Jiaxuan. "*The Big Parade.*" *Film Quarterly,* 43, no. 1 (Fall 1989), pp. 57–9.

Zhang Mingtang. "Xie Jin dianying zhi mi" [The Enigma of Xie Jin's Films]. *Dianying yishu,* no. 5 (May 1985), pp. 15–28.

Zhang Wei. "Chuantong wenhua zhiyue zhe Zhongguo dianying" [Traditional Culture Restricts Chinese Cinema]. *Dianying yishu,* no. 1 (January 1987), pp. 13–17.

"Guai lun 'Diwu dai' zhi yi: Zhang Yimou yu Chen Kaige fendao yangbiao" [Part One of Offbeat Remarks on the "Fifth Generation": Zhang Yimou and Chen Kaige Each Follow Their Separate Paths]. *Zhongguo dianying bao,* September 25, 1988.

"Xin shiqi Zhongguo dianying lilun fazhan liubian lunkuo" [The Development and Transformation of Film Theory in China During the New Period]. *Dangdai dianying,* no. 2 (February 1990), pp. 4–14.

"Yu Zhuangzhuang tan Zhuangzhuang" [Tian Zhuangzhuang on Tian Zhuangzhuang]. *Dandai dianying,* no. 1 (January 1989), pp. 37–44.

Zhang Yingjin. "Ideology of the Body in *Red Sorghum:* National Allegory, National Roots, and Third Cinema." *East–West Film Journal,* 4, no. 2 (June 1990), pp. 38–53.

"The Idyllic Country and the (Post) Modern City: Cinematic Configurations of Family in *Osmanthus Alley* and *Terrorizer.*" In Wimal Dissanayake, ed., *Melodrama in Asian Cinema* Cambridge University Press, 1993.

Zeng Naiyi. "The Art of the Chinese Film and Television." Unpublished paper, State University of New York at Binghamton, Cinema Department, February 15, 1991.

Zhong Changxiang. "*Laojin:* Cong xiaoshuo dao dianying" [*Old Well:* From Novel to Film]. *Dangdai dianying,* no. 6 (June 1987), pp. 38–47.

Zhong Dafeng. "Lun 'ying xi'" [On "Shadow Theater"]. *Beijing Dianying Xueyuan xuebao,* no. 2 (1985), pp. 54–89.

Zhong Li. "Menglong de xiandai nüxing yishi: Xin shiqi dianying nü biandao chuangzuo sixiang xinli pingxi" [The Ambiguity of Contemporary Female Consciousness: The Creative Thought and Psychological Perspectives of Women Screenwriters and Directors in the New Era of Filmmaking]. *Dangdai dianying,* no. 5 (May 1986), pp. 3–12.

Zhongguo dianying yishu bianji shi, ed. *Hua shuo "Huang tudi"* [On *Yellow Earth*]. Beijing: Zhongguo dianying chuban she, 1986.

Zhu Dake. "Xie Jin dianying moshi de quexian" [The Deficiencies of the Xie Jin Film Mode]. *Wenhui bao* (Shanghai), July 18, 1987.

Zhu Hong, ed. and trans. *The Chinese Western.* New York: Available Press, 1988.

INDEX

Printed in the United Kingdom
by Lightning Source UK Ltd.
9573700001B